FORTY DAYS ON THE MOUNTAIN

FORTY DAYS
ON THE MOUNTAIN

MEDITATIONS ON KNOWING GOD

STEPHEN E. SMALLMAN

CROSSWAY BOOKS

A PUBLISHING MINISTRY OF
GOOD NEWS PUBLISHERS
WHEATON, ILLINOIS

Cover design: Jon McGrath

Cover illustration: Veer

First printing 2007

Printed in the United States of America

ISBN 10: 1-58134-847-9

ISBN 13: 978-1-58134-847-7

Library of Congress Cataloging-in-Publication Data
Smallman, Stephen, 1940–
    Forty Days on the Mountain : Meditations on Knowing God /
Stephen E. Smallman.
        p. cm.
    ISBN 13: 978-1-58134-847-7 (tpb)
    1. Moses (Biblical leader). 2. God (Christianity)—Knowableness.
3. Spiritual life—Christianity. 4. Spiritual exercises. I. Title.
BS580.M6S495   2007
222'1206—dc22   2006026388

VP		17	16	15	14	13	12	11	10	09	08	07
15	14	13	12	11	10	9	8	7	6	5	4	3	2	1

To the congregation of McLean Presbyterian Church,
which it was my joy and privilege to serve from 1967 to 1996,
and which has supported me as its missionary since then.
As Paul wrote to the Philippian congregation:
"I thank my God in all my remembrance of you."

CONTENTS

ACKNOWLEDGEMENTS

As I explain in the Introduction, *Forty Days on the Mountain* began several years ago as a personal journal that I wrote while on a sabbatical from McLean Presbyterian Church. I appreciate the people along the way who have continued to encourage me to get it published. Among them are: Dick Strong, who passed manuscript copies along to numbers of people he ministered to; Libby Conrad, who has used it as a tool to disciple dozens of Young Life leaders; Betty Herron, who found it a great comfort during her last months on this earth; and most persistent of all, my wife, Sandy, who has encouraged me in all my writing projects but felt this was the most helpful of them all.

I appreciate the staff of Crossway Books for their friendly and professional support. In particular I thank Allan Fisher for encouraging me to submit the manuscript, and Lydia Brownback, whose insights and editorial skills have made *Forty Days* far more readable and user-friendly.

Such a book is only possible because God Almighty himself chose to make it possible that we could actually know him. May he receive all the glory if this effort can be used to help us grow in that knowledge.

INTRODUCTION

I invite you to join me as I try to capture something of what it means to know God. How can mortals like you or me—self-centered, sinful ones at that—actually think about knowing the eternal, immortal God? But that is what Moses, Paul, and countless others have desired and prayed for, and it is an opportunity that is available to us as well. In fact, that is how Jesus defined eternal life: "that they *know you* the only true God, and Jesus Christ whom you have sent" (John 17:3).

The meditations on knowing God that you are about to read grew out of a very needy time in my life. After almost twenty-five years of pastoring the same congregation (McLean Presbyterian Church, a church in suburban Washington, D.C.), I was granted an extended sabbatical. My wife, Sandy, and I, along with our youngest child, Andrew, went to a home near Denver, Colorado, for six months of rest and reflection. I reasoned that while a change of location and situation might provide physical rest, only the Lord could bring the deeper kind of rest I needed. And I was asking him to give it. To help accomplish this desire, I was drawn to Exodus 32–34, the remarkable passage recording Moses' meeting with God to intercede for the people of Israel. At the core of his dealings with God was a passion to know him, to know his presence, and even to be shown the glory of God.

Shortly after our arrival, I set apart one day each week to go to the library of Denver Theological Seminary to explore my chosen text through the various commentaries available to me. As you will see, door after door of understanding opened as I tried to enter vicariously into Moses' experience with God. It also took me all over the Scripture. I began writing down the insights I was gaining as journal entries just for my own benefit. Gradually I became convinced that I needed to find a way that would allow others to share in the blessing of what I was learning. Moses was on the mountain for forty days on two separate occasions. Since the unit of forty is very common in Scripture, I decided to divide up my thoughts in a format that would help others meditate on the knowledge of God for that same basic period of time. That is how *Forty Days on the Mountain* was born.

When I returned to the McLean congregation I felt renewed personally as well as having a new heart for the ministry.[1] Several of our members read through the manuscript of *Forty Days* and offered many helpful suggestions. They also expressed enthusiasm for what they learned. We reproduced it for limited distribution as part of our Fiftieth Anniversary Jubilee celebration. In the time since then I have returned to the themes of *Forty Days* over and over in retreats and conferences. I never fail to find that my own heart is stirred and renewed along with those who attend. I am grateful that the editors of Crossway Books are also convinced of the value of these meditations and want to pass them along to a wider readership.

WHO SHOULD READ THIS BOOK?

These meditations are written for anyone who is serious about knowing God. Individuals very new to the faith as well as those who are advanced in their knowledge have used *Forty Days*. It has been read by couples for their devotions, and it has been studied in small groups as the basis for training in spiritual leadership. The one thing all have in common is a sincere desire to know God.

Some of you reading this book might consider yourselves *seekers* rather than *believers*. I hope you will find this book life changing. But you need to recognize that I have two basic assumptions in writing. They are: (1) We can know God only because God wants us to know him. "He is there and he is not silent."[2] He has made himself known through written Scripture, revelation that was demonstrated by Moses' being commanded to write what he was told in a book.[3] (2) Knowing God ultimately comes as a result of God making himself known through his final Word—God revealed in human flesh. Authentic spirituality is anchored in the Son of God, Jesus Christ. I'm not going to try to *prove* either of these ideas—but even if you have unanswered questions (and who doesn't?) I pray that you will nevertheless patiently work through these lessons and let their truth and reality bear witness to your own heart.

HOW SHOULD YOU USE THIS BOOK?

Obviously, there are any number of settings where these meditations would be profitable for you as an individual or for a couple or a group. But there are three expectations in my mind for those who want to gain maximum benefit from reading and studying them.

THE FIRST EXPECTATION: THE USE OF SCRIPTURE

It is my assumption that *Forty Days* will be read with an open Bible. I am including a portion of the text in the *English Standard Version* of the Bible at the beginning of each meditation as well as when I quote Scripture in the meditation. You will find the meditations even more profitable if you read from the Bible you ordinarily use in reading and study. That means not only using your Bible for the "Reading for the Day" at the beginning of the meditation, but keeping it open before you as you work through my remarks. My objective is that you will try to understand the teaching of the passage before making an application.

Scripture itself is the key. Let the Spirit minister to you through the Scripture with my thoughts provoking you to think about things you might not have noticed before. I hope you will find yourself going back to reread parts of the passage or even reading other places in the Bible.

As we shall see, even at the moment when God met Moses on the mountain in answer to his bold praying, what Moses received was not an experience or a vision, but a *word*. He was then told to write these words for the benefit of the people (Ex. 34:27). The written Scripture must be central if we are to enter into genuine spirituality.

THE SECOND EXPECTATION: THE USE OF TIME

You need to be willing to give these readings and meditations time to sink in. I have tried to make each meditation fairly brief. But this was not done with the intention of a casual thought-for-the-day. Rather I have tried to walk deliberately through a very profound topic—the knowledge of God—one small step at a time. Don't be impatient; try to allow each day's lesson to sink in. Some have told me one meditation every day is too fast. There is certainly no requirement that these be read in forty consecutive days. But they will be more helpful if read in sequence and close enough together so that one day will prepare you for the next. I strongly encourage you to find a regular time in your day or week when you can have at least thirty minutes of quiet.

Time also allows you to stop and pray through what you have read and thought about. The entire passage is about Moses' meeting with God—which is the essence of prayer—and every day should end with a time of prayer and reflection. It will also be helpful to make use of a journal to record your own thoughts and prayers. Journal keeping is a time-honored aid to spiritual growth, and for very good reasons.

THE THIRD EXPECTATION: THE USE OF PLACE

For maximum benefit, I want to add a comment about the importance of place. This is, in fact, the subject of a meditation (Day 12). But several readers have encouraged me to include in my introductory words the value of locating a place (a room, a corner, a particular chair) that will serve physically as your "prayer closet." We are such harried people, and we should make use of any little thing that can aid in bringing quiet to our souls, so it is vital to have a "quiet place."

I wish I could tell you that as a result of writing these meditations I have entered fully into the knowledge of God for which I pray. But that awaits a better world. Growing up spiritually is a slow process, and I am thankful that I have been able to take a few more steps as a result of the work of preparing *Forty Days*. It is my prayer that your time with this little book and *The Book* will help you do the same.

Stephen Smallman
www.birthlineministries.com

SELECTIONS FROM
EXODUS 32-34

The next day Moses said to the people, "You have sinned a great sin. And now I will go up to the LORD; perhaps I can make atonement for your sin." So Moses returned to the LORD and said, "Alas, this people has sinned a great sin. They have made for themselves gods of gold. But now, if you will forgive their sin—but if not, please blot me out of your book that you have written." But the LORD said to Moses, "Whoever has sinned against me, I will blot out of my book. But now go, lead the people to the place about which I have spoken to you; behold, my angel shall go before you. Nevertheless, in the day when I visit, I will visit their sin upon them."

Then the LORD sent a plague on the people, because they made the calf, the one that Aaron made. . . .

The LORD said to Moses, "Depart; go up from here, you and the people whom you have brought up out of the land of Egypt, to the land of which I swore to Abraham, Isaac, and Jacob, saying, 'To your offspring I will give it.' I will send an angel before you, and I will drive out the Canaanites, the Amorites, the Hittites, the Perizzites, the Hivites, and the Jebusites. Go up to a land flowing with milk and honey; but I will not go up among you, lest I consume you on the way, for you are a stiff-necked people."

When the people heard this disastrous word, they mourned, and no one put on his ornaments. For the LORD had said to Moses, "Say to the people of Israel, 'You are a stiff-necked people; if for a single moment I should go up among you, I would consume you. So now take off your ornaments, that I may know what to do with you.'" Therefore the people of Israel stripped themselves of their ornaments, from Mount Horeb onward. . . .

Now Moses used to take the tent and pitch it outside the camp, far off from the camp, and he called it the tent of meeting. And everyone who sought the Lord would go out to the tent of meeting, which was outside the camp. Whenever Moses went out to the tent, all the people would rise up, and each would stand at his tent door, and watch Moses until he had gone into the tent. When Moses entered the tent, the pillar of cloud would descend and stand at the entrance of the tent, and the Lord would speak with Moses. And when all the people saw the pillar of cloud standing at the entrance of the tent, all the people would rise up and worship, each at his tent door. Thus the Lord used to speak to Moses face to face, as a man speaks to his friend. When Moses turned again into the camp, his assistant Joshua the son of Nun, a young man, would not depart from the tent. . . .

Moses said to the Lord, "See, you say to me, 'Bring up this people,' but you have not let me know whom you will send with me. Yet you have said, 'I know you by name, and you have also found favor in my sight.' Now therefore, if I have found favor in your sight, please show me now your ways, that I may know you in order to find favor in your sight. Consider too that this nation is your people." And he said, "My presence will go with you, and I will give you rest." And he said to him, "If your presence will not go with me, do not bring us up from here. For how shall it be known that I have found favor in your sight, I and your people? Is it not in your going with us, so that we are distinct, I and your people, from every other people on the face of the earth?"

And the Lord said to Moses, "This very thing that you have spoken I will do, for you have found favor in my sight, and I know you by name." Moses said, "Please show me your glory." And he said, "I will make all my goodness pass before you and will proclaim before you my name 'The Lord.' And I will be gracious to whom I will be gracious, and will show mercy on whom I will show mercy. But," he said, "you cannot see my face, for man shall not see me and live." And the Lord said, "Behold, there is a place by me where you shall stand on the rock, and while my glory passes by I will put you in a cleft of the rock, and I will cover you with my hand until I have passed by. Then I will take away my hand, and you shall see my back, but my face shall not be seen." . . .

The Lord said to Moses, "Cut for yourself two tablets of stone like the first, and I will write on the tablets the words that were on the first tablets, which you broke. Be ready by the morning, and come up in the morning to

Mount Sinai, and present yourself there to me on the top of the mountain. No one shall come up with you, and let no one be seen throughout all the mountain. Let no flocks or herds graze opposite that mountain." So Moses cut two tablets of stone like the first. And he rose early in the morning and went up on Mount Sinai, as the LORD had commanded him, and took in his hand two tablets of stone. The LORD descended in the cloud and stood with him there, and proclaimed the name of the LORD. The LORD passed before him and proclaimed, "The LORD, the LORD, a God merciful and gracious, slow to anger, and abounding in steadfast love and faithfulness, keeping steadfast love for thousands, forgiving iniquity and transgression and sin, but who will by no means clear the guilty, visiting the iniquity of the fathers on the children and the children's children, to the third and the fourth generation." And Moses quickly bowed his head toward the earth and worshiped. And he said, "If now I have found favor in your sight, O Lord, please let the Lord go in the midst of us, for it is a stiff-necked people, and pardon our iniquity and our sin, and take us for your inheritance." . . .

And he said, "Behold, I am making a covenant. Before all your people I will do marvels, such as have not been created in all the earth or in any nation. And all the people among whom you are shall see the work of the LORD, for it is an awesome thing that I will do with you. . . .

And the LORD said to Moses, "Write these words, for in accordance with these words I have made a covenant with you and with Israel." So he was there with the LORD forty days and forty nights. He neither ate bread nor drank water. And he wrote on the tablets the words of the covenant, the Ten Commandments. . . .

When Moses came down from Mount Sinai, with the two tablets of the testimony in his hand as he came down from the mountain, Moses did not know that the skin of his face shone because he had been talking with God. Aaron and all the people of Israel saw Moses, and behold, the skin of his face shone, and they were afraid to come near him. But Moses called to them, and Aaron and all the leaders of the congregation returned to him, and Moses talked with them. Afterward all the people of Israel came near, and he commanded them all that the LORD had spoken with him in Mount Sinai. And when Moses had finished speaking with them, he put a veil over his face.

Whenever Moses went in before the LORD to speak with him, he would remove the veil, until he came out. And when he came out and told the people of Israel what he was commanded, the people of Israel would see the face of Moses, that the skin of Moses' face was shining. And Moses would put the veil over his face again, until he went in to speak with him. —Exodus 32:30–35; 33:1–23; 34:1–10, 27–35

FORTY DAYS
ON THE MOUNTAIN

THE MEDITATIONS

DAY ONE

THE OVERVIEW

READING FOR THE DAY: EXODUS 32:30-35; 33:1-23;
34:1-10, 27-35.

*Thus the LORD used to speak to Moses face to face, as a man speaks to his
friend. . . . And he said, "My presence will go with you, and I will give you rest."
And he said to him, "If your presence will not go with me, do not bring us up
from here. For how shall it be known that I have found favor in your sight, I and
your people? Is it not in your going with us, so that we are distinct, I and your
people, from every other people on the face of the earth?" And the LORD said to
Moses, "This very thing that you have spoken I will do, for you have found favor
in my sight, and I know you by name."*

EXODUS 33:11, 14-17

The purpose of today's reading is to get focused on the basic facts of
the story that we will be studying in detail. Did you get a sense of the
intensity of Moses' prayers and the determined and almost reckless way
he approached God? He was a man with whom the Lord spoke "face to
face, as a man speaks to his friend" (33:11). He wanted to know God and
find favor in his sight (33:13). But that was not enough. Moses would not
stop praying until he secured the continued presence of God, not only
for himself, but for the people he was leading (33:15). And even that was
not enough—Moses went on to make the extraordinary request, "Please
show me your glory" (33:18).

As we approach this remarkable passage, focusing in on these few
verses gives us more than enough to think about. However, no teaching
in Scripture can be taken in isolation. Almost as though retracting a zoom
lens, we need to move our perspective back to see how this meeting with
God is set into a larger picture. For example, Israel's sin of dancing around
the golden calf (Exodus 32) is basic to understanding the passage. The
grace to be revealed shines all the brighter in contrast to the shocking
evil in the hearts of the people. But the golden calf incident also needs

to be put in context. We need to consider the whole book of Exodus to appreciate what is going on between God and Moses.

Exodus is nothing less than the story of salvation by grace alone. That doctrine is stated in the New Testament, but in Exodus it is presented in exciting narrative with dramatic pictures that have been with us from childhood. God Almighty heard the cries of the helpless children of Israel and did battle with the most powerful nation on earth to set them free. God carried them "on eagles' wings" and brought them to himself at the mountain of Sinai with the intention of making them into his "treasured possession" (19:4–5). There, from the mountain, he spoke to them and gave them ten basic "words" by which they could enjoy the liberty that he had purchased for them. He then not only obligated himself to them by way of a covenant, but he also promised his presence to a degree unknown by any nation of people on the face of the earth. All of these thoughts need to be looked into to make Moses' meeting with God all the more meaningful.

The final aspect of context that must be appreciated, if our passage is to have its full meaning, is the perspective of the New Testament. Even the exquisite glimpse of the glory of God given to Moses was only prologue to the coming of Jesus Christ and the privileges that are given to those who are in Christ. But it is important to begin our reflection with the basic facts of the passage, as well as an awareness of the larger context. Then pray with anticipation that God will be pleased to teach you experimentally (as the Puritans would say) the realities behind the facts.

DAY TWO
A GREATER GLORY

READING FOR THE DAY: EXODUS 34:29-35,
2 CORINTHIANS 3:7-18

Aaron and all the people of Israel saw Moses, and behold, the skin of his face shone, and they were afraid to come near him. . . . And when Moses had finished speaking with them, he put a veil over his face. Whenever Moses went in before the LORD to speak with him, he would remove the veil, until he came out. . . .

EXODUS 34:30, 33-34

And we all, with unveiled face, beholding the glory of the Lord, are being transformed into the same image from one degree of glory to another. For this comes from the Lord who is the Spirit.

2 CORINTHIANS 3:18

Moses' face was shining as he came down the mountain with the tablets of the testimony. He had to cover his face with a veil because the people were in awe. Did you notice that the apostle Paul gives a very different perspective on Moses' use of the veil from that which comes from a reading of Exodus alone? In Exodus we are struck by the radiance on the face of Moses that came from being in the presence of God. It caused the people to be in awe of Moses and became a powerful reminder of his unique standing before God. Paul, on the other hand, interprets that same incident to demonstrate the superiority of the new covenant ("ministry of the Spirit") over the old. The glory of the old was a fading glory in comparison to the surpassing and permanent glory of the new.

We will consider both passages in detail in later meditations, but it is important to get a taste of the teaching of the New Testament as we begin. We live today in the blessing of the new covenant, or the New Testament, as we call the record of that covenant. All of the shadows and promises that are found in the Old Testament point to the New, and specifically to their fulfillment in Jesus Christ. Therefore, as much as we benefit from the teaching of the Old Testament, it can only be fully understood and appreciated in the light of the New. The veil was taken away *historically* with the coming of Christ, and it is taken away *personally* when we turn to the Lord (2 Cor. 3:14–16). This new reality will be illustrated again and again as we proceed through these studies. It is striking to learn how often this incident and the role of Moses are mentioned in the New Testament. In each case, after due respect is given to Moses and the revelation he received, the New Testament writer goes on to show a greater fulfillment in the person of Christ.

The lesson is not only the matter of the primacy of the New Testament witness—it is also the fact that the anchor of our whole existence is found in Jesus Christ. This understanding will keep us from feeling that we are somehow meant to duplicate the experience of Moses in our own lives. There are wonderful lessons to be learned, but invariably they will cause us to focus more deeply on Jesus and the "glory that surpasses it" through our union with him.

Nevertheless, while we recognize that our union with Christ carries us to higher spiritual privilege than that of Moses or any other "saint" of the Old Testament, we must still question the actual reality of this in our own lives. Whether or not the radiance on Moses' face was relatively transient, the fact is that his time with God had changed him in a way that was apparent to others. Is our relationship with Christ apparent to others? Moses may have known God at a lesser level of revelation than we have in Christ. Yet he sustained that relationship day after day in such a way that he could be bold in his praying. Do we know that kind of boldness in our praying, since Christ Jesus as our high priest gives us even greater access? "We are very bold," says the apostle (2 Cor. 3:12). Are we? There is obviously a great deal to learn from Moses.

THE FIRST MEETING

READING FOR THE DAY: EXODUS 3:1-15

And the angel of the LORD appeared to him in a flame of fire out of the midst of a bush. He looked, and behold, the bush was burning, yet it was not consumed. And Moses said, "I will turn aside to see this great sight, why the bush is not burned." When the LORD saw that he turned aside to see, God called to him out of the bush, "Moses, Moses!" And he said, "Here I am."

EXODUS 3:2-4

Today's reading is the familiar account of Moses' meeting God at the burning bush. It was important as Moses' first meeting with God, but it is also foundational for the meetings that follow. This initial revelation began while Moses was in the desert happily tending the flocks of his father-in-law, minding his own business. I suspect that upon first leaving Egypt, Moses, like many of us who get away from the attractions of a cosmopolitan life, was restless and horrified at the prospect of spending the rest of his life in exile in the desert. But with the passage of time and the coming of his children, he most likely came to love the solitude and unhurried pace of his life and couldn't imagine how he could ever go back to the "rat race" of Egypt.

But God had other plans. The first thing to note in the passage is the fact that this initial meeting came about entirely at God's initiative. God used the burning bush as a device to arouse Moses' curiosity, and then "called" (v. 4) Moses to himself. This initiative on the part of God is the pattern throughout Scripture, from his seeking out Adam and Eve after the fall, to the call that God graciously extends to draw us to faith in Christ ("by whom you were called into the fellowship of his Son, Jesus Christ our Lord" [1 Cor. 1:9; cf. 1:20–31]). In subsequent meetings it will be Moses' seeking God, but it all goes back to God's coming to him.

A. W. Tozer's classic work, *The Pursuit of God*, begins on this same note: "We pursue God because, and only because, He has first put an urge within us that spurs us to the pursuit. . . . And it is by this very prevenient drawing that God takes from us every vestige of credit for the act of coming. The impulse to pursue God originates with God, but the outworking of that impulse is our following hard after Him; and all the time we are pursuing Him, we are already in His hand."[4] The relationship between the divine initiative and our response will always be mysterious. But a fundamental step to "the pursuit of God," as Tozer terms it, is to surrender the notion that we are the initiators, that something within us has the power to open heaven and take us into the presence of God.

It all begins with God. We already know that, deep in our hearts, if we have come to trust in Jesus. We know that God sought us, showed us our need, and gave us eyes of faith to behold our Savior. But in the actual practice of the Christian life, we constantly slide back toward the supposed self-sufficiency that took us away from God in the first place.

No matter the spiritual heights to which Moses climbed, he always knew it started when God came to him and called him to himself. We must never forget that same lesson. Reflect on this wonderful hymn of testimony:

> I sought the Lord, and afterward I knew
> he moved my soul to seek him, seeking me;
> it was not I that found, O Savior true;
> no, I was found of thee.
>
> Thou didst reach forth thy hand and mine enfold;
> I walked and sank not on the storm-vexed sea
> —'twas not so much that I on thee took hold,
> as thou, dear Lord, on me.
>
> I find, I walk, I love, but O the whole of love
> is but my answer, Lord to thee;
> for thou wert long before-hand with my soul,
> always thou lovedst me.
>
> ANONYMOUS (1878)

DAY FOUR
"I AM WHO I AM"

READING FOR THE DAY: EXODUS 3:13-15; 6:1-8

*Then Moses said to God, "If I come to the people of Israel and say to them,
'The God of your fathers has sent me to you,' and they ask me, 'What is his
name?' what shall I say to them?" God said to Moses, "I AM WHO I AM." And he
said, "Say this to the people of Israel, 'I AM has sent me to you.' . . . This is my
name forever, and thus I am to be remembered throughout all generations. . . .
Say therefore to the people of Israel, 'I am the LORD, and I will bring you out
from under the burdens of the Egyptians, and I will deliver you from slavery to
them, and I will redeem you with an outstretched arm and with great acts of
judgment.'"*

EXODUS 3:13-15; 6:6

The first part of today's reading is a continuation of Moses' meeting
with God at the burning bush. He obeyed God, returned to Egypt,
and spoke to the elders of Israel, and then he and Aaron had their first
meeting with Pharaoh. Both meetings were failures in terms of the
response Moses hoped for. The workload for the people was increased
and the elders complained bitterly. The second part of the reading takes
place as a discouraged Moses returns to God for an explanation of what
was going on (5:22–23).

God himself initiated the first meeting with Moses when he called
him to the burning bush. Now we need to try to understand just *what*
God revealed in that meeting. Essentially the purpose of the meeting was
for God to reveal his name to Moses (3:13). That sounds strange at first,
because we are used to a name being simply a tag that we use to identify
one person from another. But in Scripture, as well as in many cultures,
a name is in reality a description of a person's features or character. The
name is not just who they are, but what they are like. Taking the time to
notice what name is used for God will profoundly impact your reading
of the Bible.

In this instance God reveals his name as "the LORD."[5] It is not as

28

though he is a new God; he is the same as the God of Moses' ancestors (3:15). But as he explained in the later conversation recorded in chapter 6, there is something that those fathers did not know. "God" or even "God Almighty" (6:3) is a general name for God used by all peoples. On the other hand, when God entered into a covenant with the family of Abraham, the people he had chosen, he used a name that could only be rightfully used within the family. Throughout the Old Testament, this name is used as God deals with his covenant people. However, when Gentiles become involved, the name is no longer used, but the text reverts to the more general name, God. (See this in Daniel 2, for example).

It is important to stop and reflect on this name. The place to start is to note that the Hebrew letters for God's covenant name are YHWH. Because of the sacredness of this name to the Jews, they would not corrupt even the letters by adding vowels to the text as it came later to be copied and recopied. For that reason, the actual pronunciation of the name has been lost. If two vowels are added, it is pronounced YaHWeH, which is commonly done today. The more traditional word, YeHoWaH, or Jehovah, is derived by adding three vowels. This gets even more complicated because in most of our English translations this name appears as "LORD" written in the uppercase. Note that this is a different name for God from "Lord" in lowercase letters (which carries the sense of "Lord and Master"). Understanding this will put a whole new light on reading the Old Testament and, in particular, will help make more sense of texts such as "O LORD, our Lord, how majestic is your name in all the earth" (Ps. 8:1), i.e., "O Yahweh, our Master . . ."

Now look again at 6:2–4, where God tells Moses that he is YHWH ("the LORD"), even though he didn't reveal himself in that way to Abraham, Isaac, and Jacob when he made his covenant with them. That statement has always puzzled me. In a passage such as Genesis 15 where the LORD made the covenant with Abraham, he does come as "the LORD" and is even called that by Abraham. What does it mean then, to say they didn't know him as the LORD? The answer lies in the words that follow in 6:6–8 where the LORD described what he would do to actually fulfill the promises of his covenant. He would fight for his people to redeem them from their slavery. So Abraham had *heard* the words of the covenant, but the *reality* of the covenant promises was about to be seen in the mighty acts of God. Perhaps we could say that Abraham knew God as LORD THEOLOGICALLY, but that Moses and the people of Israel were about to come to know him as LORD EXPERIENTIALLY. It was now time for the revelation of this name in a greater fullness.

In Exodus 33:19 the Lord proclaimed his name, the LORD, to Moses in an even fuller sense. But between the revelation of chapter 6 and that of chapter 33 there had to be time and experiences to allow the earlier revelation to become a reality. Still later there would be an even more profound revelation of that "name that is above every name" (Phil. 2:9), the name of Jesus, but that, too, needed to await the proper time.

As we seek to know the Lord in a deeper sense, we have to ask ourselves if this is simply a theological or intellectual quest. Do we know experientially even the more elementary understanding of God that we already have? If not, what value would there be in a greater revelation? Somehow our theoretical and factual knowledge of God has to match up with our experience of him, or we get out of balance. It seems to me that the Lord knows that better than we, which is why he brings us step-by-step to the place where we are ready to take in the deeper lessons.

REDEMPTION BY GRACE

READING FOR THE DAY: EXODUS 6:6-8; 12:1-13

Say therefore to the people of Israel, "I am the LORD, and I will bring you out from under the burdens of the Egyptians, and I will deliver you from slavery to them, and I will redeem you with an outstretched arm and with great acts of judgment. I will take you to be my people, and I will be your God, and you shall know that I am the LORD your God, who has brought you out from under the burdens of the Egyptians. I will bring you into the land that I swore to give to Abraham, to Isaac, and to Jacob. I will give it to you for a possession. I am the LORD."

EXODUS 6:6-8

The great promises of redemption in chapter 6 are demonstrated in the terrible judgment spoken of in the reading in chapter 12 as well as in the actual death of the firstborn (12:29–32) and the crossing of the Red Sea (13:17–14:31). I have a very distinct memory of studying the story of the exodus as a graduate student. Like a light bulb going on, I realized that virtually every detail of God's deliverance of his people was a picture of "by grace you have been saved" (Eph. 2:5, 8). It was one of those moments of enlightenment that permanently affected my understanding of God. From that time on I have seen the Bible as a unity, and the God who met with Moses as the same One whom I meet through Jesus Christ. I'm sure I already understood this *theologically* (to use the terminology of the last lesson), but now this great truth became mine *experientially*.

I mention this insight because I continue to meet many Christians who have not taken this step in understanding the Old Testament. They see the Old Testament as full of wonderful stories (and puzzles), but see its teaching as that which relates to a totally different era. There are important differences to be sure, but those differences relate to a very different context, not to the character of God or the way he saves us. Grace is as fundamental to the Old Testament as it is to the New.

Now go back and read Exodus 6:6 with your own spiritual condition in mind. Aren't we also slaves and in such an oppressed condition that we are helpless to change our situation? In Ephesians 2:1–3, we are said to be dead in our trespasses and sins. The hope is not that we somehow resolve to be different, but that "God, being rich in mercy, because of the great love with which he loved us, even when we were dead in our trespasses, *made us alive* together with Christ" (Eph. 2:4–5). Do you see the very same mercy at work in the saving of Israel from its bondage—"I will deliver you from slavery to them, and I will redeem you with an outstretched arm and with great acts of judgment" (Ex. 6:6)?

The key word in that statement is the word "redeem." Redemption is virtually synonymous with salvation. However, it adds the idea of a purchase price or ransom. God did not simply take his people away; he redeemed them, and the price he paid was the blood of the innocent lamb. In the reading from chapter 12, recall that the Lord said Israel was to begin its calendar from the date of the slaying of the lamb. Their life of freedom began with their redemption through the death of the Passover lamb (12:2). Jesus is that Passover Lamb, and, just as Israel returned every year to celebrate their new beginning in freedom from slavery, so we come again and again to the communion table. There we acknowledge that we are free from the curse of sin because of the cross of Jesus.

Return to the reading in Exodus 6 and read verse 7 again. "I will take you to be my people, and I will be your God" is the essence of the covenant of grace. The Lord spoke those words to Abraham (Gen. 17:7–8), then again here in Exodus, and again as part of the new covenant (Jer. 31:33; Heb. 8:10). God Almighty himself comes to sinful people and obligates himself to be with them and to save them. And there is nothing those people did or do to deserve that level of commitment. That was true for Israel and it is true for us. The only way salvation has ever come has been through the grace of God.

A final thought from this lesson comes from verse 7 where God says, "and you shall know that I am the LORD your God." We will come back again and again to this word *know*. To know God as the LORD, the God who comes personally to save us and be with us, has many dimensions. But it begins with our acknowledging joyfully and gratefully that we have been saved by grace alone, and however unworthy we may feel, God has been pleased to save us through his Son, Jesus. We contributed nothing to that gracious act, nor can we add anything to it now. If you haven't fully appreciated that in your own experience, you can see it fully displayed in the salvation of Israel. Our God is gracious!

Amazing grace, how sweet the sound
that saved a wretch like me;
I once was lost, but now am found,
was blind, but now I see.
              JOHN NEWTON (1779)

THE TEN WORDS

READING FOR THE DAY: EXODUS 19:16-20; 20:1-21

On the morning of the third day there were thunders and lightnings and a thick cloud on the mountain and a very loud trumpet blast, so that all the people in the camp trembled. Then Moses brought the people out of the camp to meet God, and they took their stand at the foot of the mountain. Now Mount Sinai was wrapped in smoke because the LORD had descended on it in fire. The smoke of it went up like the smoke of a kiln, and the whole mountain trembled greatly. . . . The LORD came down on Mount Sinai, to the top of the mountain. And the LORD called Moses to the top of the mountain, and Moses went up.

EXODUS 19:16-18, 20

And God spoke all these words, saying, "I am the LORD your God, who brought you out of the land of Egypt, out of the house of slavery." . . . Moses said to the people, "Do not fear, for God has come to test you, that the fear of him may be before you, that you may not sin."

EXODUS 20:1-2, 20

No set of statements or commandments has been so revered and studied (or vilified) as the words we know as the Ten Commandments. And this is appropriate. These commandments, unlike any other law given to Israel, were spoken by a voice that could be heard by the people themselves. (If this does not seem to be clear in Exodus 20, it is explicitly stated in Deuteronomy 4:11–13 and 5:4, 22, where Moses recounts this event for a new generation.) It is little wonder that they were terrified and begged Moses to be the messenger through whom they would hear the Law (20:18–19). It was these same "Ten" that were recopied when Moses returned to the mountain in chapter 34. They were then placed in the ark of the covenant as a perpetual witness to the people of the character of their God.

The Old Testament abounds in laws, commands, and decrees, but these ten clearly stand out as the Law from which all the other laws are derived. In fact, the Ten are not even called "commandments" in Scripture. They are literally the "ten words," even though the usual English translation is "commandments" (see Ex. 32:16; 34:28; Deut. 4:13; 10:4, where they are also called the "covenant" or the "testimony"). There is no end of thoughts that could be offered about the Ten. But for the purpose of a deeper appreciation of what transpired in Moses' second trip up the mountain, reconsider the setting in which the Ten were given. Reflect on the fact that redemption by grace alone had occurred well before they were spoken. God's saving his people from bondage had nothing whatsoever to do with the Law. It was accomplished by his mighty power and through the sacrifice of the Passover Lamb.

In his first meeting with Moses at the base of Sinai, the Lord told him that once the people had been delivered, Moses would lead them back to the very place where they were meeting (Ex. 3:12). Now they were there, still infants in their faith, not even sure if being saved from the bondage of Egypt was better than the life they knew before. They were God's people because of a mighty act of grace done in their lives. But they didn't *know* what that meant, and they didn't know the God who had saved them. And so God graciously came to meet with them. As Moses later interpreted this event, he explained, "Has any god ever attempted to go and take a nation for himself from the midst of another nation . . . by a mighty hand and an outstretched arm. . . . To you it was shown, that you might know that the LORD is God; there is no other besides him" (Deut. 4:34–35). He made it clear that the Lord's intention in giving the "ten words" was not to be punitive, but to give them a basic direction "that it may go well with you and with your children after you" (Deut. 4:40). All of Deuteronomy 4 and 5 is a marvelous commentary on the meaning of Exodus 20 and the giving of the Law.

Once again we are encountering the God of grace and mercy. Even in the actual giving of the Ten, he began with a reminder of his unconditional love: "I am the LORD your God, who brought you out of the land of Egypt, out of the house of slavery" (Ex. 20:2). In the words that follow, he gave ten unambiguous statements that he expected to be obeyed. He spoke as a loving father would to children who need simple but firm directions for their own good (see Deut. 10:10–13). The Lord had a life of unspeakable joy and fulfillment for his people. It was his plan to make them his "treasured possession" (Ex. 19:5). But this could never be experienced until they learned to obey. Knowing God includes obedience. Here at Sinai the people of God were introduced to that essential lesson.

Do we ever get away from the need to come back to these first lessons? We are not saved by obedience; we are saved by grace. But we will only know what that means and know the God who saved us by coming to him in a spirit of obedience. There is a significant difference in the degree of freedom we have under the new covenant. Under the Law covenant, God's people were treated as little children—because that is what they were. We have "come of age" and have come into our full rights as heirs (Gal. 4:4–7). But the fact that we have been given "freedom" in Christ (Gal. 5:1) doesn't take away from the need to come to God with a childlike spirit of submission and genuine desire for obedience. "Do not use your freedom as an opportunity for the flesh, but through love serve one another. For the whole law is fulfilled in one word: 'You shall love your neighbor as yourself'" (Gal. 5:13–14).

Take some time in prayer to reaffirm your willingness to be obedient. The refrain of the familiar gospel song points the way to enjoying the salvation we have been given:

> *Trust and obey, for there's no other way*
> *to be happy in Jesus, but to trust and obey.*
> JOHN H. SAMMIS (1887)

THE PRESENCE OF GOD

READING FOR THE DAY: EXODUS 24:1-25:9

*Then he said to Moses, "Come up to the LORD . . . and worship from afar. Moses
alone shall come near to the LORD, but the others shall not come near, and the
people shall not come up with him." . . . Then Moses and Aaron, Nadab, and
Abihu, and seventy of the elders of Israel went up, and they saw the God of
Israel. There was under his feet as it were a pavement of sapphire stone, like
the very heaven for clearness. . . . The LORD said to Moses, "Speak to the people
of Israel, that they take for me a contribution. . . . And let them make me a
sanctuary, that I may dwell in their midst."*

EXODUS 24:1-2, 9-10; 25:1, 8

There is another concept that is vital to understand as we seek to
appreciate Moses' meeting with God in Exodus 32–34. That is the
idea of the "Presence" of God that is introduced in the reading for today. It
is this Presence that is the object of Moses' tenacious intercession in those
chapters. In 33:15 he prayed: "If your Presence will not go with me, do
not bring us up from here" (I will capitalize the word to make it distinct
from the truth that God is everywhere present.).

After receiving specific case law as applications of the Ten (chaps.
21–23), there is a ceremony in the presence of God sealing the covenant
relationship with blood and a meal (24:1–11). It says the elders "saw the
God of Israel" (24:10), and Peter Enns writes that this means they saw
something to do with the feet of God (see 33:20, "man shall not see me
and live"). "When meeting the heavenly King, their gaze does not rise
higher than his feet."[6] But in that meal the Lord was giving a taste of what
was to come.

Moses was then called up into Mount Sinai for forty days and nights
(24:18). During that time he was given detailed instruction about the
construction of the tabernacle (chaps. 25–31). This included not only the
furniture, but the minutest detail about the tent itself, the area around

the tent, the garments of the priests who would offer sacrifices, and even the formula for the incense to be used in tabernacle ceremonies. A first reading through all of this detail seems to call attention preeminently to the holiness of God—the Most Holy Place that could be entered only by a high priest who himself had been cleansed; the necessity of blood sacrifice done in the prescribed manner; the constant threats for any aberration, etc. The other aspect about the tabernacle that draws so much comment is that every aspect of it points in one way or another to the person and work of our ultimate high priest, Jesus Christ. But while both of these lessons are basic to the meaning of the tabernacle, there is an even more fundamental truth that must first be considered.

In his introductory words to the description of the tabernacle, the Lord says this: "And let them make me a sanctuary, *that I may dwell in their midst*" (25:8). Later he said: "There I will meet with the people of Israel, and it shall be sanctified by my glory. . . . I will dwell among the people of Israel and will be their God. And they shall know that I am the LORD their God, who brought them out of the land of Egypt that I might dwell among them. I am the LORD their God" (29:43, 45–46).

While all of the specifics of the tabernacle were to teach visibly aspects of the character of God, the fundamental reality was that he had chosen to come and literally dwell in their midst. Moses or his successors would no longer need to leave the camp and climb the mountain to talk to God—he would be in its center, living where they lived, living how they lived—in a tent. "There I will meet with you, and from above the mercy seat, from between the two cherubim that are on the ark of the testimony, I will speak with you about all that I will give you in commandment for the people of Israel" (25:22). Throughout the revelation of the building of the tabernacle, the most common term used was "the tent of meeting" (27:21; 28:43; 29:10, 42, 44, etc.). Once the camp was established and the tabernacle erected, that Presence in the center of the camp was demonstrated by the sight of a cloud by day and a pillar of fire at night (40:34–38).

What an extraordinary thing—to have the Lord of heaven and earth living among his people! As Moses later prayed, this is what distinguished the Israelites from all other people on the face of the earth (33:16). Of course they knew that he was omnipresent and that they couldn't contain him (this is the deception of idolatry—that a god is now in the possession of his owners), but they also were to understand that he had chosen to come and be with them in this unique way. It is little wonder that God's threat to withdraw his Presence and give them a general blessing instead (33:1–6) was unacceptable to Moses and the people.

This theme of the presence of God unfolds through the rest of Scripture. When the people of God arrived in the Promised Land and lived in permanent dwellings instead of tents, the Lord decreed that he, too, would live in a house. He directed David and Solomon to build the great temple in Jerusalem. It is clear from Solomon's prayer of dedication that he understood this idea of Presence (2 Chron. 6:12–42).

When we come to the New Testament, the truth of God's Presence in the midst of his people is fulfilled first of all in the person of Jesus. A literal rendering of John 1:14 is "The Word became flesh and *tabernacled* ["lived for a while" NIV] among us." But if Jesus' earthly life was the more temporary earthly dwelling of God, represented by the tabernacle, then the permanent dwelling, the temple, is found in the gathering of the church (1 Cor. 3:16–17; Eph. 2:21–22). One way to understand the term "body of Christ," as used for the church, is this concept of visible Presence.

God *still* dwells with his people. There will be unique times when we as individuals know that Presence. But the way to know that Presence in an ongoing sense is to gather with the people of God in worship, celebration, and prayer. God is there. If he is not, then there is nothing that makes us different from any other gathering of people. Let us continually seek his Presence together.

> So then you are no longer strangers and aliens, but you are fellow citizens with the saints and members of the household of God, built on the foundation of the apostles and prophets, Christ Jesus himself being the cornerstone, in whom the whole structure, being joined together, grows into a holy temple in the Lord. In him you also are being built together into a dwelling place for God by the Spirit. (Eph. 2:19–22)

SIN IS UGLY

READING FOR THE DAY: EXODUS 32:1-20

When the people saw that Moses delayed to come down from the mountain,
the people gathered themselves together to Aaron and said to him, "Up, make
us gods who shall go before us. As for this Moses, the man who brought us up
out of the land of Egypt, we do not know what has become of him." . . . And he
received the gold from their hand and fashioned it with a graving tool and made
a golden calf. . . . And the LORD said to Moses, "Go down, for your people, whom
you brought up out of the land of Egypt, have corrupted themselves. They have
turned aside quickly out of the way that I commanded them. They have made
for themselves a golden calf and have worshiped it and sacrificed to it and said,
'These are your gods, O Israel, who brought you up out of the land of Egypt!'"

EXODUS 32:1, 4, 7-8

How could they do it? Reading the infamous story of the golden calf immediately makes us very critical of the children of Israel. How could they be so stupid and short-sighted? It is true that Moses had been gone over a month, and that is a long time when you have nothing to do but wait. But wouldn't the memory of the voice of God and the extraordinary experience they had shared at the base of this mountain sustain them for even that amount of time? Furthermore, it is not as though this was the first time they had a chance to reflect on the power of God at work on their behalf. They had all witnessed the plagues, including the ones they had been protected from (Exodus 7–10). They had participated in the Passover when their own firstborn sons were spared judgment (chaps. 11–12). They had watched the Red Sea part for them and close over their enemies (chap. 14). They had seen God graciously provide manna and quail and water (chaps. 16–17). And yet, in a fairly minor crisis, their faith completely failed, and they turned against the God that saved them.

We ask, "How could *they* do it?" as we reflect on the ugliness of their rebellion, as a way of asking, "How can *we* do it?" We have experienced the abundance of God's love through Christ, but we are constantly disobeying our Lord. And, in my experience, it seems that I am especially prone to falling just after I have been given a special blessing! In terms of serious progress in the spiritual life, I seem to have a death wish. Whenever I think I'm getting close to some sort of breakthrough, I do something to ruin my chances of getting closer to God. So I find the rebellion of Israel disgusting and inexcusable—not as a statement of judgment, but as a look into a mirror. I don't like what I see. What does this say to you?

Strange as it may seem, this terrible incident is integral to the remainder of the passage. There are important lessons here. First of all, we are reminded in looking at this *mirror* that all sin is, at its core, rebellion against God. Too often we focus on the sensual aspects of this event. But the "party" was the consequence of the people's perception that they now had God in their control. An alternative translation in 32:1, 4, 8 for "gods" is "God," since the word for God is a plural word in the Hebrew, *Elohim.* In other words, Aaron probably wasn't offering them new gods, he was giving them their God in a form they could manage. Notice in verse 5 that he calls the festival to the golden calves a "feast to the LORD." And it was after doing their religious duty that they "rose up to play" (v. 6). Can it be that the grosser aspects of our flesh are always present just beneath the surface, and any movement away from the Lord allows them to appear? That seems evident in the character of societies, from the Israelites to our own culture. And this is also true for us. We need to face the reality of how ready we are to move in this direction.

We are also reminded in this passage that God who sees the ugliness of sin far more clearly than we, nevertheless, still came to dwell with his people. Sin must be dealt with, not only in terms of the immediate situation, as it was here, but in an ongoing sense, as provided through the sacrifices. But confession and forgiveness of sin did not change the root character of the people. *And yet he came!* In a very real sense, the richness of God's mercy could be seen to an even greater depth because of this uncovering of the depth of sin in the hearts of his people. This is not to suggest in any way that the sin of the people was good. But I do think that it was necessary to provide a contrasting background for the revelation that would follow.

It seems that reminders of the depth of our own sinfulness are necessary to appreciate more fully the depth and breadth of God's love for us. Paul's statement, "There is therefore now no condemnation for those who are in Christ Jesus" (Rom. 8:1), shines all the brighter in the light of the wrestling he had just done with his own depravity (Rom. 7:14–25). We need to heartily repent of our sin, but at the same time we need to give up the notion that in doing so we have made ourselves acceptable to a holy God. We are welcome in the presence of God because we are his children through our Lord and Savior Jesus Christ (see Rom. 8:1–17). One of the most fundamental battles of the spiritual life is to face the horror of sin but then, with no illusions about our own goodness, to marvel all the more at the richness of God's mercy that is ours through Jesus.

> *Nothing in my hand I bring, simply to the cross I cling;*
> *naked come to thee for dress; helpless look to thee for grace;*
> *Foul, I to the Fountain fly; wash me Savior, or I die.*
> AUGUSTUS TOPLADY (1776)

DAY NINE

INTERCESSORY PRAYER

READING FOR THE DAY: EXODUS 32:21-35; HEBREWS 4:14-16

The next day Moses said to the people, "You have sinned a great sin. And now I will go up to the LORD; perhaps I can make atonement for your sin." So Moses returned to the LORD and said, "Alas, this people has sinned a great sin. They have made for themselves gods of gold. But now, if you will forgive their sin. . . ."

EXODUS 32:30-32

Since then we have a great high priest who has passed through the heavens, Jesus, the Son of God, let us hold fast our confession. . . . Let us then with confidence draw near to the throne of grace, that we may receive mercy and find grace to help in time of need.

HEBREWS 4:14, 16

The readings today teach us the meaning of *intercessory* prayer—praying for others. One of the most challenging aspects of this study of Exodus is the intensity of Moses' intercession for Israel. But once again, the lessons learned from Moses point us to Jesus.

In Exodus 18, there is a record of the advice given by Moses' father-in-law, Jethro, as he watched Moses exhaust himself in trying to meet all the needs of the people. Moses needed to delegate most of the work to other capable men. But one duty he could *not* delegate, and the one mentioned first by Jethro, was that Moses would "represent the people before God" (18:19). That statement, along with the rest of the advice given (18:19–21), is a profound and compelling list of priorities for effective spiritual leadership. Moses' first forty days on the mountain certainly served as an example of his representing the people. But now, in the aftermath of the terrible sin of the Israelites, there comes into play another meaning of that call. In a literal, and almost physical, sense, Moses stands between God and the people. Moses so identified with the people, even in their sin, that if God was going to destroy them, then he was to be destroyed too—"please blot me out of your book that you have written"

(32:32; cf. Rom. 9:1–4 where Paul stated he was willing to accept damnation if it would mean the salvation of his people, the Jews).

It is this tenacious intercession that is the key to understanding the encounters that follow. In no case did Moses seek anything for his personal benefit. He was truly selfless in what he sought from God. And it will also become evident that God is both honored and pleased with this kind of bold prayer. We are often timid in the way we pray because, in the back of our minds, we wonder if we are not being selfish in asking for this or that blessing. And that may very well be the case! But when it comes to praying for others, we should pray with great boldness, because in the mysterious realm of prayer God Almighty is moved to act when his people pray.

The intercession of Moses is only one of dozens of examples in Scripture. This thought is also clearly confirmed in the teaching of Jesus about prayer. Consider, for example, his parable of the man who sought bread for his guests in Luke 11: "because of his *impudence* ["persistence" NIV] he will rise and give him whatever he needs" (Luke 11:8).

But in this important matter of intercessory prayer, it is crucial that we look finally, not at Moses' example or even the teaching of Jesus, but at the person of Jesus and what he does for us. The book of Hebrews, from which the second reading is taken, was written to move our minds from the lessons of the Old Testament to their fulfillment in Christ. "Therefore, holy brothers, you who share in a heavenly calling, consider Jesus, the apostle and high priest of our confession" (3:1). And, as we read in chapter 4, there is no intercession like that of Jesus'. He not only offers a kind of intercession that Moses, though willing, was unable to do ("*perhaps* I can make atonement for your sin" [32:30]), but his intercession continues to this very moment. The writer of Hebrews deliberately uses the present tense in saying we "have" a great high priest in the presence of God. Ultimately then, the mercy God bestows on the people we are praying for does not depend on our intercession but on the intercession of Jesus.

Nevertheless, it is important to notice that the application of this passage is that since Jesus is our high priest, we should "with confidence draw near to the throne of grace" so that we may receive the answers to our prayers. Therefore, knowing that Jesus is our high priest does not remove the need to pray as Moses did. It opens the way to praying with even greater confidence than he had.

FULL ATONEMENT

READING FOR THE DAY: HEBREWS 2:14-3:6; 9:11-14; 10:19-23;
EXODUS 32:30

Therefore, holy brothers, you who share in a heavenly calling, consider Jesus, the apostle and high priest of our confession, who was faithful to him who appointed him, just as Moses also was faithful in all God's house. For Jesus has been counted worthy of more glory than Moses. . . . Now Moses was faithful in all God's house as a servant, to testify to the things that were to be spoken later, but Christ is faithful over God's house as a son. And we are his house if indeed we hold fast our confidence and our boasting in our hope.

HEBREWS 3:1-3, 5-6

The next day Moses said to the people, "You have sinned a great sin. And now I will go up to the LORD; perhaps I can make atonement for your sin."

EXODUS 32:30

Reflect today on the intercession of Moses but in particular on the statement recorded in verse 30, "Perhaps I can make atonement for your sin." As dedicated an intercessor as Moses may have been, that was something *he could not do.* The Lord replied that he would render judgment when it was time (v. 34).

The idea behind atonement is that of removing an offense so there can be reconciliation with the one offended. Sin is offensive to God and puts a barrier between the sinner and God. The sense that such a barrier exists and that something needs to be done to remove it is a reality that haunts every human being—whether ancient or modern. But Moses' desire to do something to make atonement for the sins committed at Mount Sinai and the universal search for atonement both reveal the help-lessness of mankind to bring down the barrier.

In fact, they point the way to the work of Jesus Christ on the cross. That is why reading from Exodus 32 took us to readings in the letter to the Hebrews. The writer emphasized over and over, often in contrast to the ministry of Moses, that the death of Jesus provided full atonement for our sin. He did what no animal sacrifice or human priest could ever do: "that he might make atonement for the sins of the people" (2:17 NIV), "he has appeared once for all at the end of the ages to put away sin by the sacrifice of himself" (9:26); "we have been made holy through the sacrifice of the body of Jesus Christ once for all" (10:10 NIV).

Without having a true appreciation of the atonement of Christ, it is not possible to boldly seek the face of God. It is certainly possible to be an ardent seeker after God without such an understanding, but when that is the case, the seeking will include either an inappropriate presumption (the "man upstairs" kind of thinking), or an underlying fear that we are unacceptable. On one level, the teaching on atonement is so basic that anyone who has come to faith in Christ has some understanding that Jesus died for our sins. But in too many instances we tend to view the atonement as the thing that got us in the front door. Afterward, however, we are on our own, and we need to do something more to gain worthiness and favor with God. But this contradicts the burden of Hebrews: "Therefore, brothers, since we have confidence to enter the holy places by the blood of Jesus, by the new and living way that he opened for us through the curtain, that is, through his flesh, and since we have a great priest over the house of God, let us draw near with a true heart in full assurance of faith . . ." (10:19–22).

Moses *wanted* to make atonement for the sins of the people—Jesus actually did it. This glorious truth is celebrated in the Scripture; we return to it every time we come to the communion table, and it needs to be alive for us every time we pray.

> Arise, my soul arise, shake off your guilty fears;
> the bleeding sacrifice in my behalf appears:
> before the throne my Surety stands,
> my name is written on his hands.
>
> He ever lives above, for me to intercede,
> His all redeeming love, his precious blood to plead;
> His blood atoned for every race,
> and sprinkles now the throne of grace.

My God is reconciled; his pardoning voice I hear;
He owns me for his child, I can no longer fear;
with confidence I now draw nigh,
and "Father, Abba, Father!" cry.
CHARLES WESLEY (1742)

DAY ELEVEN
THE ABSENCE OF GOD

READING FOR THE DAY: EXODUS 33:1-6

The LORD said to Moses, "Depart; go up from here, you and the people whom you have brought up out of the land of Egypt, to the land of which I swore to Abraham, Isaac, and Jacob, saying, 'To your offspring I will give it.' I will send an angel before you, and I will drive out the Canaanites, the Amorites, the Hittites, the Perizzites, the Hivites, and the Jebusites. Go up to a land flowing with milk and honey; but I will not go up among you, lest I consume you on the way, for you are a stiff-necked people." When the people heard this disastrous word, they mourned, and no one put on his ornaments.

EXODUS 33:1-4

Can we be satisfied with the blessing of God if it comes without the presence of God? There is an important difference. Both Moses and the people understood that they were different, and would not accept only the Lord's blessing. There is an important lesson here.

Notice that in 33:1, the Lord reaffirmed his promise to see that they would get back to their homeland. He promised protection from all their enemies through his angel and reminded them of the bounty that was there, the "land flowing with milk and honey" (vv. 2–3). All of this had been repeatedly stated, and here it is stated again. But then the Lord said something that was a radical change in his dealing with his people. Because of their rebellious nature, he said that he would *not* be going with them (v. 3). In fact it would not be good for them if he went—"If for a single moment I should go up among you, I would consume you" (v. 5). With that horrifying prospect, the people genuinely humbled themselves in repentance (vv. 4, 6), and Moses began his determined intercession to re-secure the Presence (vv. 12–17).

It is frightening to consider that there can be blessing from God, even the material blessings of being in the land of milk and honey, without God's being there. We tend to think that obtaining those blessings indicates the presence of God. Furthermore, when we have those material blessings (health, a reasonably comfortable life, family, friends, etc.), then we are perfectly satisfied. We do not ask the hard questions about whether we are coming to know more of the actual presence of God. In terms of my calling as a pastor, I need to recognize that the church I lead can seem to be growing, prospering, and effectively ministering—all of which are certainly blessings from God—without experiencing the actual presence of the God we serve.

It is not a comforting thought, but often the Lord has to strip away the blessing in order to cause us to hunger more deeply for his presence. That must be because, in our immaturity, we have a hard time separating one from the other. A deepening spiritual maturity, therefore, includes learning to distinguish between God's blessings and God's presence and then seeking to deepen our knowledge of God irrespective of outward circumstances. Neither our comfort nor our lack of comfort is, in itself, a sign of the presence of God.

But if the more tangible thing, the blessing, is not the same as the presence of God, how can we actually know this presence? Is it a feeling? An experience? Just what does it mean to be in the presence of God? This is what is now before us in the meat of the passage.

To begin with, it seems clear that we need to have the genuine sense of horror expressed by both Moses and the people at the thought of God's absence. His presence was vastly more important to them than his blessing. As immature and rebellious as they were, they got the message. And when they got the message, they responded. They humbled themselves before God and stripped off their ornaments as a demonstration of their heartfelt repentance.

When Martin Luther posted his famous Ninety-five Theses on the door of the Wittenburg church, the movement now called the Reformation was launched. The first of Luther's theses was this: "Our Lord and Master Jesus Christ, in saying 'Repent ye . . .' meant the whole of life of the faithful to be an act of repentance."[7]

Psalm 130 was Luther's favorite; let it be your prayer of desire and of humility.

FORTY DAYS ON THE MOUNTAIN

Out of the depths I cry to you, O LORD!
*   O Lord, hear my voice!*
Let your ears be attentive
*   to the voice of my pleas for mercy!*

If you, O LORD, should mark iniquities,
*   O Lord, who could stand?*
But with you there is forgiveness,
*   that you may be feared.*

I wait for the LORD, my soul waits,
*   and in his word I hope;*
my soul waits for the Lord
*   more than watchmen for the morning,*
*   more than watchmen for the morning.*

O Israel, hope in the LORD!
*   For with the LORD there is steadfast love,*
*   and with him is plentiful redemption.*
And he will redeem Israel
*   from all his iniquities.*

THE TENT OF MEETING

READING FOR THE DAY: EXODUS 33:7-11

Now Moses used to take the tent and pitch it outside the camp, far off from the camp, and he called it the tent of meeting. And everyone who sought the LORD *would go out to the tent of meeting, which was outside the camp. Whenever Moses went out to the tent, all the people would rise up, and each would stand at his tent door, and watch Moses until he had gone into the tent. When Moses entered the tent, the pillar of cloud would descend and stand at the entrance of the tent, and the* LORD *would speak with Moses. And when all the people saw the pillar of cloud standing at the entrance of the tent, all the people would rise up and worship, each at his tent door. Thus the* LORD *used to speak to Moses face to face, as a man speaks to his friend. . . .*

EXODUS 33:7-11

Look again at the first verse of today's reading, "Now Moses *used* to take the tent and pitch it outside the camp" (33:7). The verses of this reading are written in a way that suggests this is an insertion to explain how Moses was in a place where the Lord could come to him. The verb "used" suggests the idea of a pattern that was a consistent part of Moses' life. He regularly went a short distance from the camp and set up a tent that became known as the "tent of meeting." Even though that same term was used of the tabernacle, that tent of meeting had not yet been erected. In this passage the tent was an ordinary one, but it was a place where Moses would meet with God, probably as a witness of what would come for all the people. The people could only watch as "the pillar of cloud would descend and stand at the entrance of the tent, and the LORD would speak with Moses" (v. 9). Moses would be in God's presence and talk to the Lord "face to face, as a man speaks to his friend" (v. 11).

This is what we could call *the devotional habits of Moses*. It takes us one step further in answering the question of just how, from the human side, we can know the presence of God in the profound sense revealed in Exodus 33 and 34. The steps we have already seen include: (1) an expressed horror at the prospect of his absence, and (2) a genuine repentance of the spirit of rebellion (33:4–6). To this list add: (3) a regular time of meeting with God.

We should not expect those occasional moments of profound awareness of God's presence if we are not consistently coming before him in prayer, reflection, and reading of the Word. I found this helpful paragraph in a published journal entry of the late Roman Catholic mystic Henri Nouwen called "Useless Prayers":

> The remarkable thing, however, is that sitting in the presence of God for one hour each morning—day after day, week after week, month after month—in total confusion and with myriad distractions radically changes my life. God, who loves me so much that he sent his only Son not to condemn me but to save me, does not leave me waiting in the dark too long. I might think that each hour is useless, but after thirty or sixty or ninety such useless hours, I gradually realize that I was not as alone as I thought; a very small, gentle voice has been speaking to me far beyond my noisy place. So: Be confident and trust in the Lord.[8]

In addition to the pattern of meeting with God, there is another important lesson in this record of the tent. It points to the need to have a place where we meet with God. This is not a specific holy place, such as the tabernacle was to become, but a place which emotionally and even physically tells us it is time to "be still, and know that I am God" (Ps. 46:10). For me, this has been a particular room and even a chair within that room. As I sit in that chair, I find it far easier for my spirit to calm down than if I just go to a random place to try to be still. I have found it difficult to have anything more than a superficial devotional life when I am traveling. If I am in a new location for a few days, then I can mentally identify a place to be still and reestablish my sense of meeting.

Perhaps I am strange in that need, but I suspect not. As long as we are bodies as well as spirits, the idea of *place* will be important. Was this part of Jesus' teaching that when we pray we are to enter our "closet" (Matt. 6:6 KJV)? Of course, the principal issue in that passage is the need to be private in our praying, but couldn't he also be suggesting that we need our own place to pray? Do you have a "tent of meeting," and do you regularly go there to speak with the Lord?

DAY THIRTEEN

FACE TO FACE

READING FOR THE DAY: EXODUS 33:11; JOHN 15:5-15

Thus the LORD used to speak to Moses face to face, as a man speaks to his friend. When Moses turned again into the camp, his assistant Joshua the son of Nun, a young man, would not depart from the tent.

EXODUS 33:11

"I am the vine; you are the branches. Whoever abides in me and I in him, he it is that bears much fruit, for apart from me you can do nothing. If anyone does not abide in me he is thrown away like a branch and withers; and the branches are gathered, thrown into the fire, and burned. If you abide in me, and my words abide in you, ask whatever you wish, and it will be done for you. By this my Father is glorified, that you bear much fruit and so prove to be my disciples. As the Father has loved me, so have I loved you. Abide in my love. If you keep my commandments, you will abide in my love, just as I have kept my Father's commandments and abide in his love. These things I have spoken to you, that my joy may be in you, and that your joy may be full. This is my commandment, that you love one another as I have loved you. Greater love has no one than this, that someone lay down his life for his friends. You are my friends if you do what I command you. No longer do I call you servants, for the servant does not know what his master is doing; but I have called you friends, for all that I have heard from my Father I have made known to you."

JOHN 15:5-15

Today we will consider the implications of this single sentence: "Thus the LORD used to speak to Moses face to face, as a man speaks to his friend." Is something like this possible for us? Or was this something only Moses experienced? The words of Jesus to his disciples on the night before his crucifixion, when he called them his "friends," make it clear that this is for us as well.

It should first of all be pointed out that in the case of Moses, his face-to-face meeting with the Lord was not intended to be understood in a literal, physical sense. When Moses asked for that, he was told, "you

53

cannot see my face, for man shall not see me and live" (33:20). "Face to face," refers then to the intimacy with which Moses and God communed. God was present though not visible; nevertheless, we are to have a mental picture of two old friends sitting together, looking each other in the eyes, and talking about anything that would come to mind. This was the ongoing relationship that Moses increasingly experienced with God. When the time came for Moses to press his case urgently (33:12ff), he did not come to a stranger, nor did he speak with someone whom he went to only in times of trouble and need.

Not many people in Scripture are called "friends of God." Moses was one and Abraham was another (Isa. 41:8; James 2:23). This fact deepens the meaning of Jesus' statement to his disciples, "No longer do I call you servants . . . but I have called you friends." (John 15:15). This means that the intimacy of relationship that Moses knew with God, while in some respects quite unique (Num. 12:8), is nevertheless our privilege as well, through Jesus. We, too, can know what it is to have a face-to-face relationship with the Lord.

In John 15 Jesus used another image that is not to be thought of as literal, but it is still quite remarkable in what it suggests. He called himself the vine and said that we are the branches. We are those who draw strength from Jesus so that by his energy we can bear fruit (15:5, 8). But the imagery of vine and branches also means we are intimately connected to him, are loved by him, can know his joy, and should think of him as our friend (15:9–15).

In *The Pursuit of God,* A.W. Tozer defines faith as "the gaze of a soul upon a saving God." Bring this definition to the picture of two friends sitting face-to-face and talking. It is by faith—the gaze of the soul upon a saving God—that we know he is present in the conversation. Let Tozer speak to us further on this matter:

> When we lift our inward eyes to gaze upon God we are sure to meet friendly eyes gazing back at us, for it is written that the eyes of the Lord run to and fro throughout all the earth. The sweet language of experience is "Thou God seest me." When the eyes of the soul looking out meet the eyes of God looking in, heaven has begun right here on this earth. When the habit of inwardly gazing Godward becomes fixed within us we shall be ushered onto a new level of spiritual life more in

keeping with the promises of God and the mood of the New Testament. The Triune God will be our dwelling place even while our feet walk the low road of simple duty here among men. We will have found life's summum bonum indeed.

Note that Tozer speaks of "the habit of inwardly gazing Godward." That could be thought of in terms of our *duty* or *obligation* to have regular times of communion with God. We run away from those words in our day, but there are times when we don't feel like doing something and we do it anyway—because it is our *duty*. In this instance, however, this is an obligation to meet with a friend, and it is therefore a duty we anticipate with joy, just like we anticipate an evening with a friend whom we haven't seen for some time. How do we turn our duty into a delight? A key is to embrace Tozer's remark that as we enter God's presence and by faith seek to gaze upon him, we can be sure that we will "meet friendly eyes gazing back at us." Conclude this meditation by praying the prayer Tozer wrote at the end of the chapter entitled, "The Gaze of the Soul," from which the quotations were taken:

> O Lord, I have heard a good word inviting me to look away to Thee and be satisfied. My heart longs to respond, but sin has clouded my vision till I see Thee but dimly. Be pleased to cleanse me in Thine own precious blood, and make me inwardly pure, so that I may with unveiled eyes gaze upon Thee all the days of my earthly pilgrimage. Then shall I be prepared to behold Thee in full splendor in the day when Thou shalt appear to be glorified in Thy saints and admired in all them that believe. Amen.[9]

DAY FOURTEEN
LET ME KNOW YOU

READING FOR THE DAY: EXODUS 33:12-13

Moses said to the LORD, "See, you say to me, 'Bring up this people,' but you have not let me know whom you will send with me. Yet you have said, 'I know you by name, and you have also found favor in my sight.' Now therefore, if I have found favor in your sight, please show me now your ways, that I may know you in order to find favor in your sight. Consider too that this nation is your people."

EXODUS 33:12-13

Because of our previous studies, we know that the remarkable prayers recorded in 33:12–34:3 took place in the tent of meeting just outside the camp. The Lord still was not dwelling in the midst of his people as he promised, but he was coming nearer, thanks to the powerful intercession of Moses. The people were aware of this, and they watched and worshiped as Moses met with the Lord in the tent (33:10). The prayer we read for today is Moses' response to the Lord's call for repentance in Exodus 33:5.

That the Lord threatened his absence and then came closer, and appeared to want to be asked to come even closer, should not be viewed as some kind of capriciousness on God's part. He had already declared by blood oath what he would do. But as part of his remarkable condescension, the Lord dealt with his people in a way in which they could participate as human beings. By studying Moses we can learn that God invites us to argue with him, to present our case, and to try to change his mind. Through the back and forth of these intercessions Moses was learning to know God, and his prayers became bolder and bolder. This was not the same man who tried to talk God out of a call to service just months earlier.

Notice that in verse 12 Moses quoted God's word back to him—twice. In the first instance, Moses claimed that although the Lord was sending him forth to lead the people, he hadn't said whom he would send with him. In fact, the Lord *had* said whom he was sending—it would be his angel (32:34). In a respectful way, Moses was refusing to accept the Lord's will! If they could not know the very presence of God, they would not leave (33:15–16). "I will not let you go unless you bless me," said Jacob as he wrestled with the angel of the Lord (Gen. 32:26). That same kind of determination can be seen in Moses. He would re-secure the presence of God, and he would not let go until he got it.

The second time Moses quoted God's word back to God, he referred to the assurance he had received of God's favor. The favor was to be found in that he was known by name to God. Based on the fact of God's knowledge of him, Moses went on to pray that he might "know [him] in order to find favor in [his] sight." He then concluded this part of the prayer by reminding God of his covenantal relationship with his people: "Consider too that this nation is your people." They, too, had been favored by God, not because of their inherent worthiness, but because God had chosen to favor them. Moses would not release God from his covenant. Even at the end of the full revelation that God would give him on the mountain, Moses, the most determined intercessor until Christ, returned to hold God to his promise (34:9).

The core idea throughout these studies has been the remarkable truth that God knows his people and wants them to know him. It is time to give this more concentrated attention. No form of prayer has had a greater effect on my spiritual life than the prayers throughout Scripture that we would come to know God. The striking thing is that it is always on the lips of those who *already* know God! Moses was a man with whom God spoke "face to face, as a man speaks with his friend," and yet, Moses still prayed to know him.

As we shall see, the same kind of praying is found constantly on the part of the apostle Paul. On one level, knowing God is synonymous with entering into eternal life. Jesus said, "And this is eternal life, that they know you the only true God, and Jesus Christ whom you have sent" (John 17:3). But the same word is also used of an ever-deepening relationship with God. Paul said, "I count everything as loss because of the surpassing worth of knowing Christ Jesus my Lord" (Phil. 3:8).

Thus says the LORD: "Let not the wise man boast in his wisdom, let not the mighty man boast in his might, let not the rich man boast in his riches, but let him who boasts boast in this, that he understands and knows me, that I am the LORD who practices steadfast love, justice, and righteousness in the earth. For in these things I delight, declares the LORD." (Jer. 9:23–24)

DAY FIFTEEN

GOD KNOWS US

READING FOR THE DAY: ISAIAH 43:1-13;
EXODUS 33:12-13, 17

*But now thus says the LORD, he who created you, O Jacob, he who formed you,
O Israel: "Fear not, for I have redeemed you; I have called you by name, you
are mine. When you pass through the waters, I will be with you; and through the
rivers, they shall not overwhelm you; when you walk through fire you shall not
be burned, and the flame shall not consume you. . . . Because you are precious
in my eyes, and honored, and I love you, I give men in return for you, peoples in
exchange for your life. Fear not, for I am with you. . . ."*

ISAIAH 43:1-2, 4-5

*"You have said, 'I know you by name, and you have also found favor in my
sight.' Now therefore, if I have found favor in your sight, please show me now
your ways, that I may know you." . . . And the LORD said to Moses, "This very
thing that you have spoken I will do, for you have found favor in my sight, and I
know you by name."*

EXODUS 33:12-13, 17

We are looking more closely at the prayers of Moses and others in
Scripture for a deeper knowledge of God. Through the years of
wrestling with the meaning of such prayers, I have come to the conviction
that what we are actually asking for is to enter into a knowledge that the
Lord already has of us. In Exodus 33, Moses prayed to know the Lord,
and the Lord said he would grant that request because he already knew
Moses. To say that God knew Moses by name points clearly to knowing
in the sense of relationship, not simply in the sense of information. As we
read in Jeremiah 9, if we have any boast, it is not in our wealth or wisdom
or strength. It is that we know the Lord. But an even greater boast, if such
a word is appropriate for this, is that the Lord knows us. Here is our place
to stand, our resting place.

In passage after passage in Isaiah, particularly in chapters 40–49, the Lord sets forth his divine majesty, his mighty creative power, and his faithfulness to all he has promised. And the context of those glorious statements is the fact that his people can find deepest comfort because this mighty and gracious Lord knows them so intimately that he calls them by name. This is particularly evident in the reading for today. "Fear not, for I have redeemed you; I have called you by name, you are mine. When you pass through the waters, I will be with you; and through the rivers . . . through fire . . . for I am the LORD your God . . . you are precious in my eyes, and honored, and I love you . . . everyone who is called by my name." Consider one other example from Isaiah: "Can a woman forget her nursing child, that she should have no compassion on the son of her womb? Even these may forget, yet I will not forget you. Behold, I have engraved you on the palms of my hands" (49:15–16).

These and many similar passages reveal God's love for those whom he saves and are not to be limited to Israel. The same themes can be found in the New Testament as well. In John 10 Jesus spoke of his sheep. "He calls his own sheep by name. . . . I know my own and my own know me. . . . My sheep hear my voice, and I know them, and they follow me. I give them eternal life, and they will never perish, and no one will snatch them out of my hand" (John 10:3, 14, 27–28). "We love because he first loved us" (1 John 4:19). This is not love in some undefined sense, but God's love that is personal and specific.

This gives light to the mysterious word "foreknowledge" or "foreknow," which appears several times in the New Testament (Rom. 8:29, 11:2; 1 Peter 1:2). It was not simply that God knew about us beforehand, before we believed. God knew us in the sense we have seen all through the Scripture—he knew us individually and personally, and he could call us by name. He did this long before we could call his name. This is the idea of *chosen-ness* that marked Israel's identity and marks ours as well—"What then shall we say to these things [God's foreknowledge and predestination]? If God is for us, who can be against us?" (Rom. 8:31).

It is basic, then, to recognize that our prayer for deeper knowledge is really a prayer to know him in the way that he already knows us. While

God's knowledge of us is perfect, ours will always be growing. This is evident from Paul's conclusion to his great tribute to love:

> Now we see in a mirror dimly, but then face to face. Now I know in part; then I shall know fully, even as I have been fully known. (1 Cor. 13:12)

PAUL'S GREAT PASSION

READING FOR THE DAY: PHILIPPIANS 3:1-14

Indeed, I count everything as loss because of the surpassing worth of knowing Christ Jesus my Lord. For his sake I have suffered the loss of all things and count them as rubbish, in order that I may gain Christ and be found in him, not having a righteousness of my own that comes from the law, but that which comes through faith in Christ, the righteousness from God that depends on faith—that I may know him and the power of his resurrection, and may share his sufferings, becoming like him in his death, that by any means possible I may attain the resurrection from the dead.

PHILIPPIANS 3:8-11

I have always thought of Moses and Paul as the two "giants" of Scripture—one for the Old Testament era and one for the New. Neither Moses nor Paul was the actual bearer of salvation. It was Abraham and his seed, Christ, who brought redemption. But it was Moses and then Paul who were God's instruments to set forth, in teaching and writing, the meaning of God's mighty work.

It is not at all surprising, then, to learn that Moses' great passion to know God is also found in Paul. Both of them had personal experience of God's first knowing them by name in a very specific sense. When the Lord called to Moses from the burning bush, he called out "Moses, Moses" (Ex. 3:4), just as he called out "Saul, Saul" (Acts 9:4) when he brought Saul of Tarsus to himself. This is not to suggest that God's ability to say their names was in itself extraordinary. But consider what it must have been like for those men to actually hear their names spoken by God. God knew them! Now they became passionate to know God to the greatest degree possible.

That passion to know is very evident in the reading for today. Philippians was one of four epistles Paul wrote from prison. When he wrote, Paul was facing the prospect of losing his life. But that was immaterial to the apostle, because for him "to live [was] Christ, and to die [was] gain" (Phil. 1:21). He had the same disregard for any of his impressive earthly credentials—he considered them "loss for the sake of Christ." Furthermore, everything was a loss "because of the surpassing worth of knowing Christ Jesus my Lord" (3:8). In fact, in comparison to the knowledge of Christ, everything else was considered rubbish by Paul. (In the KJV, that word *rubbish* is translated "dung.") He wanted to move as far away from his own righteousness as possible and instead be found cloaked in the righteousness of Christ, which comes through faith. Paul's hunger to know Christ included knowing the power of his resurrection and even a readiness to share in his sufferings.

In verse 12, Paul was careful to admit that he had not yet obtained this level of knowledge, but he was pressing ahead "to make it my own, because Christ Jesus has made me his own." He was striving to obtain what was already his in Christ. What Paul has in mind here is the idea of that perfect knowledge which God already had of him. He was now pressing on ("straining forward to what lies ahead") to enter that knowledge even though it would only be perfect when he met Christ ("then I shall know fully, even as I have been fully known," 1 Cor. 13:12). This was the prize (3:14) for which Paul was striving. Nothing, in life or in death, was more important to Paul than knowing God through his Son, Jesus Christ. It should not be at all surprising that he had this same passion for those whom he taught.

Paul, like Moses, was called to be a point man for the advancement of the kingdom of God. With his intelligence, skill, and drive, I can picture him easily fitting in with a top executive team in politics or industry. He could take a church or ministry and offer leadership to make it a tremendous success. But once he came to know Christ on the Damascus road, all of that potential was subservient to his passion to enter more deeply into that knowledge. Many of us, on a much more modest scale, are called to some form of leadership in the work of the kingdom. There is so much to be done, so many important tasks to be accomplished for our Master. But do we *know* the one whom we seek to serve? That is the fundamental question. Paul, both in his example and teaching, brings us back to this time and time again.

PAUL'S PRAYERS FOR KNOWLEDGE

READING FOR THE DAY: COLOSSIANS 1:9-14

And so, from the day we heard, we have not ceased to pray for you, asking that you may be filled with the knowledge of his will in all spiritual wisdom and understanding, so as to walk in a manner worthy of the Lord, fully pleasing to him, bearing fruit in every good work and increasing in the knowledge of God. May you be strengthened with all power, according to his glorious might, for all endurance and patience with joy, giving thanks to the Father, who has qualified you to share in the inheritance of the saints in light.

COLOSSIANS 1:9-12

Given Paul's great passion to know God more deeply, it should not be surprising that this was what he desired for other believers as well. When we study the prayers he recorded, that is exactly what we find. Paul's prayer for the Colossians is the first example we will consider.

The understanding of how central these prayers are became the bedrock of my own spiritual life and opened a path of discovery that continues to this day. That understanding grew out of a struggle, which I know is shared by most followers of Jesus, to live a life that seemed even remotely close to the life I felt God wanted me to live. My growing frustration was that the harder I tried, the worse I seemed to get. I was praying for help, for power, for Holy Spirit baptism, for *anything* that could help me be what I knew Christ wanted me to be. But as I read the Scriptures, I found myself drawn to the praying that the apostle Paul did for those under his care. In particular, I have been profoundly affected by the prayers in what are known as the four Prison Epistles: Ephesians, Philippians, Colossians, and Philemon. In every one of them, Paul introduced the letter by stating that he had been praying for those to whom he wrote. But beyond that general statement, he went on to say precisely what it was he had prayed for them. And while it is stated variously in the four letters, in all four instances his prayer was that they might "know" (Eph. 1:15–18; Phil. 1:9–11; Col. 1:9; Philem. 4–6).

It is significant that in all four prayers, the Greek word used for "knowledge" was an intensive word, *epignosis,* instead of the usual *gnosis.* The prefix *epi* serves to lift the idea of knowing beyond that of simply knowing *about,* a superficial acquaintance. *Epi* is used today in speaking of the epicenter of an earthquake—the center of the center. "Epi-knowl-edge," therefore, is knowing at the center of knowing. In his second great prayer in Ephesians (3:14–19), Paul prayed the paradoxical prayer that they might "know the love . . . that surpasses knowledge." Indeed, the very idea of actually knowing God would be preposterous except for the fact that he makes himself known! He has spoken, and ultimately he spoke the final Word by coming to us in the person of Jesus Christ.

The way the prayer is expressed in Colossians 1 gives an important perspective on the Christian life. Look again at verse 9 where the apostle stated that in his continuous praying for the Colossian church he was constantly asking that God would fill them "with the *knowledge* [*epignosis*] of his will in all spiritual wisdom and understanding." Those are words pertaining to the mind and heart, not to action. But note that in verse 10 he assumed, as a consequence of this knowledge, they would be able "to walk in a manner worthy of the Lord," and then he went on to describe the life that pleases God. In other words, it is the *knowing* (v. 9) that leads to the doing (vv. 10–12).

I'm afraid that for many Christians that order is reversed—it was certainly the case for me. Or perhaps it would be better to say that we are so preoccupied with the *doing* of Christianity, that we pay scant attention to the matter of *knowing.* We want to please God, but we assume that it will come about by actions. It is very clear from this passage that when Paul prayed for those Christians, he was praying, first of all, that they would know the Lord. And these prayers were offered on behalf of Christians who already "knew" the Lord.

I hope you are learning with me to dwell continuously on this great theme and to pray constantly the same prayer for ourselves and for those we are called to serve.

For this reason I bow my knees before the Father, from whom every family in heaven and on earth is named, that according to the riches of his glory he may grant you to be strengthened with power through his Spirit in your inner being, so that Christ may dwell in your hearts through faith—that you, being rooted and grounded in love, may have strength to comprehend with all the saints what is the breadth and length and height and depth, and to know the love of Christ that surpasses knowledge, that you may be filled with all the fullness of God. (Eph. 3:14–19)

KNOWING WHO WE ARE

READING FOR THE DAY: EPHESIANS 1:15-23

For this reason, because I have heard of your faith in the Lord Jesus and your love toward all the saints, I do not cease to give thanks for you, remembering you in my prayers, that the God of our Lord Jesus Christ, the Father of glory, may give you a spirit of wisdom and of revelation in the knowledge of him, having the eyes of your hearts enlightened, that you may know what is the hope to which he has called you, what are the riches of his glorious inheritance in the saints, and what is the immeasurable greatness of his power toward us who believe.

EPHESIANS 1:15-19

Consider one more prayer for the knowledge of God. In my discovery of the importance of spiritual knowledge, I was drawn to the passage we read today before I discovered that same essential prayer in the other three Prison Epistles. I have grown a great deal since then—in understanding of Scripture, in theological learning, in life experiences and, I trust, in spiritual depth. But at no point in this growth have I had to retract my conviction of the centrality of the concept of the knowledge of God. On the contrary, everything I have studied has been an extension of the discovery that began with Ephesians 1.

Notice that the familiar pattern begins with verse 15. Paul not only stated that he was praying for his readers, but he identified precisely what he prayed for them. His constant prayer was that God, the Father of the Lord Jesus Christ, would "give you a spirit of wisdom and of revelation in the knowledge [*epignosis*] of him" (v. 17). In this way the eyes of our hearts are enlightened so that we might "know" the hope to which he has called us, the riches that are ours in Christ, and the immeasurably great power that raised Christ from the dead . . . which is the very power that has raised us from spiritual death (1:18–20; 2:1–5). It is essential to note that, in terms of the three ideas of hope, riches, and power, the apostle was not praying that we would have them, or receive them. He prayed that we would know, since we are "in Christ," that they are already ours.

Now look back to 1:3–14. Those verses are an extraordinary doxology (a word of praise) in which Paul praises the God and Father of our Lord Jesus Christ, "who has blessed us in Christ with every spiritual blessing in the heavenly places." He then lists these blessings, starting with the fact that we were chosen (known) from before the creation of the world. "In love he predestined us for adoption . . . through Jesus Christ." All this was freely given to us through his beloved Son, who has redeemed us through his blood, and through whom God lavished his grace upon us as part of his grand purpose to unite all things under the lordship of Christ. And we were included "in Christ" when we heard the word of truth, the gospel, and having believed, we were sealed in him with the promised Holy Spirit. And all this was "to the praise of his glory" (vv. 6, 12, 14).

Once we comprehend the extent to which God has blessed us in Christ, we are overwhelmed with praise and humility. But that is just our problem—we don't comprehend. We have been adopted into the richest family in the universe and we are constantly lamenting our poverty! When Paul prayed for a spirit of wisdom and revelation, I believe he was praying that we would actually grasp the meaning of the praise he was offering in 1:3–14. It is hard to think of a single portion of Scripture that reveals more of the gracious work of God in salvation than those verses. But they are not simply words; they set forth the spiritual blessings that are already ours in Christ. The prayer is that we would know this in the very core of our being. And knowing in this sense will cause us to live differently, as we noted in the prayer of Colossians 1.

There is one other aspect of our knowledge of God that is evident in this passage. It is that knowing God includes a relationship with each of the persons of the divine Trinity. God the Father has blessed us with every spiritual blessing. He has done this in and through God the Son, and this is communicated to us, and sealed in our hearts, by the ministry of God the Holy Spirit. "Knowing God," therefore, means knowing the Father and the Son and the Holy Spirit. The triune nature of God is never explained in Scripture intellectually or philosophically, but it is revealed in our experience with God as he saves us. In addition to Ephesians 1, look up Ephesians 2:18, 22; 3:14–19; 4:3–5; 2 Thessalonians 2:13–14; and 1 Peter 1:1–2, and mark specific references to the three persons of the Holy Trinity at work in our salvation.[10]

It is therefore our privilege to know communion with God on a level that was not yet made known to Moses, even in the intimacy of his relationship. He prayed for the knowledge of God, and God was pleased to answer. But an ever greater knowledge awaited the coming of his Son, and that knowledge is ours. May God be pleased to give us more and more of "a spirit of wisdom and revelation" to lead us more and more into the knowledge of God.

> For God, who said, "Let light shine out of darkness," has shone in our hearts to give the light of the knowledge of the glory of God in the face of Jesus Christ. (2 Cor. 4:6)

TRUE SABBATH-REST

READING FOR THE DAY: HEBREWS 3:7-4:5

As it is said, "Today, if you hear his voice, do not harden your hearts as in the rebellion." For who were those who heard and yet rebelled? Was it not all those who left Egypt led by Moses? And with whom was he provoked for forty years? Was it not with those who sinned, whose bodies fell in the wilderness? And to whom did he swear that they would not enter his rest, but to those who were disobedient? . . . For we who have believed enter that rest.

HEBREWS 3:15-18; 4:3

The Lord said, "My Presence will go with you, and I will give you rest" (Ex. 33:14). Finally, Moses received the blessing he had so doggedly sought. He was able to remove the terrifying prospect of God's sending his people on without him. His patient intercession was rewarded, and it would be the Lord himself who would take them into the Promised Land. But our reading from Hebrews raises the question of a greater rest.

The reference to rest in Exodus 33:14 means the people of Israel dwelling in the land of their fathers, the land promised to them by an oath (cf. 33:1; Psalm 95; Heb. 3:16–19). It was to be a place where they would be free from the prospect of slavery, a place to live in peace, and preeminently, a place where they could meet with the God whose presence was in their midst. Therefore it is called a place of rest. The word *rest* comes into our English language as the word *sabbath*.

Simply a physical resting, or a cessation of activity, is not the rest, the *Sabbath*, of Scripture. That kind of rest can only be known by being in the presence of God. It is necessary to slow down physically and mentally and to find the place of quiet in order to begin to know rest, but the rest itself is not essentially physical. The Pharisees of Jesus' day had forgotten this point. They thought of the Sabbath as an entity in itself, rather than as a God-given mandate to stop one form of activity in order to allow for a quiet time to renew a sense of his presence.

So there can be a *place* of sabbath-rest, and a *time* or *day* of sabbath-rest. But the deepest form of sabbath-rest comes in answer to prayer. Moses regularly went to God in the tent of meeting and spoke with him face-to-face; he was constant in his intercession for the people, and finally he heard the word he was waiting for, "I will give you rest." God gives the real *sabbath*.

The basis for looking beyond the immediate use of the word "rest" in the Lord's response to Moses is the teaching of Hebrews 3 and 4. The writer has in view both the rest of entering the land (3:7–19) and the rest of the seventh day (4:4). However, there is more. He makes it clear that "the promise of entering his rest still stands" (4:1) and that "there remains a Sabbath rest for the people of God" (4:9). Those early forms of Sabbath point to a much more profound *sabbath*. It is a sabbath-rest to be found in trusting ourselves to Jesus Christ. *He* is the fulfillment of the Sabbath—not a time or a place, but a Person. "For we who have believed enter that rest" (4:3). Here is yet another example of how the study of Exodus 33 and 34 calls us to center our lives on Jesus. While Moses may have been anxious about finding the presence of God, we can be sure where it can be found—in the person of our Lord and Savior, our older brother, our high priest, our friend, the Lord Jesus Christ.

But there is a difference between the truth about the sabbath-rest and the actual entering into the experience of rest in Christ. In closing, reflect on the hymn that has become my favorite:

> *Jesus, I am resting, resting in the joy of what thou art;*
> *I am finding out the greatness of thy loving heart.*
> *Thou hast bid me gaze upon thee, as thy beauty fills my soul,*
> *for by thy transforming power, thou hast made me whole.*
>
> *O how great thy loving kindness, vaster, broader than the sea!*
> *O how marvelous thy goodness lavished all on me!*
> *Yes, I rest in thee, Beloved, know what wealth of grace is thine,*
> *know thy certainty of promise, and have made it mine.*
>
> *Ever lift thy face upon me as I work and wait for thee;*
> *resting 'neath thy smile, Lord Jesus, earth's dark shadows flee.*
> *Brightness of my Father's glory, sunshine of my Father's face,*
> *keep me ever trusting, resting, fill me with thy grace.*

(JEAN SOPHIA PIGOTT, 1876)

ENTERING THE REST

READING FOR THE DAY: HEBREWS 4:6-13

*Since therefore it remains for some to enter it, and those who formerly received
the good news failed to enter because of disobedience, again he appoints a
certain day, "Today," saying through David so long afterward, in the words
already quoted, "Today, if you hear his voice, do not harden your hearts."
For if Joshua had given them rest, God would not have spoken of another day
later on. So then, there remains a Sabbath rest for the people of God.*

HEBREWS 4:6-9

"So then, there remains a Sabbath rest for the people of God" (v. 9). The reading from Hebrews makes it very clear that the rest of entering the land was to find a deeper fulfillment in what we can know "today" (vv. 7–8). The word "today" (from Psalm 95) is a reference to the coming of Christ into the world. In that sense, we are living in that same *today*, as were those who first read these words from Hebrews. On one level, the writer explains, we enter that rest when we come to faith in Christ (Heb. 4:3). As we have already considered, Jesus is the rest that is promised. But there is another meaning to the word "rest." Note that the writer goes on to present the idea of sabbath-rest in Christ as an experience that is available for those who "strive to enter that rest" (v. 11). By implication, then, there are some who are trusting in Christ for salvation, but who are not experiencing the rest that is theirs through him.

This passage defines just what is meant by rest. Look again at verse 10: "for whoever has entered God's rest has also rested from his works as God did from his." There needs to be a point at which we stop insisting that our endeavors are necessary to complete the work of God in our lives. In one sense, we could never have become Christians if we didn't stop working and, by faith, simply receive the gift of salvation. But we still live under the compulsive pull to do our part. Therefore, we do not know the peace—the rest in our spirits—that comes from knowing with certainty that God is truly sovereign and active, and that in him we are complete. For most of us that requires the deeper knowledge of the grace of God that comes through time and experience with him.

The initial fulfillment of rest beautifully illustrates the process that is involved. In the spiritual pilgrimage of Israel there were two major crossing points—the Red Sea and the Jordan River. The first crossing, through the Red Sea, was a move from slavery to liberty by means of the power of God and of the blood of the Passover Lamb. God redeemed Israel by grace, just as we are saved by grace through faith.

But although redeemed, God's people did not immediately enter their rest. Instead they entered a period of wilderness, characterized by constant doubts about whether God would stand by his promises. This wilderness period was very important to their spiritual growth as, time and time again, they were given tangible evidence of God's love and his power at work on their behalf. Just as we do, the Israelites needed simple lessons in the goodness of God in the infancy of their experience with him. But the wilderness phase of their spiritual journey was prolonged unnecessarily when they faced a crisis and refused to believe that God was greater than the giants in the land (Numbers 13–14; Psalm 95). God was ready to give them rest, but they would not have it on his terms. Consequently, for a whole generation they wandered aimlessly until he brought them again to a time of entering in under the leadership of Joshua.

The second crossing of Israel was the crossing of the Jordan. They moved from the wilderness to rest in the land of promise. This represents the experience of those who already have experienced the grace of salvation, moving from the wilderness of doubt and struggle to a place of knowing the Lord. It is a knowing that allows them to rest in the strength of his presence and promises.

It is important to note that once Israel crossed into the Promised Land, they didn't stop sinning nor did all of their doubts go away. They were finally in the place where God wanted them to be, but life went on with its ups and downs. In the same way, the rest promised in Scripture is not to be thought of as entering some kind of sinless state (or heaven, as pictured in so many gospel songs). When we enter the sabbath-rest, we live our lives for Christ as we always have, with varied successes or failures. But there is a difference—deep within our spirits we know that God really is God, and that his love through Jesus is real. It is that knowledge that sustains us, no matter what the circumstances may bring (see Paul's spirit of rest in Phil. 4:11–13).

"Let us strive to enter that rest." That striving, ironically, is to learn to stop working on our own and to learn more and more of the gracious character of God. This is what God was about to teach Moses.

YOU MUST GO WITH US

READING FOR THE DAY: EXODUS 33:12-17; LUKE 11:1-13

"For how shall it be known that I have found favor in your sight, I and your people? Is it not in your going with us, so that we are distinct, I and your people, from every other people on the face of the earth?" And the LORD said to Moses, "This very thing that you have spoken I will do, for you have found favor in my sight, and I know you by name."

EXODUS 33:16-17

"And I tell you, ask, and it will be given to you; seek, and you will find; knock, and it will be opened to you. For everyone who asks receives, and the one who seeks finds, and to the one who knocks it will be opened."

LUKE 11:9-10

Every time during the past several years that I have had to face a personal change or a change for the church I was serving as a pastor, I have gone back and prayed these words based on today's passage: "Lord, if your presence doesn't go with us, please don't allow us to make a move, because it is only your presence that makes us different from anyone else." It is so easy to jump at anything new (and in the ministry of the church that usually means something bigger with a greater opportunity to be a witness) without honestly and patiently seeking the face of God. It is frightening to realize that with our slick fund-raising techniques and skill in marketing the church, we know how to make a ministry "successful" whether the Lord is there or not! So we need to pray these words more than ever before.

Notice that Moses offered this prayer after the Lord had just said that his presence would go with him (v. 14). At first, Moses wouldn't take no for an answer; now he seemed to be unwilling to take a yes, or at least to take the answer at face value. It was almost as though he didn't know when to stop asking and to start offering thanks.

But there is another possible explanation: Peter Enns, in his commentary on Exodus, points out that the "you" in verse 14 is singular. It could have a plural sense, but it could also mean that the Lord was still expressing his intention to start over again with Moses as the founder of his chosen people (32:10). "In other words, the argument of Exodus 33:12–16 serves the singular purpose of ensuring that the people will not be left behind."[11] In the ESV there is a change in person in verse 15 that reflects a literal reading of the original, "If your presence will not go with *me*, do not bring *us* up from here." Perhaps the Lord was promising his presence to all the people by promising it to Moses—but Moses would not take that for granted. In the statements that follow, Moses makes it clear that anything the Lord will do for Moses, he must also do for his people.

Before we find fault with Moses' tenacity (his *impudence* to use the words of Luke 11:8), note the Lord's response in Exodus 33:17: "This very thing that you have spoken I will do, for you have found favor in my sight, and I know you by name." In addition to knowing him, the Lord says that he was actually pleased with him, and in this setting it means he was pleased with the way Moses prayed.

This is both a confirmation and an illustration of Jesus' teaching about prayer in Luke 11. After teaching his disciples to pray the Lord's Prayer, he told the parable of the persistent friend. Jesus then applied the parable by giving a command to do the kind of determined praying that Moses did. "*Keep on* asking, seeking, knocking" is the sense of the verb in Greek. Then Jesus very emphatically reassured his disciples that this kind of praying is pleasing to God. He used the powerful analogy of the love of human fathers to that of the infinite love of the heavenly Father (vv. 11–13). If we are pleased to hear from our children and love to give them the best that we are able, how much more will that be true of God.

In the light of Moses' prayers for the presence of God with the people, it is worth noting that the "good gift" to be given by the Father, to those who ask, is the Holy Spirit. Surely, of all the things we can and should pray about and for, this request is by far the most significant. In one sense, that prayer was offered by Jesus to the Father, who answered by sending the "Helper, to be with you forever" (John 14:16–18). But we need to pray persistently for a sensitivity to that presence. This is what Paul meant in Ephesians 5:18 when he gave the command, "Be filled with the Spirit." As with Jesus' command to pray, in Luke 11:9, this command has an ongoing sense of "be being filled," "keep being filled." It is also the plural—"you together," "you the church, be continuously filled with the presence of the Spirit." After all, as Moses told the Lord, that is what makes a gathering of people distinctly the people of God—God is in their midst. If we lose this, we are no different from any other assembly. We need to pray constantly for a continuous experience of the Spirit's presence and power in our lives and in the churches we are part of. The old saying is true, "You have all of the Holy Spirit, but does the Holy Spirit have all of you?"

DAY TWENTY-TWO

SHOW ME YOUR GLORY

READING FOR THE DAY: EXODUS 33:18-20

Moses said, "Please show me your glory." And he said, "I will make all my
goodness pass before you and will proclaim before you my name 'The LORD.'
And I will be gracious to whom I will be gracious, and will show mercy on whom
I will show mercy. But," he said, "you cannot see my face, for man shall not see
me and live."

EXODUS 33:18-20

M oses said, "Please, show me your glory." This request actually
to behold God's glory is one of the boldest in all of Scripture.
"Glory" in this context refers to a revelation of what theologians call
the *essence* of God. That is, whatever it is that makes God, *God*, is God's
glory. Once the tabernacle was actually erected, the Scripture says that
"the cloud covered the tent of meeting, and the glory of the LORD filled
the tabernacle" (Ex. 40:34). Later in Israel's history, the same expression
would be used of the filling of the temple (1 Kings 8:1). This was the
purest expression of the majesty of God, and it would dwell between
the outstretched wings of the cherubim in the Most Holy Place.

Once a year the high priest was to come into this Most Holy
Place with the blood of the lamb to make atonement for the sins of
the people. He fully expected to be struck dead if there was anything
unacceptable to God (Leviticus 16). Isaiah found himself in the
presence of this glory, and he fell on his face in terror. He said, "Woe
is me! For I am lost . . . for my eyes have seen the King, the LORD
of Hosts" (Isa. 6:5). And yet, this is the glory that Moses prayed he
might see. Perhaps he didn't fully understand what he was asking for,
but I am more inclined to think that he did understand and that his
passion to know God was unbounded. He knew he had found favor
in God's eyes and he wanted more.

But he was asking for more than God would give. The Lord didn't

78

deny his request, but note in verse 19 that there is a very significant change in what will be revealed. Moses asked to see God's glory, and the Lord said he would cause all his *goodness* to pass in front of him. If "glory" refers to the expression of essence or majesty of God, "goodness" refers to his benefits, the good things he bestows on those he blesses. Those benefits unfold as God proclaims his name (33:19), which he does in 34:5–7. As those verses make clear, God's proclaiming his name means explaining his character—the way he works and the things he does.

This distinction can be very helpful as we try to understand just what it is we are seeking when we pray to know more of God. If it means seeking for the glory of God, then the image in my mind is that of some sort of abstract grasping for light. On the other hand, knowing the goodness of God is something tangible. I can take aspects of that goodness and dwell on them. The psalmist did this in Psalm 103:2: "Bless the LORD, O my soul, and forget not all his benefits," which he then proceeded to list through the rest of the psalm. One medieval mystic wrote of knowing God as the "Cloud of the Unknowing." I have a great deal of respect for the contemplative tradition, but I believe the concept of "cloud" seriously misses the point of our text.

There certainly is an indefinable, unknowable majesty about God. But that is not the aspect of his nature that he has chosen to reveal, either to Moses or to us. He wants us to know his *goodness*. Seeking for what God clearly does not choose to reveal can open the way to some of the forms of thinking and meditation that are characteristic of the various Eastern religions, including the so-called New Age movement. That is why we must let the Scripture restrain as well as direct us in our spiritual pilgrimage.

Actually, it is not quite accurate to say that the Lord would not reveal his glory to Moses. It is better to say that it was not *time* for Moses to see that glory. He certainly experienced a greater measure of glory when he was taken into the very presence of God at death. And in a spectacular manifestation of glory, his prayer was finally answered on the Mount of Transfiguration when he, along with Elijah and three of the disciples, saw Jesus in all of his majesty. Jesus was praying and "his face changed, and his clothes became as bright as a flash of lightning"

(Luke 9:28–31 NIV). That is the glory that we, too, will someday know. But it is not time.

The Puritan commentator Matthew Henry added a remark to his discussion of this passage that appears in a source I cannot recall, and it is a fitting word with which to conclude: "In the meantime, let us adore the height of what we do know and the depth of what we do not."

THE CLEFT OF THE ROCK

READING FOR THE DAY: EXODUS 33:18-23

And the LORD said, "Behold, there is a place by me where you shall stand on the rock, and while my glory passes by I will put you in a cleft of the rock, and I will cover you with my hand until I have passed by. Then I will take away my hand, and you shall see my back, but my face shall not be seen."

EXODUS 33:21-23

The truth of God's sovereignty stands out in the concluding verses of chapter 33. In the next chapter the scene shifts to the mountain, but in the reading for today Moses was still in the tent of meeting that had been pitched on the outskirts of the camp. When the Lord said, "I will be gracious to whom I will be gracious, and will show mercy on whom I will show mercy" (v. 19), he was making it clear that Moses would learn of the goodness of God only because the Lord was pleased to reveal it. Neither Moses nor any of us have any right to know God. In fact, if we got our rights, it would actually be judgment. The apostle Paul quoted this statement in a rigorous defense of the sovereignty of God and concluded, "So then it depends not on human will or exertion, but on God, who has mercy" (Rom. 9:16).

There is much to be said for boldness in prayer and for believing that God is honored when we ask him for great things. But the fact remains that God is God. He is the Almighty Sovereign, Ruler of all of his creation. Although he graciously welcomes us into his presence and condescends in remarkable ways to accommodate our weaknesses, we must never forget who he is.

But God is not aloof or capricious. He is good, and he is merciful. Even though Moses was asking too much when he asked to see God's glory, the Lord was honored by such a bold prayer and provided a way for Moses to take in all that he would choose to reveal of himself. The contrast between God's *glory* and his *goodness* was given to Moses in terms of the difference between seeing the "face" of God, which was not permitted (v. 20), and seeing the "back" or "afterglow" of God (v. 23).

The phrase "cleft of the rock" (v. 22) is a poetic one that excites the imagination. One can picture Moses on the mountain gaining an ever greater awareness of the approaching majesty. The term "glory" can also be translated *heaviness*. And, as Moses sensed the Lord in his glory coming closer, there must have been that inward sense of pressure that all of us have felt in those "heavy" moments. Then, at just the right time, Moses would have been gently pushed back into a crevice where a rock had split and a shadow would cover his vision. He knew that he was closer to the glory than any mortal had ever known in his earthly existence! The experience of that moment would have been overwhelming—but it was also unique and personal. It is important to note that what was to endure was the spoken word of God, "I will proclaim before you my name," which Moses was later to write in a book. What has been given to us is not the experience but the Word, as a means for us to know God for ourselves.

But in reflecting on the experience of Moses, it is encouraging to note that it was the Lord who provided that opportunity for Moses to know more of God himself. The Lord said he would direct him to the rock on which he should stand, and "while my glory passes by I will put you in a cleft of the rock, and I will cover you with my hand until I have passed by. Then I will take away my hand, and you shall see my back" (33:22–23). This was the Lord *actively* revealing himself to Moses. It is hard to believe that God will go to such lengths to let us know him. We may acknowledge this truth theologically, and it is certainly evident in the fact of Jesus' coming to be among us. Nevertheless, it is still hard to grasp in a personal way, *but it is true!* "Rock of Ages, cleft for me, let me hide myself in thee."

> Lord, I freely acknowledge your sovereignty and bow before you as Lord of all creation. Now, give me wisdom and understanding to acknowledge just as freely your willingness to let me know you in all of your goodness.

DAY TWENTY-FOUR
THE VOICE OF GOD

READING FOR THE DAY: EXODUS 34:1-5; 1 KINGS 19:1-13

*The LORD said to Moses, "Cut for yourself two tablets of stone like the first,
and I will write on the tablets the words that were on the first tablets, which
you broke." . . . The LORD descended in the cloud and stood with him there, and
proclaimed the name of the LORD.*

EXODUS 34:1, 5

*And after the fire the sound of a low whisper. And when Elijah heard it,
he wrapped his face in his cloak and went out and stood at the entrance of the
cave. And behold, there came a voice to him and said, "What are you doing
here, Elijah?"*

1 KINGS 19:12-13

We are part of a very experience-centered generation. That experience orientation can mean the search for perfect health, self-esteem, "possibility thinking," or the quest for "the spiritual life" with very little concern for defining what is spiritual. But the root of all of these varied desires is the need to experience life with relatively little regard for the substance behind the experience. Given the fact that this is the environment in which we are living, we need to recognize how easily we can put our quest to know God into the same sort of framework.

This is why today's reading is critical to our series of meditations. Moses was to prepare to receive that which could be *written down*. First came the tablets for the Ten Commandments, but there was more. Before he returned to the people, he was told to "write these words" (34:27–28) which would have included all that God said. When we finally come to the actual encounter on the mountain, what Moses was given was not a feeling or some sort of indefinable experience; he was given a *word*. He heard the voice of God who "proclaimed the name of the LORD." This is not to deny that Moses had a profound experience in God's presence. He did, and his face shone as a consequence (34:29). That was deeply

personal to Moses. But what endured, to be passed on to future generations, was the written record of the voice of God. *The substance behind the
experience was the Word of God.*

The account of Elijah on this same mountain has striking similarities.
After being directed to go to Sinai for a time apart, Elijah traveled "forty
days and forty nights to Horeb, the mount of God" (1 Kings 19:8). After
a night's rest in a cave, he was told by the Lord to "'Go out and stand on
the mount before the LORD.' And behold, the LORD passed by." Then came
a powerful wind, but that was not where the Lord was to be found. Nor
was he in an earthquake or a fire that followed. But finally there came
a "low whisper" (I love the *King James* phrase, a "still small voice"), and
Elijah knew that God was present in the voice. He covered his face and
went out to listen (19:11–13). As was true for Moses, the substance of
Elijah's experience was the voice—*the Word of God.*

All of this brings us back to the Bible as the basis for our spiritual
pilgrimage, if that pilgrimage is to lead us to a true knowledge of God. We
must learn to be still and listen for the voice of God. But as we do so, it
will come to us from the pages of Scripture and will be brought to living
reality through the witness of the Holy Spirit.

GRACE OR JUDGMENT

READING FOR THE DAY: EXODUS 34:4-7

The LORD passed before him and proclaimed, "The LORD, the LORD, a God merciful and gracious, slow to anger, and abounding in steadfast love and faithfulness, keeping steadfast love for thousands, forgiving iniquity and transgression and sin, but who will by no means clear the guilty, visiting the iniquity of the fathers on the children and the children's children, to the third and the fourth generation."

EXODUS 34:6-7

We have come to the high point of Exodus 32–34. The Lord actually proclaimed his name to Moses. This means that the Lord explained or revealed his character to Moses, and through Moses to us. Martin Luther called this the "sermon on the Name of God." It was God's answer to Moses' prayer to be shown God's glory. However, as we have seen, the Lord answered it the way he saw fit, not necessarily in terms of what Moses expected.

This is the third of the great moments of revelation of God's name in Exodus. The first revelation of God's name was at the burning bush (Ex. 3:14–15; 6:2–8), and then there was additional revelation the first time he wrote down the Ten Commandments (20:1–6). In the first instance the Lord announced his name and declared that he, as the Lord, would be faithful to the covenant he made with their fathers to deliver his people from bondage. By the time they got to Mount Sinai to receive the Ten, the people had experienced that deliverance, as the Lord reminded them in the first words he spoke from the mountain, "I am the LORD your God, who brought you out of Egypt, out of the land of slavery." The emphasis in this second revelation would seem to be on the people's obligation in the covenant relationship. The element of judgment and the Lord's jealousy and justice are very evident in this passage.

But by the time the Lord came to further reveal himself in Exodus

34, the people and Moses had both had significant spiritual experiences. They had witnessed the fearsome majesty of God, they had all actually heard his voice, and they had known the potential for their own depravity. Now, they were ready to receive a deeper understanding of the nature of the God who had saved and disciplined them.

This illustrates my conviction that, however ardently we may seek for a greater knowledge of God, it will only come at the pace God determines. And it will come in ways such that our experiences will allow us to incorporate the greater revelations meaningfully into our lives. In the case of Moses and the Israelites, it was this time that the Lord chose to explain more fully who he is.

Before we consider the treasury of particular words and phrases, consider the overall message. The Lord emphatically revealed himself, first and foremost, as a God of grace, love, and mercy. Far too often our first instinct is to think of God in terms of his sovereignty and majesty. And when we consider our own sinfulness, we add to that impression the fearful sense of his holiness and judgment. These attributes are certainly true about God, and they were impressed on the people of Israel as well. But in this passage we have *God himself* telling us what he wants us to know about him, and this is what he says first: "a God merciful and gracious, slow to anger, and abounding in steadfast love and faithfulness, keeping steadfast love for thousands, forgiving iniquity and transgression and sin" (34:6–7a). Then he went on to speak of his justice, for that is just as much a part of his name as the mercy. His justice is also part of "all of his goodness" (33:19). But it seems evident, from the order in which he revealed his character, that it was his intention that we first of all focus on the fact that he is a gracious and merciful God.

And if that was true for Moses, consider how this wonderful truth has been brought to even greater fulfillment in the coming of Jesus. As we have seen, the covenant name, the LORD, has its highest meaning in the name of Jesus. And because of Jesus, God has a new name. It is "Father." In fact, as children adopted into the household of God, we call him "Abba" (Rom. 8:15; Gal. 4:6), the most intimate word for Father.

Let these next several meditations be times of rejoicing as all of the goodness of God passes in front of us.

Enter his gates with thanksgiving,
*   and his courts with praise!*
Give thanks to him; bless his name!

For the LORD is good;
*   his steadfast love endures forever,*
and his faithfulness to all generations. (Ps. 100:4–5)

GOD IS GOOD

READING FOR THE DAY: LAMENTATIONS 3:16-33

"The LORD is my portion," says my soul, "therefore I will hope in him. The LORD is good to those who wait for him, to the soul who seeks him. . . . For the Lord will not cast off forever, but, though he cause grief, he will have compassion according to the abundance of his steadfast love."

LAMENTATIONS 3:24-25, 31-32

The LORD passed before him and proclaimed, 'The LORD, the LORD, a God merciful and gracious, slow to anger, and abounding in steadfast love and faithfulness, keeping steadfast love for thousands, forgiving iniquity and transgression and sin'" (Ex. 34:6–7). It was an unusually rewarding experience to take the words found in Exodus 34:6–7 and, using the cross-reference part of my study Bible, to trace the themes all over Scripture. This Exodus passage is actually quoted in seven other Old Testament passages (Num. 14:18; Neh. 9:17; Ps. 86:15; 103:7–8; 145:8; Joel 2:13; Jonah 4:2). In the next four meditations we will see how God's people held on to the various aspects of the goodness of God to sustain them in the midst of whatever life had to offer—whether good times or bad times. As you read the suggested Scripture portions, watch for the constant reference to the goodness, or steadfast love, or faithfulness of God. These are not simply abstract ideas, but ways in which a good and merciful God has cared for his people.

One important truth that the Scripture lessons make abundantly clear is that the goodness and graciousness of God do not mean some guarantee of an easy or comfortable life. In fact, it seems that it is out of the ashes of defeat and in times of affliction, the affirmation of the goodness of God is all the sweeter. This thought is basic to a full appreciation of the reading for today.

The book of Lamentations was written by Jeremiah as he walked through the rubble of Jerusalem, the city of God. His entire ministry had been devoted to warning of judgment unless the people turned back to God. But in spite of all of his efforts, that judgment had come and the Babylonian armies had ruined his beloved city. Jeremiah wrote at a time of despair, "Remember my affliction and my wanderings, the wormwood and the gall! My soul continually remembers it and is bowed down within me" (3:19–20). And it is in this setting, not in a time of prosperity, that he recognized his only hope—the truth of the goodness of God.

> But this I call to mind, and therefore I have hope: The steadfast love of the LORD never ceases; his mercies never come to an end; they are new every morning; great is your faithfulness. . . . For the LORD will not cast off forever, but, though he cause grief, he will have compassion according to the abundance of his steadfast love. (3:21–23, 31–32)

Take a moment to recall some period of great difficulty. Perhaps for you it is the present. Although we struggle for explanations, almost invariably deliverance from a sense of despair comes when, like Jeremiah, we rest in the hope of God's love and goodness.

One of the most difficult times that I ever passed through was dealing with the death of my father. God used Psalm 13 to give me a sense of peace, and as I turned to that psalm again and again, I realized that its power was rooted in an affirmation of the goodness of God.

> *How long, O LORD? Will you forget me forever?*
> *How long will you hide your face from me?*
> *How long must I take counsel in my soul*
> *and have sorrow in my heart all the day?*
> *How long shall my enemy be exalted over me?*
>
> *Consider and answer me, O LORD my God;*
> *light up my eyes, lest I sleep the sleep of death,*
> *lest my enemy say, "I have prevailed over him,"*
> *lest my foes rejoice because I am shaken.*
>
> *But I have trusted in your steadfast love;*
> *my heart shall rejoice in your salvation.*
> *I will sing to the LORD,*
> *because he has dealt bountifully with me.* (Psalm 13)

GOD IS PATIENT

READING FOR THE DAY: NEHEMIAH 9:5-37; EXODUS 34:6-7

"They refused to obey and were not mindful of the wonders that you performed among them. . . . But you are a God ready to forgive, gracious and merciful, slow to anger and abounding in steadfast love, and did not forsake them. . . . Many years you bore with them and warned them by your Spirit through your prophets. Yet they would not give ear. Therefore you gave them into the hand of the peoples of the lands. Nevertheless, in your great mercies you did not make an end of them or forsake them, for you are a gracious and merciful God."

NEHEMIAH 9:17, 30-31

The LORD passed before him and proclaimed, "The LORD, the LORD, a God merciful and gracious, slow to anger, and abounding in steadfast love and faithfulness, keeping steadfast love for thousands, forgiving iniquity and transgression and sin."

EXODUS 34:6-7

The reading for today takes us to the time of Israel's return from exile in Babylon. Even after the terrible judgment that was described by Jeremiah, the people continued to need godly leaders to bring them to repentance and renewal. In the return from the exile God used Ezra and Nehemiah for that purpose. The priest Ezra is called by the Jews the "second Moses." Just as Moses brought order to the people of God after their deliverance from Egypt, so Ezra reorganized the people after their deliverance from Babylon.

The long prayer of confession in today's reading grew out of a time of renewal led by Ezra and Nehemiah. They had gathered the people together and, for an entire day, read to them the Law. "They read from the book, from the Law of God, clearly, and they gave the sense, so that the people understood the reading" (Neh. 8:8). Not surprisingly, the account says that as the people heard the Law read, they began to "mourn and weep." But Nehemiah told them to stop weeping and instead to prepare a feast—"Do not be grieved, *for the joy of the* LORD *is your strength*" (8:10). Nehemiah wanted them to understand that while the Law clearly condemned much of what they had been doing, ultimately their hope rested in the compassionate and merciful nature of God, not on the level of their obedience. This was not to ignore or excuse their sin, for an extensive confession of that sin was prepared and signed (9:38). But woven throughout the confession was a total resting upon the goodness of God.

The aspect of God's goodness that was of particular importance to the people was God's *patience*. To use the time-honored word from the *King James Version*, he is "long-suffering." That is a picturesque word and summarizes the way the Lord dealt with his people over their long history of willfulness and disobedience. "But they and our fathers acted presumptuously and stiffened their neck and did not obey your commandments. They refused to obey and were not mindful of the wonders that you performed among them, but they stiffened their neck and appointed a leader to return to their slavery in Egypt. But you are a God ready to forgive, gracious and merciful, slow to anger and abounding in steadfast love [Note: this is a direct quotation of Exodus 34:6], and did not forsake them" (9:16–17).

And so they moved through their history—"Even when they had made for themselves a golden calf . . . you in your great mercies did not forsake them in the wilderness" (vv.18–19); "and delighted themselves in your great goodness" (v. 25); "and according to your great mercies you gave them saviors" (v. 27); "you heard from heaven, and many times you delivered them according to your mercies" (v. 28); "Nevertheless, in your great mercies you did not make an end of them or forsake them, for you are a gracious and merciful God" (v. 31). Based on this knowledge of their long-suffering God, they prayed for forgiveness to "the great, the mighty, and the awesome God, *who keeps covenant and steadfast love*" (v. 32).

For some reason it is easier to apply this great lesson to others than to our own stories. The Lord could be patient with Israel, but then we wonder how he can put up with our disobedience time after time after time. But just like the people under Ezra, we need to look back and celebrate the fact that it has been God's perseverance, not ours, that has kept us on the path. Our strength, like theirs, is the "joy of the LORD." And in a contemplation of the goodness and patience of God who is "slow to anger," we will be brought to a true place of repentance. All of this brings new meaning to the statement of Paul:

> Or do you presume on the riches of his kindness and forbearance and patience, not knowing that God's kindness is meant to lead you to repentance? (Rom. 2:4)

DAY TWENTY-EIGHT
GOD IS LOYAL

READING FOR THE DAY: PSALM 107:1-9, 15, 21, 31-32, 43;
118:1-4, 28-29; EXODUS 34:6-7

*Oh give thanks to the L*ORD*, for he is good,*
for his steadfast love endures forever!
*Let the redeemed of the L*ORD *say so,*
whom he has redeemed from trouble.

PSALM 107:1-2

You are my God, and I will give thanks to you;
you are my God; I will extol you.
*Oh give thanks to the L*ORD*, for he is good;*
for his steadfast love endures forever!

PSALM 118:28-29

There is a wonderful aspect of the goodness of God that is celebrated throughout the Scripture. In Hebrew the word for this is *hesed*, and it has such a rich meaning that it is translated in various ways. The word appears twice in God's revelation to Moses, and in the ESV it is translated "steadfast love"—"abounding in *steadfast love*" and "keeping *steadfast love* for thousands." In the reading for today, the psalmist calls on us to "give thanks to the LORD, for he is good; for his *steadfast love* endures forever!" (Ps. 107:1; 118:1, 29). Later in Psalm 107 the refrain is repeated over and over, "Let them thank the LORD for his *steadfast love*" (vv. 8, 15, 21, 31). Psalm 136 is a litany in which every one of the twenty-six thoughts is answered with "for his *steadfast love* endures forever." In other versions this word is translated as "love," "lovingkindness," "mercy," and "constancy."

The idea behind *hesed* is a particular kind of love. It is love that produces loyalty. That is why there was no redundancy for the Lord to reveal himself as the God who is both merciful and gracious, and the God who is "abounding in steadfast love [*hesed*]." As a way to emphasize the

93

constancy of that love, he added that he keeps or maintains "steadfast love [*hesed*] for thousands." The "thousands" probably refers not just to thousands of individuals, but to "a thousand generations" (Ex. 20:6 NIV). The people of God understood that once he made a promise or commitment, it was contrary to his nature to go back on his word. Love, in this sense, is rooted in the whole idea of his covenant. It is, therefore, integral to the revelation of his covenant name, the LORD.

If a single word must be used, "love" is probably better than "loyalty," because the sense of *hesed* includes the wonderful fact that the Lord *desires* to be in this covenant relationship. He is not simply fulfilling a contract that he would break if he hadn't committed to keeping it, even though there are times when he expresses himself as if that were the case.

Those of us who are married can identify with that feeling. We willingly and joyfully enter into the covenant known as marriage. There grows up a loyalty between a husband and wife that makes the covenant more than just a legally binding contract. But there are occasions when the relationship is strained. At those times, it is the unbreakable nature of the covenant that sustains the marriage until a reconciliation restores the joyful aspect of the loyalty. Magnify the loyalty within the marriage vow to an infinite degree and we begin to understand the depth of God's loyal love, his steadfast love. It is love that endures a thousand generations.

Is it any wonder that of all the characteristics of God's goodness that Israel celebrated, this is perhaps the one they rejoiced in the most? And, as it is with so many of the truths revealed in the Old Testament, the nature of God's steadfast love is brought to an even higher fulfillment in the person and work of Jesus Christ. Consider this word from Hebrews:

> So when God desired to show more convincingly to the heirs of the promise the unchangeable character of his purpose, he guaranteed it with an oath, so that by two unchangeable things, in which it is impossible for God to lie [God's nature and his covenant promise], we who have fled for refuge might have strong encouragement to hold fast to the hope set before us. We have this as a sure and steadfast anchor of the soul, a hope that enters into the inner place behind the curtain, where Jesus has gone as a forerunner on our behalf. (Heb. 6:17–20)

I will extol you, my God and King,
  and bless your name forever and ever.
Every day I will bless you
  and praise your name forever and ever. . . .

The LORD is gracious and merciful,
  slow to anger and abounding in steadfast love.
The LORD is good to all,
  and his mercy is over all that he has made. (Ps. 145:1–2, 8–9)

FORGIVENESS OF SIN

READING FOR THE DAY: PSALM 103; EXODUS 34:6-7

Bless the LORD, O my soul,
and all that is within me,
bless his holy name!

Bless the LORD, O my soul,
and forget not all his benefits,
who forgives all your iniquity,
who heals all your diseases,
who redeems your life from the pit,
who crowns you with steadfast love and mercy. . . .

For as high as the heavens are above the earth,
so great is his steadfast love toward those who fear him;
as far as the east is from the west,
so far does he remove our transgressions from us.

PSALM 103:1-4, 11-12

The psalm of David that we read today is one of the favorites of the people of God. We are called to praise the Lord from the very depths of our souls. One of the most important ways to give praise to our wonderful God is to "forget not all his benefits" (v. 2). David recited a list of the benefits that have come to us from the Lord who is "merciful and gracious, slow to anger and abounding in steadfast love [love, mercy, lovingkindness, covenant loyalty—*hesed*]" (v. 8). Remarkably, Exodus 34:6 is quoted yet another time.

Of all the benefits listed, the one David celebrated most passionately was the forgiveness of sin. It was not only the first benefit he mentioned (v. 3), but he returned to it after the citation of Exodus 34:6. The Lord's slowness to anger means that "he does not deal with us according to our sins, nor repay us according to our iniquities" (v. 10). Furthermore, "as far as the east is from the west, so far does he remove our transgressions from us" (v. 12), and like a compassionate father toward his children, so the Lord "shows compassion" and "remembers that we are dust" (v. 14). He understands our weakness and the depth of our rebellion far better than we do. Try to let your mind linger on those wonderful words. Perhaps we have come to take them for granted.

David certainly didn't take for granted the forgiveness of sin. On many occasions he had sought forgiveness but none more ardently than after his sin with Bathsheba came to light. "Have mercy on me, O God, according to your steadfast love [*hesed*]; according to your abundant mercy blot out my transgressions. Wash me thoroughly from my iniquity, and cleanse me from my sin" (Ps. 51:1–2).

Nor would the children of Israel have taken for granted forgiveness of sin. We need to remember the context of the passage in Exodus. The people had defied everything that God had told them. To be sure, they were judged for their sin (we will consider the matter of justice next), but Moses was being told that once the sin had been dealt with, *it was over*. With an emphatic statement, the Lord said that he would forgive "iniquity and transgression and sin," a description of the very things that had just gone on in the camp.

And of all people, we cannot take for granted the forgiveness of sin. We stand before God cleansed and welcomed with the same depth of compassion with which the prodigal son was welcomed home. If ever we are tempted to think of that as a minor "benefit," all we need to do is stop and consider the price that was paid. Think of our Lord Jesus on the cross. "For our sake he made him to be sin who knew no sin, so that in him we might become the righteousness of God" (2 Cor. 5:21). "In him we have redemption through his blood, the forgiveness of our trespasses, according to the riches of his grace" (Eph. 1:7).

Is this more than a doctrinal concept for you? Do you truly know yourself to be forgiven through the merits of Christ? I know that this is a serious struggle for many who love the Lord. After living this long in the faith, we should be more victorious over our flesh. But then we need to reflect not only on the work of Christ but also to remember that God knows far more of our "wickedness, rebellion, and sin" than we ever will—and he is the one who declares us forgiven. This is why the communion is called the "Eucharist"—the thanksgiving. We must come again and again to celebrate this mercy of God.

> *Blessed is the one whose transgression is forgiven,*
> > *whose sin is covered.*
> *Blessed is the man against whom the LORD counts no iniquity,*
> > *and in whose spirit there is no deceit.*
>
> *For when I kept silent, my bones wasted away*
> > *through my groaning all day long.*
> *For day and night your hand was heavy upon me;*
> > *my strength was dried up as by the heat of summer.*
>
> *I acknowledged my sin to you*
> > *and I did not cover my iniquity;*
> *I said, "I will confess my transgressions to the LORD,"*
> > *and you forgave the iniquity of my sin.* (Ps. 32:1–5, a psalm of David)

GOD IS JUST

READING FOR THE DAY: EXODUS 34:4-7; 20:1-6

So Moses cut two tablets of stone like the first. And he rose early in the morning and went up on Mount Sinai, as the LORD had commanded him, and took in his hand two tablets of stone. The LORD descended in the cloud and stood with him there, and proclaimed the name of the LORD. The LORD passed before him and proclaimed, "The LORD, the LORD, a God merciful and gracious, slow to anger, and abounding in steadfast love and faithfulness, keeping steadfast love for thousands, forgiving iniquity and transgression and sin, but who will by no means clear the guilty, visiting the iniquity of the fathers on the children and the children's children, to the third and the fourth generation."

EXODUS 34:4-7

As the revelation of God's name moves to the issue of "punishing the guilty," it is tempting to think that we have completed the unveiling of the goodness of God, which has been the theme of the last several meditations. But this cannot be so. The Lord said to Moses that in proclaiming his name to him, he would "make *all* [his] goodness pass before [him]" (33:19). The justice of God is an aspect of his goodness. It is absolutely essential to the working of the universe God created and pronounced "very good." What kind of world would this be if there were no standards, no right and wrong? (We are rapidly finding out!) It is our gracious and merciful God who has established and declared those standards. The fact that he holds the world to those standards is the essence of justice. Another of the "benefits" for which we give praise to God is that "the LORD works righteousness and justice for all who are oppressed" (Ps. 103:6). Our good God is righteous and administers justice. He "will by no means clear the guilty."

It is striking, however, to note the difference in the way the Lord spoke the first time he gave the Ten Commandments (Exodus 20) and the way he made himself known as he prepared to give them a second time. There is a reversal in the order of judgment and grace (cf. 20:5–6 and 34:6–7). As we have already noted, the revelation of chapter 34 came out of an experience of both judgment and grace. Many commentators suggest that this kind of experience meant that Israel was ready to hear the message of grace and compassion—without taking it as a *carte blanche* to do anything they wanted.

I believe most of us pass through a similar stage of growth as we begin to understand more of the nature of God (at least this was true for me). In the most initial phases of our spiritual lives, we are filled with the joy of forgiveness and the privilege of being a child of God. But then as we get more serious about actually living out our faith, we come face-to-face with the depth of our sinfulness. We know we are forgiven, but we become convinced that we must overcome the flesh in order to please God. Not only are we dealing with our weakness, but as we read the Scripture in a more disciplined way, we also begin to see more and more of the majesty, holiness, and sovereignty of God. If God is so mysterious and almighty but is also just in his dealing with me, then who am I?

That is a very uncomfortable place to be, but at the same time I believe it is quite necessary for our growth. We, too, need to come to the mountain of God, as it smokes and belches fire, and recognize that our God is the Almighty. He is Lord of all creation and in his infinite justice he does not ignore those who rebel against him. Here is the place for the fear of God (Ex. 20:20). In our feel-good evangelical world, the unwillingness of many to faithfully proclaim God as holy and just not only tends to trivialize God, but it also keeps people at a level of spiritual immaturity. They are happy only with a God who makes them feel comfortable—and that is not the God who reveals himself in the Scripture.

Once we have gotten *that* message, however, I believe it is then time to hear the word of grace from Exodus 34. That is how God himself wants us to know him, when we are ready to receive this word. For those of us living under the new covenant, I think this is particularly important. It is not that God has reversed justice and grace, but justice has been *fulfilled* in Jesus' death on the cross. In Jesus we have come into the fullness of what God created us to be. Therefore, it is time to enjoy our freedom, not cower under the demands of the law.

Reflect on these words of the apostle Paul from the eighth chapter of

Romans. They come immediately after he spoke of the agony of spirit that resulted when he held his life up to the demands of the law (7:15–23).

> There is therefore now no condemnation for those who are in Christ Jesus. For the law of the Spirit of life has set you free in Christ Jesus from the law of sin and death. For God has done what the law, weakened by the flesh, could not do. By sending his own Son in the likeness of sinful flesh and for sin, he condemned sin in the flesh, in order that the righteous requirement of the law might be fulfilled in us, who walk not according to the flesh but according to the Spirit. (Rom. 8:1–4)

THE SINS OF THE FATHERS

READING FOR THE DAY: NUMBERS 14:17-35

*"The LORD is slow to anger and abounding in steadfast love, forgiving iniquity
and transgression, but he will by no means clear the guilty, visiting the iniquity
of the fathers on the children, to the third and the fourth generation." . . . Then
the LORD said, "I have pardoned, according to your word. But truly, as I live . . .
none of the men who have seen my glory and my signs that I did in Egypt and
in the wilderness, and yet have put me to the test these ten times and have not
obeyed my voice, shall see the land that I swore to give to their fathers."*

NUMBERS 14:18, 20-23

The last phrase to consider in the Lord's proclamation of his name to
Moses is the haunting phrase, "he visits the sins of the fathers upon
the children to the third and fourth generations" (KJV). This was repeated
from the first giving of the commandments (Ex. 20:5). It is cited again
in Numbers 14:18 and in Jeremiah 32:18 (where it is paraphrased, "you
repay the guilt of fathers to their children after them"). The words have
long captured the attention of literary people, and the expression "sins of
the fathers" can be found as a title for novels and plays.

What could this mean? Is the Lord saying that his anger over sin
cannot be satisfied unless four generations feel his judgment? Is this what
he means when he says he is a "jealous God" (Ex. 20:25; 34:14)? Doesn't
this contradict the teaching that every person is accountable for his or her
sins? For a long time I have wrestled with the meaning of that statement.
And it is my strong conviction that far from revealing a capriciousness
in the character of God, it is essentially a revelation about the character
of sin. We tend to treat sin too casually, as though it applies only to the
moment and has few, if any, consequences. In the frightening words of
this verse, our gracious and compassionate God is trying to tell us that sin
does have serious consequences. And in many cases, those consequences
will pass from generation to generation.

The reading today is an excellent illustration of this principle at work. The context of Numbers 14 is the report of the spies who scouted out the Promised Land. The great majority of the people rejected Joshua and Caleb and believed those spies who were convinced that it would be impossible to overcome the people of great heights ("giants") and their fortified cities (Num. 13:26–33). Not only was this a failure of nerve, but it was the last straw in the people's unwillingness to trust God. This time, even when Moses claimed the Lord's Exodus 34 promise of forgiveness (Num. 14:17–20), and the Lord did forgive them, there were serious consequences. The rebellion of the Israelites caused the Lord to declare that the entire generation would die off before he would bring his people into the land (Num. 14:21–23). What is significant for this lesson is the statement in 14:33 that not only would the rebellious people die for their sin, but also *"your children* shall be shepherds in the wilderness forty years and shall suffer *for your faithlessness."* In the very nature of the situation, the children would be forced to share in the suffering that was a consequence of their parents' sin. This is life, and it is important that we recognize it.

The world seems to have a better handle on this biblical principle than many believers do. It is not an overstatement to say that much of modern psychology is founded on a serious regard for the "sins of the fathers." In many respects it has perverted the concept, but that doesn't deny the importance of looking back for generations to understand how the sins of the fathers have emotionally or even physically handicapped the children, who in turn pass them on to their children. It is becoming clear, for example, that the great majority of those who abuse children were themselves abused. And consider the important research that has been done on the consequences of parents' alcoholism on children.

In my experience with counseling couples who are about to marry, I have learned to take a great deal of time to talk through the home environments in which the prospective partners grew up. In the conversation, I commonly hear that the problems experienced in his or her home were experienced also in the homes of their grandparents (the "third generation"). My objective in this exercise is not to offer some kind of proscription about what kind of marriage they will have based on how their forefathers' actions have cursed (or blessed) them. Rather, it is to gain a realistic understanding of the "sins of the fathers." That way the couple can know, in more specific ways, how to pray for, and apply, grace.

The "sins of the fathers" is a statement of law. That is, it is the Lord telling us the nature of the world as he created it. When we defy that created order, we will suffer consequences and, tragically, so will our children. But that is not to say this is how it *must* be. We have trusted God to graciously remove the most serious consequence of our sin—judgment. We should, therefore, also trust him to graciously break that terrible chain of one generation bringing a curse on the next. We often say, "By God's grace I will . . ." That should not be a casual statement. To invoke the grace of God is probably the most important thing we can do to see changes in our lives.

> But he said to me, "My grace is sufficient for you, for my power is made perfect in weakness." Therefore I will boast all the more gladly of my weaknesses, so that the power of Christ may rest upon me. (2 Cor. 12:9)

MOSES WORSHIPED

READING FOR THE DAY: EXODUS 34:8-9

And Moses quickly bowed his head toward the earth and worshiped. And he said, "If now I have found favor in your sight, O Lord, please let the Lord go in the midst of us, for it is a stiff-necked people, and pardon our iniquity and our sin, and take us for your inheritance."

EXODUS 34:8-9

A nd Moses quickly bowed his head toward the earth and worshiped." What else could he have done? He was in the cleft of the rock with only the shadow of God's hand shielding him from the very essence of God's glory. His prayer to be shown God's glory was answered as much as it could be in mortal existence. He was coming to know the Lord in all his goodness. I don't think Moses had to deliberately plan some sort of response. There could be only one thing to do at this sacred moment—he bowed low and worshiped!

When Elijah heard the voice of God on this same mountain, "he wrapped his face in his cloak and went out and stood at the entrance of the cave" (1 Kings 19:13). When Job finally met God after crying out for a hearing, he worshiped. "I had heard of you by the hearing of the ear, but now my eye sees you; therefore I despise myself, and repent in dust and ashes" (Job 42:5–6). Isaiah could only fall on his face in humility in the presence of the glory of God (Isa. 6:1–5). The wise men, on entering the house and seeing the child Jesus, "fell down and worshiped him" (Matt. 2:11). When Thomas finally met the risen Christ, he could only worship and say, "My Lord and my God!" (John 20:28). When John saw the glorified Christ on the island of Patmos, he said, "I fell at his feet as though dead" (Rev. 1:17). And the picture of heaven that is opened to us throughout Revelation is that of continuous worship: "Day and night they never cease to say, 'Holy, holy, holy, is the Lord God Almighty, who was and is and is to come!'" (4:8). "The twenty-four elders fall down before him who is seated on the throne and worship him who lives forever and ever" (4:10). "And the four living creatures said, 'Amen!' and the elders fell down and worshiped" (Rev. 5:14).

From these examples in Scripture, it would seem that while there is singing and praise and expressions of repentance, the most essential element of worship is silence and humble submission. We are told in Psalm 46:10, "Be still, and know that I am God." That thought should encourage us because although it is hard, it is something we can do. Our worship may not always come as a result of a dramatic encounter. In fact, that will rarely be the case; but learning to be still in the presence of God puts us in the same place as the great worshipers of Scripture. Jesus taught that our Father is actually seeking for true worshipers, those who worship "in spirit and in truth" (John 4:23–24).

Henri Nouwen has a great deal to say about the importance of learning to be quiet before God. He says, "This asks for much discipline and risk taking because we always seem to have something more urgent to do and 'just sitting there' and 'doing nothing' often disturbs us more than it helps. But there is no way around this. Being useless and silent in the presence of our God belongs to the core of all prayer."[12]

Lord, help me to learn to be still and to know that you are God!

DAY THIRTY-THREE
COVENANT RENEWAL

READING FOR THE DAY: EXODUS 34:8-11; JEREMIAH 31:31-34

And Moses quickly bowed his head toward the earth and worshiped. And he said, "If now I have found favor in your sight, O Lord, please let the Lord go in the midst of us, for it is a stiff-necked people, and pardon our iniquity and our sin, and take us for your inheritance." And he said, "Behold, I am making a covenant. Before all your people I will do marvels, such as have not been created in all the earth or in any nation. And all the people among whom you are shall see the work of the LORD, for it is an awesome thing that I will do with you. Observe what I command you this day. Behold, I will drive out before you the Amorites, the Canaanites, the Hittites, the Perizzites, the Hivites, and the Jebusites."

EXODUS 34:8-11

"Behold, the days are coming, declares the LORD, when I will make a new covenant with the house of Israel and the house of Judah."

JEREMIAH 31:31

Without question, Moses was personally fulfilled through his meeting with God. What more could any human being ask than to have such an encounter? But that wasn't enough for Moses, as we learn from the first part of today's reading. He was also called to be a leader and, therefore, even in his worship, he sought once again to be assured of the presence of the Lord with the people. Acknowledging what the Lord had already said about the people (that they were "stiff-necked," [Ex. 33:5]), Moses also quoted the very words the Lord had just used (34:7) and asked pardon for their iniquity and their sin. In what was probably a reference to the Lord's words before the first giving of the Ten (19:5), Moses laid claim to Israel's being God's "inheritance" (33:9).

The answer Moses received was more than he or the people had any right to expect. In the earlier promise, the Lord had said, "Now therefore, if you will indeed obey my voice and keep my covenant, you shall be my treasured possession among all peoples" (19:5). Israel had neither obeyed God's voice nor kept the covenant—they had not even come close! But in a declaration that was totally consistent with his gracious nature and his great plan of redemption, the Lord said he was "making a covenant" with them (33:10). Actually, this would be a renewal of the covenant made when Moses went up to the mountain the first time. The various laws that followed can all be found in chapters 21–23.

To appreciate the significance of this moment it is helpful to note that the literal translation of the phrase "make a covenant" in 34:10 is "*cut* a covenant." (This is true for other places where the term appears, as well.) That meant that the Lord was once again prepared to go beyond merely promising to be their God—he would seal that promise with blood! (Ex. 24:1–8 was the actual covenant ceremony.) The blood oath was a common form of establishing covenants or treaties in the ancient world. Often people would cut themselves to seal their commitment to their gods. But in this instance it was the Lord *himself* who did the cutting; it was a sign that he would absolutely stand behind the commitments he had made to his people. The idea of *hesed* love is rooted in God's willingness to make covenants in spite of, not because of, the response of his people. The Lord went on to say that his covenanted commitment to them would cause him to "do marvels, such as have not been created in all the earth or in any nation. And all the people among whom you are shall see the work of the LORD, for it is an awesome thing that I will do with you" (34:10; see also Deut. 4:32–40).

The God who reveals himself in Scripture is a covenant-making and a covenant-keeping God. For many of us who come to faith in Christ with little or no biblical background, faith is a matter of *our* commitment. We "accept Jesus as our personal Savior," or words to that effect. This is something we have decided to do. While that is true on one level, there is a foundation under our commitment—it is God's covenant. Underneath my acceptance of Jesus is an eternal covenant, sealed by blood, through which God willed to save me.

As is very clear in today's reading from Jeremiah 31, the covenant was not just part of the Old Testament; it was the framework through which God would save the world. The numerous New Testament references to this passage (Hebrews 8, in particular) make it clear that when the

Lord spoke of making a new covenant with Judah and Israel, he meant a covenant with the *whole* people of God, not the Hebrew nation in a purely physical sense. "People" now includes those of all races. When Jesus instituted the communion supper, he said, "This is my blood of *the covenant* [modern translations do not have the word "new" before "covenant"], which is poured out for many for the forgiveness of sins" (Matt. 26:28). The book of Hebrews ends with the benediction, "Now may the God of peace who brought again from the dead our Lord Jesus, the great shepherd of the sheep, by the blood of *the eternal covenant . . ."* (13:20). Ultimately, there is not an old or a new covenant, but *the* covenant which God has sealed through the blood of his own Son. This is the foundation of our eternal salvation.

> *A debtor to mercy alone, of covenant mercy I sing;*
> *Nor fear, with Thy righteousness on, my person and off'ring to bring.*
> *The terrors of law and of God with me can have nothing to do;*
> *My Savior's obedience and blood hide all my transgressions from view.*
>
> *The work which His goodness began, the arm of His strength will complete;*
> *His promise is Yea and Amen, and never was forfeited yet.*
> *Things future, nor things that are now, nor things below or above,*
> *Can make Him His purpose forgo, or sever my soul from His love.*
> AUGUSTUS M. TOPLADY

COVENANT RULES

READING FOR THE DAY: EXODUS 34:10-26

"Take care, lest you make a covenant with the inhabitants of the land to which you go, lest it become a snare in your midst. You shall tear down their altars and break their pillars and cut down their Asherim (for you shall worship no other god, for the LORD, whose name is Jealous, is a jealous God), lest you make a covenant with the inhabitants of the land, and when they whore after their gods and sacrifice to their gods and you are invited, you eat of his sacrifice, and you take of their daughters for your sons, and their daughters whore after their gods and make your sons whore after their gods."

EXODUS 34:12-16

It would be tempting to set aside these verses we read today as having no meaning for our studies. But, as usually happens, a more careful reflection will make us think otherwise. The specific laws (an expanded version can be found in Exodus 21–23) certainly pertain to Israel in its unique setting. But considered in the context of the renewal of the covenant, there are some very important lessons.

In studies of the Lord's willingness to enter into covenants with his people, most theologians are careful to point out that God's covenants are *unilateral*, not *bilateral*. That means that when God makes, or cuts, a covenant, it is not negotiated in the way we would think of in a contract—each party has an obligation, and the contract is void if either party does not measure up. Rather, it is a commitment the Lord makes and keeps, and its fulfillment is dependent on his power. Ultimately then, the hope of Israel, as well as our hope, rests in the power and mercy of God, not in our obedience or in keeping our part of the bargain.

However, this resting in the strength and mercy of the Lord should not obscure the important truth that God always expects a response to his giving of the covenant. By faith, we believe in the truth of God's promise, and in thankfulness for his grace, we pledge our obedience. That pattern holds whether we are living under the old or new covenant. In the reading for today, there was a clear call for Israel to separate from those things that would pull them away from the Lord. They were also to build disciplines into their daily lives that would continually renew their faith. That is totally consistent with the teaching of the New Testament to "put off your old self" and "put on the new self" (Eph. 4:22–24; Col. 3:9).

In the first place, there needed to be a willingness to be separate from the world (34:12–17). Twice the Lord commanded his people not to enter treaties or covenants with the unbelieving and pagan peoples that would be around them. Of particular concern was the covenant of marriage (v. 16). God's stipulation was not to keep Israel from *associating* with other nations, but it was a prohibition against actually *participating* in their false worship. That is where formal treaties would inevitably lead. Through his covenant, the Lord had pledged his loyalty to his people, and he expected the same of them. That is the sense in which he is "jealous" (v. 17). These commands to remain separate were tied directly to obedience to the first two commandments (vv. 14, 17). Clearly, a willingness to step away from surrounding paganism is at the core of the obedient life. In a letter to new Christians who were unsure of their faith, the apostle John said: "Do not love the world or the things in the world. If anyone loves the world, the love of the Father is not in him" (1 John 2:15).

In addition to the matter of separation from the world, there is a second overall emphasis. Our reading makes it clear that obedience to the covenant called for a discipline of ordering life in a way that allowed a continuous focus on God and his goodness (Ex. 34:18–26). The weekly and annual cycle of feasts and offerings served as a wonderful means of filling up the personal and family life of Israel with times of worship and remembrance. The Lord was careful to show that separation *from* the world was not an end in itself. But it would allow his people to be separated *unto* him so that they could enjoy the delights of being God's own "treasured possession" (19:5). We miss out on the actual enjoyment of God because we have so much "junk" in our lives. As we have seen already, such separation is the essence of sabbath-rest.

Knowing God and obeying God are not separate issues. To know God in the sense that we have been studying means that we will respond sincerely to the God of our salvation and say, "All that the LORD has spoken we will do" (19:8; 24:3). That will drive us to Christ, who alone can truly obey, but a new life in Christ gives us a desire to obey.

> He is the propitiation for our sins, and not for ours only but also for the sins of the whole world. And by this we know that we have come to know him, if we keep his commandments. Whoever says "I know him" but does not keep his commandments is a liar, and the truth is not in him, but whoever keeps his word, in him truly the love of God is perfected. By this we may know that we are in him: whoever says he abides in him ought to walk in the same way in which he walked. (1 John 2:2–6)

WRITE IT DOWN

READING FOR THE DAY: EXODUS 34:27-28;
DEUTERONOMY 31:7-13, 23-27

And the LORD said to Moses, "Write these words, for in accordance with these words I have made a covenant with you and with Israel."

EXODUS 34:27

When Moses had finished writing the words of this law in a book to the very end, Moses commanded the Levites who carried the ark of the covenant of the LORD, "Take this Book of the Law and put it by the side of the ark of the covenant of the LORD your God, that it may be there for a witness against you."

DEUTERONOMY 31:24-26

Both of today's readings make it clear that God's intention was not only to speak to the Israelites, but also that his words actually be written down so that they can be read and understood and passed along to future generations. We are rightfully called, "the people of the book," and that book is the Bible.

Have you noticed that the phrase "Holy Bible" has disappeared from the front covers of many newer editions of Scripture (the ESV is a happy exception!)? Instead, what we typically find is the name of the particular translation, or brand, of Bible. That discovery filled me with real sadness, because it is hard to think of a more apt word for the Bible than "holy." I hope it doesn't suggest that we who gladly accept the label "Bible-believing Christian" have lost a sense of reverence for the Book even as we strive to make it more and more useful.

As a book, the Bible is paper and ink like any other book. However, the words that are presented to our eyes—not just the substance—but the *very words* are the words that the Lord directed Moses and the other human authors to write down. Those words have been lovingly written, copied, preserved, translated, and passed from generation to generation.

Because of this gift, we have been able to read and enter into the actual encounter of the Lord God with the man Moses.

God instructed, "Write these words" (34:27). This seems to be the first specific directive to do so. (Of course, God himself began the process by writing down the Ten Commandments.) It is entirely possible that the actual written Scripture began at this point. Exodus was probably the first book to be fully written out, and sometime in the years before his death, we can assume Moses wrote Genesis as well as the other three "Books of Moses," as they are called. Moses was writing up until the day of his death, as is evident from Deuteronomy 31:11–13, where Moses directed that the people be assembled to hear the reading of the Law. It was through reading what had been written down and preserved that God's will could be made known to the children and to all succeeding generations. This established the pattern by which God would make his truth known.

When Moses died, it was as though his "holy" pen was passed to prophets and poets and teachers who continued to put into writing the words of God. As Peter explained, "Men spoke from God as they were carried along by the Holy Spirit" (2 Peter 1:21). Paul called the Scriptures "breathed out by God" (2 Tim. 3:16), placing the written Word on the same level as the very breath that created the universe. Jesus himself built virtually everything he taught and did on the words of Scripture. He then promised the Holy Spirit to enable the apostles to recall and accurately record his words (John 16:12–15). The elders of the early church prayed, "Sovereign Lord . . . who through the mouth of our father David, your servant, said by the Holy Spirit . . . ," and they quoted from Psalm 2 (Acts 4:24–25). That may be the most concise explanation of the inspiration of Scripture to be found. God spoke by *the Holy Spirit,* through *the mouth* of his human servants *and it was written down* and preserved.

Examples can be multiplied to serve as a reminder that we indeed have a *holy* Bible. But now it is our responsibility and privilege to open this treasure and let it speak. Come to the Bible with reverence—but come! This is not a buried treasure or museum of the past. The Bible lives because God, whose very nature it is to communicate, lives. Read again from A. W. Tozer:

The Bible is the inevitable outcome of God's continuous speech. It is the infallible declaration of His mind for us, put into our familiar human words. I think a new world will arise out of the religious mists when we approach our Bible with the idea that it is not only a book which was once spoken, but a book which is now speaking. The prophets habitually said, "This saith the Lord." They meant their hearers to understand that God's speaking is in the continuous present.

If you would follow on to know the Lord, come at once to the open Bible expecting it to speak to you. Do not come with the notion that it is a thing which you may push around at your convenience. It is more than a thing, it is a voice, a word, the very Word of the living God.[13]

MOSES' SHINING FACE

READING FOR THE DAY: EXODUS 34:29-35

When Moses came down from Mount Sinai, with the two tablets of the testimony in his hand as he came down from the mountain, Moses did not know that the skin of his face shone because he had been talking with God. Aaron and all the people of Israel saw Moses, and behold, the skin of his face shone, and they were afraid to come near him. But Moses called to them, and Aaron and all the leaders of the congregation returned to him, and Moses talked with them.

EXODUS 34:29-31

The passage we have been studying began with Moses' coming down from Sinai to find an orgy of idolatry and sensuality. As it concludes, Moses again returns to the people after forty days on the mountain. This time they were waiting to receive what he would bring them from the Lord their God. It is a quiet and fitting end to the study of this remarkable encounter.

As he returned to the camp, he brought two things with him. In his *hands*, he brought the Ten Commandments. Significantly, they are called here, as well as in several other places, "the testimony" (Ex. 16:34; 31:18; 32:15). God bears witness to his person and will through the written Word. But secondly, on his *face*, Moses brought a small taste of the glory that he had been experiencing. Moses was unaware of this second gift, but the people immediately knew it and felt afraid.

The word translated "shone" (the NIV uses the word "radiant") is not the usual word for an external or physical shining (in Ps. 69:31 it means *horn*). It may point to the fact that the radiance coming from Moses was not primarily something *seen*, as it was something *sensed* by those in his presence. Without consciously trying to do so, he was reflecting to the people something of "all the goodness" of God. His time with God had changed him. Notice from the passage that Moses immediately reassured the people, and they came back to him (v. 31).

My initial reading of this incident left me with the mental picture of Moses walking around the camp wearing a veil while people avoided him. But the passage makes it clear that Moses would remove the veil during the times he taught the people the Word of God (vv. 32–33). So a more accurate picture is that of people who were initially awestruck, eagerly crowding around Moses whenever he would teach them. The combination of the authoritative word and the reflection of the majesty of God in Moses' face must have been irresistible. And when they would ask Moses to tell them more about God, the reality behind his words could have been felt as well as heard. The people in that camp could have used the words spoken by the two disciples who met Jesus on the road to Emmaus, "Did not our hearts burn within us while he talked to us on the road, while he opened to us the Scriptures?" (Luke 24:32).

As a pastor and preacher, my personal definition of effective preaching has been taken from that beautiful meeting in Luke 24. It has been my desire to have the enabling to open the Scripture in such a way that people would encounter the risen Christ and know the "burning of the heart." However I am *not* the risen Christ, and therefore this incident in Exodus 34 may be a better model to consider. Moses, too, was a sinful person. But before he brought the people the Word of God, he had spent enough time in the presence of God that something of that presence rubbed off as he taught. Furthermore, we read that Moses regularly returned to the presence of God so that the radiance was constantly being renewed (vv. 34–35). The opportunity to spend forty days on a mountain with God is a rare privilege, but a "tent of meeting"—a prayer closet—is always available.

Those same realities—the written Word and the presence of the living God—are with us now when a man of God opens the Bible to preach. Both are critically important. The Word without the reality of God is sterile; a sense of God's presence without the Word to explain it can be an undefined spirituality. But when the two come together there is teaching that moves the soul.

> Glorious Father, we pray for those called to the ministry of teaching and preaching your holy Word. Grant that they may never give forth that Word without also sharing some measure of the glory they have experienced in your presence. As you did for Moses, give them the desire and the determination to wait before you on behalf of the people you have called them to lead.

THE RADIANCE OF GOD'S GLORY

READING FOR THE DAY: 2 CORINTHIANS 3:7-18; HEBREWS 1:1-3

Now if the ministry of death, carved in letters on stone, came with such glory that the Israelites could not gaze at Moses' face because of its glory, which was being brought to an end, will not the ministry of the Spirit have even more glory? . . . Since we have such a hope, we are very bold, not like Moses, who would put a veil over his face so that the Israelites might not gaze at the outcome of what was being brought to an end. But their minds were hardened. For to this day, when they read the old covenant, that same veil remains unlifted, because only through Christ is it taken away. Yes, to this day whenever Moses is read a veil lies over their hearts. But when one turns to the Lord, the veil is removed. Now the Lord is the Spirit, and where the Spirit of the Lord is, there is freedom.

2 CORINTHIANS 3:7-8, 12-17

As we noted in the meditation for Day 2, the encounter between Moses and the Lord, glorious as that was, has an even greater fulfillment. In 2 Corinthians 3 and 4, the apostle Paul uses the imagery of the veil over Moses' face to explain the privileges that belong to those who live under the new covenant (3:6), which he also calls "the ministry of the Spirit" (3:8). The concluding meditations will focus on this New Testament commentary on Moses' experience and the application that the apostle makes to our own experience in Christ.

It is striking to note Paul's preoccupation with the idea of "glory" in 2 Corinthians 3 and 4. In 3:7–11 the word appears *ten times* and then six more times by the end of chapter 4. Recall that the boldest of all of Moses' prayers was when he asked, "Please, show me your glory." What Moses received in answer to his prayer was a marvelous revelation of all of God's goodness as he proclaimed to him his name, the LORD. But Moses could not behold God's glory. He could see God's back but not his face (33:18–23). In the context of Exodus and the Old Testament revelation, this meant that no human could ever actually see the very essence of

God's being. But God also withheld showing Moses his glory as a witness to a greater fulfillment yet to come. And it is that fulfillment Paul has in mind as he compares the glory with which the old covenant came—and it certainly was glorious—with the "glory that surpasses it" of "what is permanent" (2 Cor. 3:10–11).

And what is this surpassing (super-abounding, excellent) glory? For one thing, it is the fact that the power behind the new covenant is the Holy Spirit rather than written laws (3:6–8, 17; see also Ezek. 36:26–27). But there was more. Paul wanted his readers, then and now, to focus their attention on the person of Jesus Christ. The language of this passage makes it clear that in Jesus Christ we can know what Moses was unable to see, even though he sought it passionately. The idea of the veil shifts from a picture of the fading glory on the face of Moses to that which hides people from seeing the truth. "Only through Christ is it taken away . . . when one turns to the Lord, the veil is removed" (3:14, 16). And what do we see when the veil is taken away? In Jesus, we, with unveiled faces, behold *the glory of the Lord* (3:18). The "glory of the Lord" resides in Jesus! Paul even uses the word "face" in the same way it was used in Exodus 33, where God's face was the same as his glory. We have "the light of the knowledge of the *glory* of God in the *face* of Jesus Christ" (4:6).

Familiar texts take on new depth of meaning with this perspective. "And the Word became flesh and dwelt among us, and we have seen his *glory, glory* as of the only Son from the Father, full of grace and truth" (John 1:14). Note the precise wording of Hebrews 1:3: "He is the *radiance* of the *glory of God*." The word translated "radiance" here in the ESV has various translations in other versions, but the idea is always that of something bright and visible. In the coming of Jesus, that which has been invisible now can be seen. The word "radiance" also brings us back to the radiance on the face of Moses. Not only was it a "radiance [that] was fading away" (2 Cor. 3:13, NIV), but it was only a *reflection* of the glory of God—Jesus' radiance *is* that very glory.

> Brightness of my Father's glory, Sunshine of my Father's face,
> keep me ever trusting, resting, fill me with thy grace.
> Jesus, I am resting, resting in the joy of what thou art;
> I am finding out the greatness of thy loving heart.
> JEAN SOPHIA PIGOTT (1876)

THE TRANSFORMING VISION

READING FOR THE DAY: 2 CORINTHIANS 3:18-4:6

And we all, with unveiled face, beholding the glory of the Lord, are being trans-formed into the same image from one degree of glory to another. For this comes from the Lord who is the Spirit. . . . And even if our gospel is veiled, it is veiled only to those who are perishing. In their case the god of this world has blinded the minds of the unbelievers, to keep them from seeing the light of the gospel of the glory of Christ, who is the image of God. . . . For God, who said, "Let light shine out of darkness," has shone in our hearts to give the light of the knowledge of the glory of God in the face of Jesus Christ.

2 CORINTHIANS 3:18; 4:3-4, 6

Once it is understood that Jesus is the ultimate revelation of God's glory, we then need to consider *how* we are actually transformed so as to partake in that glory. That is the teaching of 2 Corinthians 3:18. Note that the verse speaks of a process that is presently going on in the life of a believer, and not the final, eternal glory that appears later in the passage (4:17). We "*are being* transformed into the same image from one degree of glory to another" (lit., "from glory to glory"). The word "trans-formed" comes directly from the Greek into English as *metamorphosis*, the process by which a caterpillar or other creature is changed from within to be radically altered in character and appearance. It is the same word that appears in Romans 12:2 where Paul exhorts, "Do not be conformed to this world, but be transformed by the renewal of your mind."

Paul tells just how this transformation will take place. It happens as we behold, as in a mirror, the glory of the Lord. (The word translated "behold" in the ESV or "reflect" in the NIV conveys only parts of this idea.) Visualize the common experience of looking into a mirror in such a way that you are able to see someone who is behind you or off to the side. We say that we see the person, when, in the most literal sense, what we are seeing is a reflection. Like Moses or any other mortal, we cannot directly view the glory of God. We do see, however, an exact reflection of that glory when we see Jesus.

The actual mirror through which we see the glory of God in Jesus is the gospel. In 2 Corinthians 4:4, Paul returns to the imagery of the veil to explain that if the gospel is veiled, it is because "the god of this world has blinded the minds [veiled the eyes] of the unbelievers, to keep them from seeing the light of the gospel of the glory of Christ, who is the image of God." The removal of the veil—our spiritual blindness—was not an act of our wills, but a supernatural work of God. As he says in 4:6, the very same power that created light in the first place, brought light to our souls. In the beginning God said, "Let there be light, and there was light"—the word of creation. And God now says, "Let there be life, and there is life"—the word of the *new* creation!

Reread 4:6 thoughtfully and linger over every word, for it is an explanation of what the Lord did when he took away the veil. Because of God's regenerating power, we came to understand the gospel, and in believing it we were brought into "the light of the knowledge of the glory of God in the face of Jesus Christ." What Paul wants us to realize is that if we will look closely at the gospel, what we see is not only the message of sins forgiven, but a mirror in which we see Jesus. And in the face of Jesus, we have the knowledge of the glory of God. It was the gracious work of God that opened the gospel to us. That same grace, working through the power of the Holy Spirit (it "comes from the Lord, who is the Spirit," 3:18), is causing us to be transformed into the image of the Jesus we discovered in the gospel.

All the themes that we have been considering converge at this point: Moses' (and Paul's) passion to know God, his prayer to see God's glory, the revelation of God's name, the assurance of God's presence, God's gift of rest, and the radiance of Moses' face. All of these find fulfillment in Jesus. And as we behold this glory found in Jesus, we are "being transformed into the same image." We are being made to be like Christ one step at a time—"from one degree of glory to another" ("with an ever-increasing glory" NIV). Moses was only able to anticipate God's glory; we actually partake of it through the work of the Spirit within.

We struggle with the idea that our primary responsibility in this transforming process (usually defined as *sanctification*) is to fix our minds and hearts on Jesus. Our instinct is to look for something to do, some set of rules to follow. But to lapse into that kind of thinking would not only deny the teaching of this passage, but virtually every other teaching about sanctification in the New Testament. Romans 12:2, referred to earlier, says that we are to be transformed "by the renewal of your mind." The chapter in Colossians on the practical outworking of the Christian life begins, "If then you have been raised with Christ, seek the things that are above, where Christ is. . . . For you have died, and your life is now hidden with Christ in God" (Col. 3:1, 3). There are very specific dos and don'ts that follow, and they are very important to the Christian life, but the basis of the new behavior is a focus on the exalted Christ. This is consistent with our study of prayers for the "knowledge of God." Out of the *knowing*—the heart set on Jesus—will come the *doing*. Peter said, "His divine power has granted to us all things that pertain to life and godliness, *through the knowledge of him* who called us to his own glory and excellence" (2 Peter 1:3).

Moses "endured as *seeing* him who is invisible" (Heb. 11:27). That same vision sustained Paul, and it will be more than sufficient for us as well.

> *Thou hast bid me gaze upon Thee, and Thy beauty fills my soul,*
> *for by Thy transforming power, thou hast made me whole.*
> *Jesus, I am resting, resting in the joy of what thou art;*
> *I am finding out the greatness of thy loving heart.*
> JEAN SOPHIA PIGOTT (1876)

PRESENT WEAKNESS

READING FOR THE DAY: 2 CORINTHIANS 4:7-18

But we have this treasure in jars of clay, to show that the surpassing power belongs to God and not to us. We are afflicted in every way, but not crushed; perplexed, but not driven to despair; persecuted, but not forsaken; struck down, but not destroyed; always carrying in the body the death of Jesus, so that the life of Jesus may also be manifested in our bodies. . . . For this light momentary affliction is preparing for us an eternal weight of glory beyond all comparison, as we look not to the things that are seen but to the things that are unseen. For the things that are seen are transient, but the things that are unseen are eternal.

2 CORINTHIANS 4:7-10, 17-18

After filling our minds with thoughts of partaking of the divine glory and being transformed into the very likeness of Christ (3:18), the apostle Paul makes it clear that this is going on in the midst of real life. We must not isolate this wonderful teaching from our daily experience.

Paul reminds us that we are fragile beings—"jars of clay." Paul certainly had in mind both the physical weakness of our mortal bodies and the weakness of our flesh—that part of our being that relentlessly pulls us toward pride and selfishness. We are in these clay pots and will be until we go to be with Christ. Paul was resigned to this, and he said that it is supposed to be this way "to show that the surpassing power belongs to God and not to us." Paul could even rejoice in his "thorn in the flesh" so that he could know more about the sufficiency of God's grace. "Therefore I will boast all the more gladly of my weakness, so that the power of Christ may rest upon me" (2 Cor. 12:9). Since Paul never disclosed just what this "thorn" was, we should feel free to insert our own "thorn" into our reading of that verse as we apply these truths to our lives.

In addition to the matter of human frailty, the apostle also had in mind the outward circumstances of life (2 Cor. 4:8–10; cf. 6:3–10; 11:21–28). Life was not fair to Paul. In clear terms he told the

Corinthians that he was afflicted in every way, perplexed, persecuted, and struck down. In addition to the hardships of service for Christ, it appears from the way he wrote that he also experienced their criticism for being willing to endure those hardships (3:12; 11:16–20). It seems that the Corinthians were looking for evidence that following Christ leads only to the good life. Paul's difficulties, they reasoned, were surely his own fault. Most of us entertain the same kinds of thoughts when we try to explain our difficulties or those of others. "What is wrong with me [or them]?" we ask. But Paul saw no need to "lose heart" (4:1, 16), and he could look beyond his weaknesses and circumstances because he possessed a treasure.

The context makes it clear what Paul meant by "this treasure" (4:7). Through the Spirit of the Lord, the veil had been taken away and he was liberated (3:16–17). He was liberated from his earth-bound perspective on life and could, therefore, see Jesus. He was the risen and exalted Lord Jesus (4:13–14), and Paul knew that he was already partaking of "the glory of God in the face of Jesus" (4:6; cf. 3:18). This was his treasure. Therefore, Paul saw no need to lose heart, because living meant ministry and the sharing of his treasure with more and more people (4:5, 15).

In the concluding meditation we will consider the final and eternal glory. But first recognize that our treasure, like Paul's, is more than sufficient for *this* life as well. I believe there has been a serious misrepresentation of biblical teaching in the common idea that our treasure is merely a home in heaven, so we endure this life and its troubles by dwelling on thoughts of heaven. Since few of us really live this way, we struggle with our lack of spirituality. But, in fact, our treasure is Jesus! We can live this life with joy and purpose because it is a course that *he* has laid out for us. Our "light momentary affliction" (4:17) is of no real consequence, for when we look past it, we see Jesus.

The privilege of living for Jesus in even the most difficult circumstances is summarized beautifully in Hebrews 12:

> Therefore, since we are surrounded by so great a cloud of witnesses [Moses and all the other heroes of faith named in chap. 11], let us also lay aside every weight, and sin which clings so closely, and let us

run with endurance the race that is set before us, looking to Jesus, the founder and perfecter of our faith, who for the joy that was set before him endured the cross, despising the shame, and is seated at the right hand of the throne of God. Consider him who endured from sinners such hostility against himself, so that you may not grow weary or faint-hearted. (Heb. 12:1–3)

ETERNAL GLORY

READING FOR THE DAY: 2 CORINTHIANS 4:16-18;
COLOSSIANS 3:1-4

If then you have been raised with Christ, seek the things that are above, where
Christ is, seated at the right hand of God. Set your minds on things that are
above, not on things that are on earth. For you have died, and your life is hidden
with Christ in God. When Christ who is your life appears, then you also will
appear with him in glory.

COLOSSIANS 3:1-4

Our "forty days on the mountain" will conclude with more thoughts
about glory. Moses prayed to see the glory of God and was allowed
to come close enough to see the Lord's back but not his face. In our day
of the new covenant, through the ministry of the Spirit, we see "the glory
of God in the face of Jesus Christ" (4:6). But it is a poor reflection—a dim
mirror (1 Cor. 13:12)—because of the distortions of our flesh. However,
if even that reflection is transforming us "into his likeness with ever
increasing glory," imagine what it will be like when we are present with
Christ in the fullness of his majesty and glory!

It is the anticipation of that greater glory that animated the faith and
life of the apostle Paul, and it should do the same for us. "So we do not
lose heart," he said to the Corinthians (2 Cor. 4:16). The deterioration of
the outward man is unimportant, and his light momentary affliction is
only a stepping stone to eternal glory. This could be a reality because he
did not look "to the things that are seen but to the things that are unseen."
The unseen, which is eternal, is the risen and exalted Christ along with
the anticipation of being with him for eternity (4:18).

Notice that Paul's thoughts in Colossians 3 parallel those of 2
Corinthians 4. We are to set our hearts and minds on "the things that
are above, where Christ is, seated at the right hand of God." That
doesn't mean we are to think solely about what is waiting for us in

"heaven," but to focus on Christ himself in his exaltation. That is where the most essential part of our being is hidden. In the future there will come a time when "Christ who is [our] life" will appear, and then we will appear with him and share in his glory. The entire discussion of the Christian life that follows (Col. 3:5–4:1) builds on this fundamental perspective on life.

These texts challenge the common perception of defining life as simply waiting to go to heaven. Personally, I have to be honest and say that such a definition of life is not a strong motivator for me to follow Christ. I'm sure it reflects something of my earth-bound vision, but I hope it also reflects a desire to be faithful to biblical teaching. When Paul and other New Testament authors speak of heaven or things above or what is unseen, the terms refer essentially to the presence of Christ at the right hand of the Father. Focusing on heaven in that sense *is* tremendously satisfying. Furthermore, the anticipation of actually being in that presence, with all barriers removed, is a very exciting prospect—whether it comes as a consequence of death, or at the day of Christ's return.

The late C. S. Lewis had a very Christ-centered perspective of heaven, and he moves our imagination to see more of the future glory before us. The following are a series of quotations taken from his sermon, "The Weight of Glory," delivered in 1941. In the earlier part of the sermon Lewis wrestled with the question of the worthiness of longing for heaven. But then he reviews the biblical promises and reflects on the meaning of glory.

> At present we are on the outside of the world, the wrong side of the door. We discern the freshness and purity of the morning, but they do not make us fresh and pure. We cannot mingle with the splendors we see. But all the leaves of the New Testament are rustling with the rumor that it will not always be so. Some day, God willing, we shall get in. . . . We are summoned to pass in through Nature, beyond her, into that splendor which she fitfully reflects. And in there, in beyond Nature, we shall eat of the tree of life. At present, if we are reborn in Christ, the spirit in us lives directly on God; but the mind, and, still more, the body receives life from Him at a thousand removes . . . What would it be to taste at the fountainhead that stream of which even these lower reaches prove so intoxicating? Yet that, I believe, is what lies before us.

The whole man is to live at the fountain of joy. Meanwhile the cross comes before the crown and tomorrow is a Monday morning. A cleft has opened in the pitiless walls of the world, and we are invited to follow our great Captain inside. The following Him is, of course, the essential point.[14]

THE NEXT FORTY DAYS

It is my prayer that after reading through *Forty Days on the Mountain* you have a new desire to grow in your knowledge of God. Moses' encounter with the Lord is a doorway we can step through onto a path of discovery, but the path of knowing more of God is one we will be following for the rest of our lives. Here are a few thoughts about specific steps you could take as you go through the doorway.

The most important step is to continue (or perhaps begin) a consistent reading of the Bible itself. Set a schedule for yourself or make use of the many published helps that are available. Crossway offers the reading plan of Robert Murray M'Cheyne in outline form as well as the two-volume guide to M'Cheyne's plan by D. A. Carson, *For the Love of God*. I also recommend the material of Scripture Union in Valley Forge, Pennsylvania, called *Encounter with God*. It is a daily guided Scripture reading that includes a brief meditation on the passage for the day, similar to the format that I followed.

It is important that we appreciate the value of our hymnals as aids in devotion, including the Bible's own hymnal, the book of Psalms. I try to actually sing or say the psalms or hymns quietly rather than to just read them. For me at least, this seems to engage my attention to a greater degree.

Reading *Forty Days* is an introduction to Christian spirituality. It is tragic that in our frantic culture, many overlook the wonderful treasure house in the writings of men and women who have sought to enter more deeply into the knowledge of God. What follows are suggestions for further reading by those authors who have been helpful to me. I offer this list with the understanding that those who have been helpful to me will not necessarily have the same impact on you.

I first of all highly recommend the writing of A. W. Tozer. The book I quoted in the meditations, *The Pursuit of God*, is a book of extraordinary depth, and I never find it stale with repeated readings. I profited recently from Tozer's *The Knowledge of the Holy*, a series of meditations on the attributes of God.

For more substantial books to strengthen your understanding of God, I recommend *Knowing God* by J. I. Packer. This is not a devotional reading, but the investment in reading will be very rewarding. You should also become acquainted with the excellent work of John Piper (many books published by Crossway). He will teach you about "Christian hedonism"—finding the highest possible joy through seeking God.

It should be apparent from your reading of the meditations that I appreciate the writing of Henri Nouwen. I have found him refreshing because he writes from the perspective of a different tradition—that of Roman Catholicism. But that difference will also give occasional caution about some of his views. Most of his writings (such as *Road from Daybreak*) are published journals. I have particularly enjoyed this form of writing because it can be read in small bites.

If you want to dig into Exodus itself, I recommend two recent commentaries that are scholarly and yet written to encourage believers rather than simply to exhaust the meaning of the text. They are *Exodus: Saved for God's Glory* by Philip Ryken (Crossway, 2005) and *Exodus* in the NIV Application Commentary series by Peter Enns (Zondervan, 2000).

Finally, keep in mind that coming to know God is not just a personal quest. If we are to grow, we must be hearing the Scripture preached and experiencing the fellowship of the saints in a healthy church. Spiritual maturity comes about as "we all attain to the unity of the faith and of the knowledge of the Son of God. . . . We are to grow up in every way into him who is the head, into Christ" (Eph. 4:13, 15).

NOTES

1. Read about the remarkable confirmation of God's hand when I returned from the sabbatical, in "Kathy's Story," Chap. 1 of my book *Spiritual Birthline: Understanding How We Experience the New Birth* (Wheaton, IL: Crossway, 2006).

2. A phrase coined by Francis Schaeffer, who wrote a book by the same title, *He Is There and He Is Not Silent* (Wheaton, IL: Tyndale, 1972).

3. I use the masculine pronoun to refer to God without apology. This is because it is what the Scripture uses for God. This is not to insist that God is male, but simply that our language is limited and it is how God has chosen to reveal himself.

4. A. W. Tozer, *The Pursuit of God* (Camp Hill, PA: Christian Publications, 1982), 11–12.

5. See Peter Enns's comment that "I AM" was not intended to be a name for God, but to reinforce the fact that Moses was speaking to the God who had already made himself known to the patriarchs (Peter Enns, *Exodus–The NIV Application Commentary,* [Grand Rapids: Zondervan, 2000]), 106.

6. Ibid., 491.

7. Henry Bettenson, ed., *Documents of the Christian Church* (London: Oxford University Press, 1963), 260.

8. Henri Nouwen, *Road to Daybreak* (New York: Image Books, 1990), 30.

9. A. W. Tozer, *The Pursuit of God,* 90–97.

10. See my booklet, *What Is True Conversion?* (Phillipsburg, NJ: P&R, 2005), where I explain that our experience of God is the reverse of our usual explanation of him. We first encounter God in the person of the Holy Spirit, who leads us to saving faith in God the Son, through whom we come to know God as our Father.

11. Peter Enns, *Exodus,* 581.

12. Henri Nouwen, *Reaching Out* (New York: Doubleday, 1975), 97.

13. A. W. Tozer, *The Pursuit of God,* 82–83.

14. C. S. Lewis, *The Weight of Glory and Other Addresses* (San Francisco: HarperCollins, 2001), 39–45.

PERSONAL REFLECTIONS

PERSONAL REFLECTIONS

PERSONAL REFLECTIONS

PERSONAL REFLECTIONS

PERSONAL REFLECTIONS

PERSONAL REFLECTIONS

PERSONAL REFLECTIONS

PERSONAL REFLECTIONS

PERSONAL REFLECTIONS

PERSONAL REFLECTIONS

PERSONAL REFLECTIONS

PERSONAL REFLECTIONS

PERSONAL REFLECTIONS

ONE *night* STAND

NEW YORK TIMES BESTSELLING AUTHORS

J. S. COOPER & HELEN COOPER

ACKNOWLEDGMENTS

Thank you to all of my readers for supporting my books in 2014. I write because of you. And I couldn't think of a better job to have.

Thanks to my editor Emma Mack for making time to edit my books, even when I am behind. Thanks to Louisa Maggio for the beautiful cover she made for the book. I love it so much.

Thanks to Tanya Kay Skaggs, Katrina Jaekley, Stacy Hahn, Cilicia White, Tianna Croy, Chanteal Justice, Kathy Shreve, Lisa Miller, Kelly Sloane for all your help reading this book and providing feedback chapter by chapter as I wrote Xander and Liv's story.

And last, but not least, thanks be to God for all of my blessings.

THAT · night

THE PREQUEL

Prologue

"YOU CAN STILL CALL ME Mr. Tongue if you want." He grinned at me and licked his lips deliberately, the tip of his tongue gliding back and forth, and reminding me of the night we'd spent together. The sinful night that I'd never forget. Only he wasn't supposed to be here. In my parents' house. Sitting on my couch. The couch I'd watched TV on for years. He wasn't supposed to be talking to my parents. He wasn't supposed to be looking so sexy. I didn't even know his name.

One night stands are meant to be fun. They're meant to be exciting. They're meant to be adventurous experiments in lovemaking that don't follow you home. I don't consider myself a whore or cheap. I mean I have standards for the guys I want to date and hook up with. I even have a chart of things I look for in a guy. I don't just drop my panties for any guy with a cute smile, handsome face and a wallet full of cash. I've slept with men that had no cash, missing teeth and even one that was prematurely balding, but they were all boyfriends. Yes, I've had questionable taste in men, but that's a story for another day. One I'm not particularly proud of. In fact I still cringe when I remember the guy with the missing teeth going down on me. It made for an unusual experience.

I know you might not believe that I have standards now. Especially considering how quickly I dropped my panties for the mysterious stranger at my friends' wedding. The mysterious stranger that was now standing in front of me. You might want to believe that I drop my panties for any man that asks, but trust me I don't. Mr. Tongue was the exception to the rule. I dropped my panties without a second thought when I saw him. Well, actually that's a bit of a lie. *I* didn't exactly drop my panties. He took them off with his teeth. His cute, perfectly straight, sharp pearly-white teeth. Oh shit, my body can still remember his teeth grazing my skin as he pulled my white lace panties off. Honestly, in that moment I couldn't stop him or myself. It was one of those magical moments that you see in movies. The chemistry was perfect between us, our bodies were on fire and all I could think about was him and his mouth; even though we were just one room away from a packed church. I never thought anything like that would happen to me. I got caught up in the moment. I mean it's not every day you make eye contact with a green eyed stranger, and he leads you to a back room in a church (God, forgive me). It's not every day that you meet a man: a gorgeous, sexy, virile stud of a man, and okay, yes he was slightly obnoxious, but I didn't care. It's not every day a hot stud has got you on the floor, with your dress riding up around your waist as he pulls your panties off with his teeth. And let's not forget his tongue. Oh my God, his tongue did things to me that I cannot repeat. Things, I didn't even know existed. Like multiple orgasms in minutes, yes, I said minutes. Like one right after the other. And all from his tongue: pink, long and extremely flexible. Who knew tongues could be so flexible? Not me. And of course, he knew he'd blown my world. The grin on his face and the glint in his eye told me that he knew he was the shit. Smug, cocky bastard. As I stared at him in front of me, I knew that he could still remember that day as well. I could see it in the glint of his eye as I tried to keep my breathing under control. What had he done to me then, and why was he here now?

I'd only been slightly embarrassed as I'd climaxed on his mouth. The way he'd eagerly licked up my juices from his lips had made me feel slightly dirty. I didn't care though. I was still too busy trying to catch my breath as I jumped up from the ground, and pulled my dress back down. I started panicking as I heard the organist playing "Here Comes the Bride". I had to get back to my pew in the church quickly and that also meant panty less as he didn't want to give them back (and yeah, I thought that was kind of hot). I know, I have no shame. I walked back into the church that day feeling like a harlot. I'd let some nameless, random smug man go down on me, right before a wedding. Who did that?

That wasn't even the worst of it. I went home with him too. And when I say went home, I mean to his hotel suite. His very expensive, very impressive suite at the Marriott downtown (he was most probably paying my month's rent for a long weekend). We went to his hotel room and this time he used more than his tongue. And this time, I did more than lie back with my legs in the air and his face firmly planted down smack bang in the center. It was a night of fireworks. A night of explosive sex that blew my world and everything that I thought I knew about sex. I was ruined for the next boring man I dated. No longer would I be happy with quick foreplay and some push in and out missionary action. I'd never had sex so hot and I suppose that's the beauty of one night stands. You hook up and do all the things you're too self-conscious to normally do. Neither one of us had expectations. We didn't even exchange names. And that's why I left early the next morning and hurried out of the room, head held as high as I could as I did the walk of shame through the hotel lobby, my smeared mascara and messy hair telling my tale to everyone that viewed me.

I didn't care though. I'd experienced the best sex of my life and with the hottest man I'd ever met. That does something to your ego. I felt like a million dollars and I was pretty sure I'd rocked his world as well. He wouldn't forget me anytime soon; especially as he had the scratch and bite marks to remind him of our night for the next few days. It didn't even matter that he'd seemed like he could be an arrogant asshole; the way he'd bossed me around the bed. I even kind of liked his take charge alphaness. It was good in the bedroom, though I knew in everyday life, he'd annoy me, but that didn't matter. He wasn't someone I ever had to deal with again.

I was wrong though. Because you know how life goes. When you're riding high and feeling like you're on top of everything, something always happens to bring you back down to earth. That's what happened to me this weekend when I came home to visit my parents. The weekend after the wedding when I hooked up with Mr. Tongue. Yes, my one night stand didn't seem so hot and innocent when I turned up at my parents' house and saw him sitting on my parents couch. Miracle Tongue or as he called himself Mr. Tongue had nearly given me a heart attack when I'd seen him sitting there in front of me my parents couch, sipping Earl Grey Tea. The moment he looked up at me, his green eyes laughing, was a moment I'll never forget. It was the moment that stopped my heart for what seemed like minutes. It was the moment that reminded me why I'd never had a one-night stand before. I stood there for a few seconds, before he stood up and walked over to me, a huge grin on his face.

"Hello," he grinned at me as he reached his hand out to me. "Nice to meet you, my name is Xander."

"I'm Liv." I said softly, my face red as I shook his hand.

"Nice to meet you Liv." His eyes teased me as my parents stood there watching us.

"You too." I swallowed hard. What was he doing here?

"Oh, you have something on your ear." He leaned forward and brushed something off of my ear as he whispered quietly. "Now I have a name to put to the face when I think about our night together." He said and I felt the tip of his tongue on my earlobe. I pulled back in shock and glanced at him and then back at my parents.

"What are you doing here?" I asked softly, needing an answer. This was too much of a coincidence. Of course the answer wasn't the fairytale answer that I was secretly hoping for. He hadn't tracked me down because he couldn't forget me. He hadn't come to woo me. No, of course my journey into the land of one night stands couldn't be so perfect. Of course, my journey into one night stands ended up being one complicated mess. I should have known that for me it wouldn't be one night of fun. I should have known that one night stands never end at one night and they always turn into a whole bunch of trouble.

"What would you like me to be doing here?" He laughed and ran his hands through his jet black hair. Hair I knew was silky soft to the touch. Hair that I'd grabbed and pulled. I bit my lower lip as I stood there, in shock. If I'd known the reason why he was there, I would have run away. If I'd known who he was at the wedding I would have said no. But of course, I wasn't privy to that information. So of course my one night stand changed everything I thought I knew about my life and who I was. My one night stand had a name. And that was Xander James. And Xander James was about to make everything in my life a whole lot more complicated. Because Xander James was a lot more man than just being Mr. Tongue, Xander James was a man that took what he wanted when he wanted it, no questions asked. And now that he'd seen me again. I was at the top of his list of wants.

1

ONE WEEK EARLIER

"LIV, I WILL GIVE YOU one hundred dollars if you hook up with someone at the wedding reception tomorrow." Alice grinned at me and held up five twenties in her hand. "Five big ones, baby."

"Five big ones would mean five hundred dollars, not one hundred dollars." I rolled my eyes. "Twenties aren't considered big ones."

"They are to me."

"Not to me."

"Liv." Alice sighed. "Stop trying to change the subject. You going to do it or what?" She paused. "I dare you."

My eyes narrowed as I stared at her. Alice knew that I wasn't one to back down from a dare. "What do I have to do?"

"Just make out with a guy." She grinned. "Any guy."

"Any guy?"

"Well a guy at the reception. It has to be a wedding hookup."

"Joanna will kill me." I shook my head and laughed.

"That's the point." She giggled and collapsed onto my bed.

"Oh Alice." I sighed and sat down next to her. Joanna was our roommate from college. The three of us had lived together for the last three years. And we'd been shocked when Joanna had informed us she was getting married, two months after we graduated. To Alice's ex-boyfriend.

"If you hook up with Luke, I'll give you five hundred."

"I'm not hooking up with your ex." I made a face and then slapped my mouth. "Sorry."

"Why are you sorry?" Alice shrugged. "You're a good friend."

"I can't believe she's marrying him and invited us to the wedding."

"She's a bitch." Alice nodded.

"We don't have to go." I said hopefully. I really didn't want to go to this wedding. I had a really bad feeling that something was going to go awfully wrong.

"We have to go." Alice licked her lips. "And we're going to be crazy."

"I don't know if I want to be crazy." I made a face and sighed. I didn't want to be crazy, but I knew for Alice's sake I'd be as crazy as I could be. Which would be hard, considering my background.

I'm the good girl in my family. The youngest in a family of five kids; I have three brothers and one sister. All of whom are crazy and out of control. You don't have a family of crazy siblings and end up crazy. You end up as a good kid. You end up as the kid that the parents are thankful for. You end up as a goody two shoes. I've been a goody two shoes all my life. Up until college. I went away to college determined to have some fun. And fun, I had. Though it wasn't the sexing a different hot guy every week, sort of fun. It was the smoking a joint in a dark room with three of my friends and talking about hot guys sort of fun. Don't get me wrong, I wanted to be one of those confident girls that just goes out and gets laid with whomever she wanted. Only, I didn't have the sort of personality that permitted that.

Instead, I had two long-term relationships, with two average safe guys, with some average and safe sex. I graduated with a bachelor's degree as a single, twenty two year old feeling like I was just as boring as I'd been when I'd started school. I was determined for that to change, once and for all. Even if that meant making a spectacle of myself at Joanna's wedding.

"DON'T FORGET, FIVE BIG ONES baby." Alice grinned at me as we walked into the church the next afternoon; both of us slightly tipsy from the free mimosas we'd had with our breakfast. "Just think of all the things you can do with the money."

"$100 isn't going to make me a millionaire." I rolled my eyes at her as I laughed. "I thought you'd forgotten about that stupid proposition."

"I had, but then I just saw Luke and Joanna and I wanted to gag." She made a face. "It would make me feel a lot better knowing that someone hooked up at her wedding." She grinned. "It would be like this dirty little joke that no one knew about, but me."

"Well, I'd know and the guy would know as well." We stood next to the pews awkwardly and continued talking. "Also, I don't think this is an appropriate conversation to have in front of God."

"God isn't happy with Joanna either." Alice made a face and then sighed. "Forgive me, Father for I have sinned." She quickly made the sign of a cross and screwed up her nose. "Fine, don't hook up with anyone and don't make me feel better."

"My hooking up with someone shouldn't make you feel better anyways, Alice." I laughed and then looked around. "Should we sit? I feel like we're kind of early."

"Yeah, I guess." She shrugged. "Or we could just ditch and go and get some more mimosas? That sounds like an even better plan."

"We can't ditch." I laughed at the suggestion, though I wasn't altogether sold on having to sit through the wedding of two people I didn't really like.

"Please." Alice made a hopeful face at me and I laughed again as she made a drinking motion. This time my head fell back as I laughed and I could feel someone staring at me. I looked to the left and there I saw a tall, brooding man with dark hair and a frown on his face about two hundred yards away from us. I attempted to give him a smile, but instead of smiling back, he gave me a disdainful eyebrow raise and looked away.

"That guy is an asshole." I whispered to Alice, the laughter gone from my voice.

"What guy?" She turned around and looked towards the entrance of the church, but the rude man had gone and a group of older women were walking towards us.

"There was a guy up there just now, who was looking at me as if I were some commoner on his estate or something." I could feel my face flushing red with anger as I remembered his superior look. "I'm not sure who he thinks he is, but I don't think there's anything wrong with laughing in a church."

"Yeah, that's weird." Alice nodded. "Maybe he's related to Joanna or something, I think her entire family is full of snobs. No one is good enough for her."

"I don't get why he was glaring at me." I said again. "I wasn't doing anything wrong."

"Forget him, he most probably needs to get laid." Alice said loudly and I groaned as I saw a priest behind her.

"Good Afternoon Father." I said meekly, my face burning in shame now.

"Good Afternoon." His eyes burned into mine and I knew that he'd heard Alice and was thinking that both of us needed to go to some sort of confession; even though neither one of us was Catholic. He continued walking past us and I grabbed Alice's arm.

"Let's go outside and wait until it fills up a bit. I feel like we're just making a spectacle of ourselves."

"Sex with the group would be making a spectacle of myself, not just standing here." She rolled her eyes and I felt a wave of compassion towards her.

"Are you okay? This must be hard?"

"My ex-boyfriend is marrying my ex roommate and friend, what's to be upset about?" Alice sighed and then shook her head. "I don't really care. He had a small dick. That's Joanna's problem now."

"Hahaha." I started laughing again and this time, tears were rolling down my face. I wasn't sure why I found it so funny, but I suspect that the mimosas had worked their magic and I was feeling more relaxed than usual. "You never told me that Luke wasn't good in bed."

"He was good with his tongue." She grinned. "That was good enough."

"Hmm," I scratched my head. "Let me think." I closed my eyes and tried to think about a guy going down on me versus a guy entering me. "Cock or tongue, what do I prefer?" I giggled and then opened my eyes. Alice's face looked stiff and I turned to the right of me and saw the brooding man from earlier, standing right next to Alice. His green eyes looked amused as he stared at me. He was gorgeous and I was having a hard time breathing as I realized what I'd just said, out loud. I wanted to groan, but kept my mouth shut as I stared at him. His lips looked pink and soft and he had a light, dark beard, that looked sexy as hell on him, and I wasn't even a girl that was into facial hair. I could feel my face burning up as I stared at him. All I could think about was his beard and I wondered if it would tickle me if he went down on me. I wanted to slap myself for my inappropriate thoughts. That was it, no more mimosas in the morning.

"Did you make up your mind?" The man said slowly, his voice a deep, husky growl that made me think of dark rooms and handcuffs.

"Make up my mind about what?" I squeaked out, knowing exactly what he was talking about.

"Your preference." He grinned and licked his lips slowly. My eyes followed his long tongue and I knew he was teasing me, but I didn't care.

"Yes." I said softly and flicked my long brown hair back.

"And?" He leaned forward, his eyes letting me know he was attracted to me. I looked at Alice and she was grinning at the two of us as she took a step back.

"And that's for me to know." I smiled at him sweetly, though my stomach was churning.

"What if I want to find out?" His eyes gazed into mine, searching and he touched my shoulder lightly.

"What if you do?" I shrugged and he stepped back with a smile and nodded.

"You'll find out."

"I'll find out what?" My heart was racing as I studied his chest. I could tell, even though he was wearing a suit, that he was well-built.

"You'll find out what happens when I want to know something."

"Okay…" My voice trailed off.

"Okay then." He grinned, a cocky smile, and licked his lips again. "I'll see you later." And with that he walked away.

"What was that?" I whispered to Alice, my body trembling slightly from my encounter.

"I have no idea what just happened, but that guy was sexy as hell." Alice looked behind her. "I wouldn't mind his tongue or his—"

"Alice." I laughed as I cut her off. "I think we should change the subject."

"Why?" She sighed. "You can't tell me you didn't think he was hot."

"I can't tell you that, no." I laughed and thought about the guy's green eyes and dark hair. I repositioned my legs as I remembered his pink tongue. "He's the sort of guy, it would be hard to say no too."

"Yeah, it would be very hard to say no to him." She agreed and we just stood there for a few minutes, both of us thinking about the guy. I should have known that that wasn't going to be the last I saw of him that day. I mean, he'd basically warned me that he'd be back and on the prowl. Maybe I didn't pay attention to him or care because I was up for it myself. It had been so long since I'd dated anyone, and I'd never done anything risqué or crazy. I'd never just hooked up with a guy, but now I was in a drought and hooking up didn't seem so bad. I didn't even care that he seemed like a snob or an obnoxious asshole. It wasn't like I was going to date him. Not at all. And it wasn't even me that initiated anything. Though, I was hoping that I'd bump into him again when I left the pew to go and look for some water.

"Get me a bottle as well." Alice handed me a five dollar note. "And don't take all day. I don't want to be sitting here by myself for long."

"Fine." I hurried out of the church and looked around the now packed lobby at all of the guests that were arriving. I was disappointed when I didn't see my handsome stranger and was about to turn back around, when I felt two hands on my waist.

"So did you decide?" His voice whispered in my ear as his hands ran down my hips. I'm not even sure what got into me, maybe it was liquid courage, but I slowly turned around and faced him.

"I'm a big fan of the tongue." I licked my lips then and swallowed hard as I stared at him. I couldn't believe that I was being so blatantly obvious with a stranger.

"That's a good thing then." He grinned and leaned down so that his lips were almost against mine, "I've been told that I'm very good with my tongue."

"Oh?" I said nervously.

"Oh yes." He winked at me and grabbed my hand before leading me down a small corridor. I followed behind him, a loud roar in my ears, but I couldn't stop. Not now. Not when every fiber of my being was on fire, and awaiting his touch. This man was sex personified and what would it hurt, to just make out with him.

"You're so sexy." He whispered as he opened a door, pulled me into the room with him and then closed it. He pushed me back and I felt his lips on mine. "I'm going to show you just how talented I am."

"Shhh." I kissed him back hard, my tongue entering his mouth as my hands worked their way around his neck. Bells were ringing in my head as waves of heat spread through my entire body as he sucked on my tongue. The drought was officially ending and I couldn't be happier about it.

His hands were firm and teasing as they ran down my body and up my dress, his fingers grazing my skin as they reached for the prize. His fingers lightly rubbed against my panties and I stilled for a second, pulling back and looking at him before my legs crumbled beneath me.

"Lace panties?" He grinned, his eyes challenging mine as he lightly played with the feminine material.

"Yes." I nodded and moaned as he slipped a finger inside.

"Is it your wedding?"

"Does it have to be my wedding to wear lace panties?" I groaned as I bit my lower lip.

"I suppose not." He winked. "Just like it doesn't have to be your wedding if you want to hook up at the church." His eyes laughed into mine and I knew that he was making fun of our situation.

"If you'd rather not." I made to get up and his face came towards mine again, an intense light in his eyes as he gazed into mine.

"I rather would." He muttered right before his lips came crashing down on mine. This time they weren't soft and they weren't teasing. They were demanding and straight to the point. This man wanted to dominate me. His tongue sought entry into my mouth and he sucked on my tongue with such finesse that I had to grab onto his shoulders to stop myself from falling to the ground. His lips tasted sweet and salty, like honey roasted peanuts and I grabbed his face so that I could deepen the kiss as well. My fingers ran across his stubble and I was amazed at how soft his skin felt beneath the prickly hair. He lifted me up slightly and then lowered me to the ground.

"What are you doing?" I moaned, as he pulled my formal dress up.

"What you want me to do." He bent down and I felt his tongue running up the inside of my thigh. My body tingled all over and all I could think was how glad I was that I'd shaved above the knee that morning. I was never going to do the below the knee shaving trick anymore. Not when occasions like this could possible happen. My body trembled as his teeth made contact with my panties. My now very moist panties. I leaned back and cried out as his perfect teeth grabbed a hold of the crotch of my panties and pulled them down.

"Should we be doing this?" I moaned as I glanced up at him. I watched as he slipped my panties off of my ankles and pushed them into his pocket.

"I think the question should be would we regret it if we didn't?"

"We don't even know each other."

"Does that matter?" He undid the top button of his shirt and loosened his black tie slightly. "I know that as soon as I saw you, I wanted to get to know you."

"You want to get to know me, but you don't want me to know your name?"

"No names, no questions." He looked at me intently. "Is that okay with you?"

"It's okay with me, if it's okay with you." I whispered, my heart thudding. I didn't even know what I was saying. I just knew that I wanted him to be touching me again.

"Good." He said simply as he grabbed my legs and spread them. "Now let me show you how I reward good girls." He buried his face into my pussy and his tongue licked my clit eagerly. An involuntary gasp escaped my lips as I felt his tongue sliding inside of me. My legs clenched on his face and I grabbed a hold of his shoulders as he moved his tongue in and out of me. I lay there with my head on the ground and my legs spread and all I could think about was the fact that anyone could walk into the room and catch us, fornicating, on the ground. Though, technically we weren't fornicating. I have to admit that the thought both scared me and turned me on. I had released my inner slut. Or rather Mr. Miracle Tongue had released it.

"Come for me baby," He whispered as he slid in and out of me with speed, his tongue feeling as thick and long as some men's dicks. I know, I know, it's a weird thing to think about, but he knew how to work it. I wondered what it would be like to have sex with him. I was pretty confident that he would be dynamite in bed.

"Bite my shoulder." He growled as I started screaming. I did as he commanded and bit down on his shoulder and shirt to stop the whole church from hearing my climax. However my neck felt slightly strained so I moved back slightly. He kissed my clit before licking up my juices and moving up slightly, and I kissed his neck. "You taste so good, like honey." He grunted against me and I felt his fingers rubbing me gently as I moved my lips to his neck and sucked. "You're going to leave bite marks on my neck." His eyes peered up at me, dark with lust and I laughed.

"I want to leave my mark on you." I growled back at him, surprising myself with the voracity in my tone. Where had this passionate aggressive girl come from? I want to leave my mark on you? Who said that? Who was I turning into? Was I some sort of vampire now? Or werewolf? Or just some sad freak who said weird things.

"You've already left your mark on me." He said huskily as he licked his lips. "You've left a lot more than your mark."

I laughed awkwardly then. I mean how do you not? Not when you're me. I'm the awkward one. I always have been. Just because now I wasn't as awkward, I was still awkward inside. I think that was why I reached for his belt and undid it slowly and seductively. Well, I tried to at least. I got the button undone, but then when I got to the zipper, I had issues.

"It won't go down." I mumbled as I looked up in his face. I could see that he was trying to stop himself from laughing.

"Maybe because my zipper knows that if it goes down, we won't be leaving this room for at least two hours." He winked at me and jumped up. "And then we'll both miss the wedding and that wouldn't be good, would it?"

"I guess not." I agreed and took his offered hand and let him pull me up. I pulled my dress down and stood there in front of him, not sure what to do.

"But that doesn't mean, we can't meet up tonight."

"Tonight?" I squeaked out, surprised at his suggestion and not knowing what to say. That would be it then. I'd officially ended my two years drought. I'd be having sex again. And with a hot stud. My stomach jumped for joy at the thought.

"Yes tonight." His voice was smooth. "You. Me. My hotel room. Champagne. Strawberries. My bed." He cocked his head to the side and smiled. "I think you know what comes next?"

"Steak and fries?" I joked and he laughed lightly.

"Yeah. Steak and fries." He pulled me towards him and kissed me gently, his fingers running through my hair. "You'll have to teach me that move." He whispered in my ear as he kissed the side of my face.

"Oh it's not a position." I said stupidly.

"We'll just have to make it a position then, won't we?" He stared into my eyes with such a possessive look, that I couldn't help but feel thrilled.

"If you want." I nodded, my head still up in the clouds of confusion and denial.

"We should go back into the church." He grinned. "Someone's playing 'Here Comes the Bride' again."

"Yeah, we should head in." I nodded as I hurried towards the door.

"You go first." He stayed where he was. "I'll come in after you."

"Okay." I opened the door and hurried out of the room, my body flushed with blood from my orgasms. Had I really just let a strange man go down on me? My brain was still in total disbelief and I laughed to myself as I walked into the church. Not only had I just let Mr. Miracle Tongue go down on me, but I was planning on letting him do a lot more to me later that evening.

"DID YOU JUST MAKE OUT with that guy?" Alice's face was positively giddy as she stared at me. I felt like I was doing the walk of shame as I made my way down the aisle and I knew that I'd have to donate all five of the twenties that Alice was going to eventually give me.

"No." I sat in the pew next to her, knowing full well that my lipstick was pretty much gone and that my hair was a hot mess.

"Oh my God, did you have sex with him?" Alice's jaw dropped.

"No I did not have sex with him." I squeaked out and the people in the row in front of us turned around to look at me.

"Shh." The old lady directly in front of us glared at me. "This is a wedding, not a night club."

"Sorry." I gave her a weak smile, but she turned back to the front. "Alice." I glared at her.

"Don't blame me, you had sex in a church. I can't believe it." She laughed. "You're so going to hell."

"I'm not going to hell." I pat my hair down. "We didn't have sex."

"What did you do then?" She grinned as the organist started playing 'Here Comes the Bride' once again and we all stood up.

"You don't want to know." I blushed as I straightened my dress. My inner thighs were still tingling.

"So what's his name?"

"Whose name?"

"Liv." Alice rolled her eyes and I avoided her gaze as I watched the groom and his best man walk up the aisle.

"Shouldn't they have played this song once he was already by the altar and the bride was walking down the aisle?" I made a face as we continued to listen to 'Here Comes the Bride'. "How many times are they going to play this song?"

"Liv, I don't care what they do at my ex's wedding." Alice's face dropped and I could see in her eyes that she was more hurt than she'd let on about this wedding.

"I don't know his name." I breathed out quietly. "But we can call him Mr. Miracle Tongue."

"Mr. Tongue?" Alice blurted out just as the music stopped and it felt like the whole church was looking at us. I turned to look around and I saw him standing at the back of the church with a wicked smile on his face as he grinned and straightened his jacket. He'd heard. I was almost positive of it. Oh why, oh why did I always have to be so uncool in these sort of situations?

2

"THIS IS MY HOTEL ROOM." He closed the door behind me with a slam. It was as if the door were trying to tell me that I was not leaving, at least not tonight.

"It's nice." I looked around, barely breathing. The room was huge and decorated like it was a Pottery Barn display. "Is this the penthouse?"

"Junior Penthouse." He nodded as he stepped towards me.

"Very nice." I swallowed hard.

"Are we done with the small talk?" His arms went around my waist and pulled me towards him.

"I didn't know that we were—"

"Shh." His lips touched mine gently as he kissed me. "Let's not waste our time with talking."

"I don't even know your name." I pulled away from him slightly.

"Does it matter?" He replied, his eyes light, as his hands fell to my ass.

"I guess not." My face burned in shame. Not because he didn't care about my name, but rather because I didn't really care about his either. I was going to sleep with him either way. We both knew that. His tongue had been the appetizer and now I was ready for the real thing. I knew his main course was going to fill me up. I giggled at my thoughts. I wasn't sure when I'd become so dirty minded, but I loved it.

"What's so funny?" He pulled me towards him and I felt his hardness against my stomach. Oh boy, I'd ordered an extra big helping and I hadn't even realized it.

"Just thinking about dinner." I said inanely, feeling like a fool.

"Steak and fries." He licked his lips slowly. "I've got a steak in my pants that wouldn't mind being eaten?"

"Oh?" I raised my eyebrows at him and he burst out laughing.

"Okay, that sounded a lot cooler in my mind."

"I sure hope so." I laughed. "Because it didn't sound as cool out loud."

"Are you saying I'm not cool?" He teased me as I followed him into the living room of his hotel room.

"I'm saying that you're no John Travolta in Grease. You know, you're not cool like Danny."

"Well, I take that as a compliment, Sandy." He popped open a bottle of champagne. "A glass?"

"Yes, thanks." I took the offered glass and sat down on the couch and took a small sip. *This isn't awkward at all*, I thought to myself as I sat there staring at him. I was still in my dress and he was still in his suit, only his jacket was gone. His white shirt clung to his frame as if it were a second skin and I was dying to see his chest. I knew he had to be toned. I could tell from the way his biceps bulged in his shirt. The only question in my mind was does he have a six pack or an eight pack?

"What are you thinking?" He sat next to me on the couch and stared over at me. "Your dress is very beautiful by the way."

"Uhm thanks." I took another sip of champagne. Oh my God, why was he so hot? "I'm just thinking that you're really cute."

"Thank you." He put his glass down and moved closer to me. "Do you want to know what I'm thinking?"

"What's that?"

"I'm wondering what you're going to look like without that dress on. I'm wondering how quickly I can make you come tonight. I'm wondering if you're going to try and mark me again. I'm wondering if your breasts taste as sweet as your pussy."

"Oh." I squeaked out, my face hot at his words. He was not playing and I loved it.

"Am I making you uncomfortable?" He stroked the side of my face softly.

"No." I shook my head as his fingers ran across my lips and he pushed his index finger into my mouth. I sucked on his finger gently and he stared into my eyes intently as I nibbled. He pulled it out slowly and then stuck it into my glass of champagne, his eyes never leaving mine, before putting his finger back in my mouth. I sucked hard this time, licking the champagne off with my tongue. The expression on his face changed as I moved closer to him and rubbed my hand over his crotch as I sucked his finger. I smiled as I felt the bulge in his pants. He was turned on already. It made me feel powerful to know I could do that to a man as handsome as he was. It didn't even matter to me that this was a one night stand. It didn't matter that it was just sex.

"You enjoy being a tease?" He pulled his finger out of my mouth and his hands fell to my breasts. "Stand up and take your dress off." He commanded me and I looked over at him in surprise.

"What?" I asked, still rubbing his now hard cock.

"Take your dress off."

"The magic word?"

"My cock is hard." He grinned as his eyes challenged me.

"I was thinking more like please." I licked my lips and stood up in front of him.

"There's no time for pleases, just thank you's."

"Thank you's?"

"When I make you come, you can thank me." He looked smug. "Each and every time."

"Each and every time?" I swallowed hard as I reached up to pull a strap down.

"Each. And. Every. Time." He said pronouncing each word carefully and clearly as he stood up.

"I see." My hand froze on my upper arm as I gazed at him, his body exuding confidence and power. This was a man that was used to getting what he wanted. A man that would normally annoy me.

"Don't worry. I have enough condoms." He grinned and nodded towards the table.

"You planned this?" I frowned. Had it been his plan to seduce someone at the wedding? Did it not even matter who I was.

"No." He smirked, his eyes firm as he gazed at me. "I didn't plan this. In fact this is rather inconvenient for me."

"This is inconvenient for you?"

"Yes." He nodded, his hand now on top of mine and guiding my dress strap down. "I really have other things to be worrying about right now."

"Instead of hooking up you mean?"

"Correct. This wasn't a part of the plan."

"I see." I said slightly sullenly, though I was happy that I wasn't just the girl for the night.

"It wasn't part of my plan for this weekend, but I'm adaptable when I'm around a beautiful girl." He moved in closer to me and reached for my other bra strap. "What happened to your friend by the way?"

"My friend?"

"The loud girl you were with at the wedding?"

"Oh Alice." I laughed. "She went home."

"I hope she's not mad that I stole you away for the night."

"No, she's not mad." I shook my head and grinned. "She's happy that I'm getting laid."

"Oh?" He reached behind me and I felt my zipper being pulled down.

"I'm not the sort of girl that normally has a one night stand."

"Oh?" He paused and frowned as he looked at me. "This isn't going to be —"

"Don't worry." I cut him off. "I don't think this is anything more than one night."

"I don't want you to get the wrong impression." He pulled the front of my dress down to my waist and stared at my bra covered breasts and whistled.

"Trust me, I'm not getting any impression."

"Good." He nodded, his hands now undoing my bra. "I'm not the sort of man that you want to get involved with."

"Good to know." I gasped as his fingers pinched my nipples. "I'm not the sort of girl you want to get involved with either." I moaned as he leaned forward and took my left nipple in his mouth and sucked. "Ooh." I cried out and pulled his hair.

"Why's that?"

"Why's what?" I groaned as he pulled his mouth away.

"Why don't I want to get involved with you?" His eyes looked into mine curiously.

"I'm trouble." I lied and pushed his head back down to my other breast.

"Oh really?" He grinned and his eyes flashed with some indistinguishable emotion as he took my other nipple into his mouth.

"Oh yeah." I lied again and closed my eyes. "I'm trouble with a capital T."

"I like girls that are full of trouble." He mumbled against my skin. "I like to make bad girls good." He nibbled on my nipple and sucked so hard that I felt a jolt of desire flash from my head to my toes.

"Then you better get started." I giggled and he picked me up in his arms and carried me to the bed.

"Oh, I'm ready to get started alright." He dropped me on the bed and then leaned forward and pulled my dress all of the way off. He groaned as he stared at my naked body, the lust in his eyes evident. "No panties, you little slut." He grinned at me.

"You took my panties." I protested as he laughed. "And I'm not a slut."

"I'm not a pimp so I don't care." He pulled his tie off and started unbuttoning his shirt.

"Six." I muttered to myself with a half-smile.

"What?" He frowned at me as he undid his belt buckle.

"You have a six pack, not an eight pack." I pointed at his stomach as I squirmed on the bed.

"Does that matter?" He fell on the bed next to me and grabbed my hand and ran it down his chest and abs.

"Hmmm, let me think." I ran my fingers across his chest and I felt the heat emanating from his skin seeping into mine. Holy shit, he was perfection in a six foot two bottle.

"Don't think too long." He growled as he pulled his pants down and threw them on the ground. Now he was lying next to me in only a pair of white briefs and I wasn't sure if I could stand it. "So what's your favorite position?" He asked me softly as he rolled over on his side and stared at me, his fingers running down the side of my body.

"Huh?" I swallowed hard, gazing up at him, as my body trembled at his touch.

"Your favorite position." He smiled down at me sweetly. "You have beautiful brown eyes. You know that right?"

"Uhm, thanks." I touched his cheek. "And you have gorgeous green eyes, that sometimes look blue and sometimes look black."

"Like water on a dark troubled night?" He studied my face for a few seconds and then smiled.

"No, I was more thinking of blue purple violets on an Autumn day." I stroked his cheek. "Or a forest at midnight."

"Nah, there's nothing fall-like about me. I'm all stormy troubled waters." He leaned down and kissed me. "Troubled, troubled waters." He muttered against my lips as his hand slid down my legs.

I didn't bother to ask him what he meant. I mean what was the point? We weren't here to get to know each other. I wasn't his therapist and he wasn't my boyfriend. This wasn't some deep, meaningful night. This was about having fun. I ran my fingers down his back and wrapped my legs around his waist as he lay on top of me. I could feel his erection pressing into me hard and I groaned.

"Do that again." He muttered as his fingers played with my breasts.

"Do what again?" I squirmed against him and moaned.

"That." He growled and pulled away from me. I watched as he pulled his briefs off and his hardness sprung out of his briefs, powerful and confident. I shouldn't have been surprised at how thick and hard it looked, but I couldn't stop myself from licking my lips. "You like?" He grinned and raised an eyebrow at me.

"I don't think I can lie." I giggled as he grabbed me and pulled me on top of him so that I was straddling him. I could feel his hardness between my legs.

"You're so wet." He groaned as I rubbed myself back and forth on him.

"Shh." I leaned forward and kissed him. "No more talking."

"No more talking?" His eyes narrowed.

"No more talking." I put my finger against his lips. "Just make love to me."

"Make love to you?" He smirked as his hands made their way to my waist and up to my breasts, squeezing them together softly.

"Fuck me." I whispered down at him as I continued my slow grind on top of him.

"Fuck you?" He smirked.

"Yes." I nodded with a small smile. "That's what you wanted right?"

He didn't answer me. Instead he reached to the nightstand and grabbed a packet and ripped it open. I watched him pull the condom out and I moved to the side so that he could slide it on. I stared at him then, pushed his hands back to the mattress and moved forward and up, sitting down gently on him, my eyes never leaving his, as he filled me up. In that moment, I felt more alive than I'd ever felt in my life. I felt like I was flying, soaring through the sky and nothing could stop me. I moved back and forth gently, but he wasn't having any of that. His hands moved my hips back and forth quickly so that I was truly riding him like some sort of Texas Cowgirl.

The rest of the night passed in a blur of different positions. I'd never been with a man that could get hard again so quickly after orgasming. He was like Superman. I'd have to nickname him Superman with the miracle tongue. He had me on the bed, on the couch, in the shower, on the floor. He fucked me hard, slow and in-between. He pleasured me with his fingers, his tongue and his cock and I screamed and shouted as if I were on a rollercoaster; which I suppose I was. I was on the rollercoaster ride of my life. I knew I'd be sore the next day, but I didn't care. We finally fell asleep at about four am. I awoke at five, needing to go to the bathroom and that's when I decided to leave. I grabbed my dress and pulled it on slowly as I stared at his sleeping body on the bed. He was a fine specimen of a man. And he was obviously a dog if he was so quick to have a one night stand, but I knew that was unfair of me as I'd chosen to have a one night stand as well. I crept out of his room, feeling high on life and incredibly satisfied. I'd had my first one night stand and it had been everything I'd thought it would be. In fact, it had been even better than I had thought it would be. I wished I could tell my ex Shane about what I'd done. I wanted to call him and tell him that he'd been wrong about me. I wasn't a prude. I wasn't scared of sex. I was a confident, sexy woman. I'd just fucked a hot stranger and felt like a million bucks. I wasn't ashamed at all. I didn't even care that I didn't know his name and it didn't matter. I'd never see him again. I'd gotten mine and he'd gotten his and now we could both move on with our lives.

3

"IT'S SO ANNOYING THAT I always have to go home just because Gabby wants to act like a dutiful perfect daughter." I groaned into the phone as I drove home to my parents' house. "I don't see why I'm always required to go as well."

"You'll be happy to see your parents." Alice laughed. "Plus you might meet another guy and have another night of hot sex."

"Yeah sure." I laughed. "Unlikely." I flushed as I thought about my one night stand. "Plus, I'm not going to make it a habit."

"I can't believe you didn't even get his name." Alice laughed. "I know I dared you, but I didn't think you'd go through with it."

"I didn't sleep with him because you dared me, Alice." I giggled. "And I didn't get his name because it didn't matter. It's not like he wanted mine." I thought back to the Mr. Miracle Tongue and the fact that I had no name to match his gorgeous face. "He made it very clear that it was just going to be a night of hot sex and that was it."

"I'm sure you could have stayed for a second night."

"I'm glad I left." I smiled into the phone. "If anything I left him wanting more. If I'd stayed until he woke up and waited to see what he was going to say, I would have looked like a desperate loser."

"No, you might have gotten morning sex."

"I didn't need morning sex. We had enough sex to last me for months." I lied. I would have loved to have had morning sex with him. He'd been a terrific lover and I'd spent every night of the week thinking about him and the things he'd done to me.

"It's just sad. You can't even contact him."

"It's better that way." I sighed. "Alice, he said he wasn't expecting anything to happen that weekend either. I think his life is complicated. I don't think he was looking for anything other than a night."

"Oh well, sucks for him." Alice said cheerily. "When are you back? Tomorrow night?"

"Yeah, I should be," I sighed, thinking about how I was going to have to act like the perfect daughter. "I just hope that Gabby doesn't have more exciting news to share." I groaned. The last couple of times I'd been home, she'd gotten into a PhD program, she'd adopted a stray dog, and she'd won a local volunteering award. It was just too much to compete with. I had no such accolades to share.

"If she shares any more exciting news, you should share yours as well." Alice giggled.

"What news?"

"The fact that you got laid last week to a very, very hot man."

"Yeah, I'm going to share that." I laughed. "I'd give my dad a heart attack."

"It would be funny to see their faces though."

"No, it wouldn't be." I groaned as I pulled up the driveway. "Hey, I'm home. I'll talk to you later, okay?"

"Sure have fun." Alice said and hung up as I turned off the engine and then got out of my car.

"Just smile, Liv." I muttered to myself as I grabbed my bag. "It won't be so bad. Who cares what great news Gabby has now. Grin, pretend to be happy and leave as soon as you can." I mumbled and walked to the front door.

"Liv, you're here." My mom opened the door before I could even ring the doorbell. "We've been waiting for you."

"I'm here." I grinned at her and made a face. "No need to sit around and wait anymore."

"That's not funny, young lady." She shook her head. "Now come in."

"I'm coming." I rolled my eyes, dropped my bag in the hallway and took a deep breath. I already knew it was going to be a long weekend. My mom was wearing one of her Sunday Church dresses. That meant she was excited and that whatever Gabby had done must be special. Maybe she'd saved someone from dying. Maybe she's found a cure to the common cold. Maybe she was moving to the North Pole. I grinned then. That would actually be amazing news.

"Are you listening to me Liv?" My mom frowned as we walked into the living room.

"Of course, mother." I smiled at her and took a deep breath.

"I want you to meet our guest." She nodded towards the couch and that's when time stood still. It literally stood still, as I saw miracle tongue sitting on the couch with my dad, a cup of tea in his hand.

"Hello." He stood up and smiled at me, as if he hadn't just had a one night stand with me the weekend before.

"Hello." I said softly, my face red. Oh my God, why was here? Had he told my parents? Oh God, why me?

"Hello, nice to meet you. My name is Xander." He walked over and shook my hand.

"I'm Liv." I shook his hand as if I didn't know him, but I knew he had to have felt the jolt of electricity that had passed through us as we touched.

"Nice to meet you Liv." His eyes teased me. I wanted to ask him why he was here, but my parents were there, watching us. I didn't think they'd appreciate me asking him if he was some sort of stalker.

"You too." I squeaked out.

"You have something on your ear." He leaned forward and I felt his fingers brushing the top of my ear. Then I felt his breath in my ear drum. "Now I have a name to put to the face when I think of our night together." He said huskily and I felt the tip of his tongue on my earlobe.

"What are you doing here?" I said softly, a smile plastered on my face for my parents benefit. Had he tracked me down because he wanted this to be more than one night? My heart thudded as I wondered about his appearance. Had I made that big of an impression on him?

"What would you like me to be doing here?" He asked softly, his eyes not leaving mine as he studied my face.

"I…" I stumbled as I stared at him, all of a sudden feeling faint and excited at the same time.

"Liv, I see you've met Xander." My sister Gabby ran into the room, a huge smile on her face and her blonde hair bobbing around her shoulders. Of course she looked as perfect as she always looked, not a hair out of place.

"Yes." I nodded. "I've met him." I smiled awkwardly and looked to the door and watched as another man walked into the room.

"This is Xander's brother, Henry." Gabby nodded towards the other guy, who looked like a more handsome and sweeter version of Xander.

"Hi." I smiled at him warmly. "It's nice to meet you Henry." Then I looked back at Gabby, confusion setting in. "Not to sound rude, but why are they both here?"

"Mom and dad didn't tell you?" Gabby looked excited as she grinned at me and then at our proud parents.

"No, that's why I'm asking." I was impatient in my confusion.

"I'm engaged." She squealed and showed me her engagement finger. A huge diamond sparkled on her finger and I stared at it feeling very impressed, if not slightly jealous.

"Congratulations." I gave her a quick hug and turned to Henry. "And to you too. I'm happy to welcome you to the family." I grinned as I gave him a hug as well. I could feel Xanders' eyes on me and my stomach flipped. Oh my, had I just slept with my sister's fiancé's brother? Oops. I flushed as I stepped back from Henry.

"Oh no, the congratulations aren't to me." Henry laughed. "I'm not the one that's engaged."

"What?" My face turned white as I turned to look at Xander. Oh my God, no!

"Henry's not my fiancé silly." Gabby laughed and I watched as she put her arm through Xander's and grinned at me. "Xander's my future husband to be."

"Oh." My eyes widened and I took a step back as I felt the world spinning around me. Oh my God, it was worse than I'd thought.

"Yes." Xander's eyes searched mine. "It was supposed to be a surprise."

"Aren't you happy for me, Liv?" Gabby bounced up and down and I felt sick to my stomach. "We're all going to be one happy family."

"Uh yeah." I nodded demurely. Should I tell her? My brain was screaming at me. What could I say? I had sex with your fiancé last week. "Congrats. That's amazing news." I looked back at Xander and his eyes were still on mine.

"You were right." He said softly as he walked over to me and I glared at him.

"About?" I said softly as Gabby walked over to talk to Henry with my parents.

"You are trouble with a capital T." He winked at me as his hand ran down my back and over my ass gently. "A big capital T."

"Don't touch me." I hissed and stepped back. "You're engaged to my sister."

"It's not what you think." He said slowly, his eyes piercing into mine.

"I think you're engaged to my sister, what part of that do I have incorrect?"

"Come to my room tonight and I'll tell you." He smiled a confident smile and took a step back. "I'll tell you all the things you want to know." My breath caught as he brushed my hair back and leaned forward. "And I'll show you all the things you've been missing since last week as well."

"How dare you?" I gasped.

"I dare many things Liv Taylor." The smile was gone from his face as he stared at me. "You'll see that this is just the beginning of the many things I dare to do."

1

I'M A LOSER. NO, REALLY I am. And it's not just because I slept with my sister's fiancé. I mean that wasn't my fault. I didn't even know that she was dating anyone. It's not my fault that my Mr. Miracle Tongue is going to be her husband. Oh my God, it will never feel right saying that. Saying the words my 'sister's husband' knowing that he's my one night stand, is awful. Slightly titillating, but still awful. I know, I know, I'm awful. How can I think that's even vaguely exciting? How can a part of me still feel so alive knowing that the man in the living room was my lover; albeit for one night, but still we had sex a lot in that night. And when I say a lot, I mean a lot. Though, I suppose it's not a good idea for me to brag about that right now. Or the fact that when I rode him like a Texan Cowgirl, he held my hips and told me to "ride this cowboy all night".

That's not even the worst part. When I got to my bedroom after hurrying out of the living room, I ran to the mirror to check my makeup. Yes, I wanted to make sure that I'd looked good when I'd seen Xander again. And oh my

God, what sort of name is Xander? Is he a Greek God wanna-be? Or maybe a Roman God wanna-be? Or maybe he thinks he's a super hero. Or his parents thought he was going to be a super hero. I mean, who calls their kid Xander? I mean, I wouldn't mind playing superheroes with him. I'd quite like to see him in a mask and cape, like some sexy Batman.

But yeah that's an inappropriate thought as well. Nearly as inappropriate as the way I'd checked my makeup and then checked my overnight bag to see if I'd brought anything even remotely sexy to wear. And when I say sexy, I mean subtly sexy. Not obvious. Just like a quick peek-a boo sort of thing. I told you I'm a loser. Instead of praying for some sort of redemption for hooking up with my sister's fiancé (I can barely even say the word without throwing up), I was looking to see if I had any cute clothes. What's worse is that I felt disappointed when I realized I didn't have anything remotely cute or sexy. All I had was some jeans, not skinny either, and some baggy, loose fitting tops. Nothing that was going to wow anyone. Which should have been good right? I mean, what sort of self-respecting woman wants to impress her sisters fiancé with a tight top exposing her ample cleavage? None I tell you. No good sister would be hoping to look hot in front of her sister's man.

I can barely believe it by the way. How is Mr. Miracle Tongue engaged to my sister? How do they even know each other? And what sort of cheating dog was he if he'd cheated on her with me? This was such a mess. How was I going to go to their wedding, knowing that I'd had sex with the groom at the last wedding we'd both attended? And would he be expecting a repeat, like some sort of sick reunion sex. Was wedding sex going to be our thing? I groaned at the stupidity of my thoughts. We had no 'thing'. We had a one-night stand that was now made more complicated by the fact that he was a dirty scoundrel.

I needed to speak to Xander and Gabby separately so that I could find out exactly what their story was. Maybe everything wasn't as bad as it seemed. Maybe they weren't really engaged. Maybe Gabby had hired him as an April Fools joke. Yeah, it wasn't April, but Gabby was kooky about jokes. She was always pulling bad practical jokes and her timing was atrocious. This had to be a joke. A really, really bad joke. I would tell her off for it, but then it would all be okay. We'd all be able to laugh about it. And she wouldn't be upset to know that I'd spent the last weekend in a hotel room with Xander. I tried to ignore the fact that it was a pretty impossible joke for her to pull, seeing as she didn't know I'd slept with Xander. I rubbed my forehead and fell down to my bed. I was pretty confident this wasn't a joke. I was pretty confident that I was in the middle of a really bad situation and I had no idea how to get out of it. I didn't know what to tell Gabby or if I should even tell her anything. I mean what she didn't know wouldn't hurt her, right?

She didn't have to know that I'd ridden Xander like I was galloping on a stallion across a field at sunset. She didn't have to know that I'd slapped his ass over and over again, until you could see red handprints imprinted on his flesh. She didn't have to know that he'd called me his sexy cowgirl and that I'd spoken in a Southern accent while telling him to fuck me harder. My face was going red just thinking about that night. I walked to the bathroom quickly so I could wash my face with cold water. I didn't want to think about the things he'd done to me. Or what I'd done to him with the ice cubes that had been delivered to the room with the bottles of water we'd ordered at 3am. I stared in the mirror at my reflection and I could see the embarrassment in my eyes as I thought about the fact that I had sucked on my sister's fiancés balls and liked it. There was no way I was going to tell her about that.

I WASN'T SURPRISED TO HEAR the knocking on my door. There could be any number of people on the other side and I didn't want to talk to any of them. I just wanted to call Alice and tell her what had happened. She'd know what I should do. She'd be able to give me advice and tell me everything was going to be okay. Though, I knew everything wasn't going to be okay and I knew what I had to do. There was really only one solution. And that was to do nothing. I should pretend that I'd never met him. That was what I should do.

Bang Bang.

The person banged on the door louder this time and my stomach curdled in fear and anxiety. *You sucked on his balls, Liv. How are you going to tell Gabby that?*

"Who is it?" My stomach rumbled as I waited for an answer.

"Mr. Tongue." He said lightly and deliciously. I could picture the look of amusement in his green eyes, even though I couldn't see them. "Can I come in?" He said, this time speaking slightly louder.

Shit! I groaned inwardly, though I have to admit a thrill of excitement curled my toes up. It was him on the other side of the door wanting to come in. And he was Xander. Shit, Mr. Tongue had a name. A sexy, delicious sounding name and I was drowning in fear and anticipation of speaking to him again.

"Liv?" He said and knocked again.

"Yes?" I squeaked out, not moving, my hands pressed against the door.

"Can I come in?"

"Why?" I swallowed hard. I wasn't sure I trusted either of us in my bedroom alone. Not after our last time in a private room. Shit, we didn't even need a private room to get down and dirty. I was willing to be his sexy cowgirl anywhere.

"Can we have this conversation in your room and not through the door?" He laughed. "Unless you'd prefer me to say what I have to say about what happened at the wedding through the —"

"Come in." I hurried to open the door and pulled his arm into the room. "What do you think you're doing?" I glared at him.

"Getting you to open the door to your room." He grinned at me, his eyes looking as merry as I'd imagined them to be.

"Why would you want to come into my room?" I glared at him again as I closed the door behind him quickly. "This is very inappropriate." My face was bright red as I stared at him with my hands on my hips. Why did he have to be so handsome? Why did he make butterflies flutter in my stomach? His green eyes were dark and vivid and reminded me of a forest at twilight, full of secrets and scary delights. I knew I shouldn't venture in to explore the hidden depths beckoning to me, but I just couldn't stop myself from continuing to explore.

"I thought we should talk." He ran his hands through his perfectly silky hair and my eyes followed his fingertips as they glided back and forth. The movement reminded me of other places they had rubbed gently and a tantalizing heat spread through my stomach and downwards.

"You think?" I stared at him with wide angry eyes. I wanted to let him see that I was not okay with what he'd done.

"I know this is somewhat awkward." He smiled. *Obnoxious jerk! How could he be smiling right now?*

"You think?" I said again.

"But I think we can work through this."

"You think?" I said sarcastically and I watched as a huge smile spread across his face, making him even more handsome than before.

"Yes, I do think." He said and then paused. "Do you know any other phrases, Liv?"

"Like what?" I said sarcastically. "I know another phrase. One you might not want to hear. One that goes a bit like I slept with my sister's dirty dog fiancé and I don't know what he's doing in my room?"

"I know that you most probably have questions."

"Yeah, just a few." My voice rose and I shook my head at him as I poked him in the chest. *Wrong move! Why did I touch him?* My finger tingled from the connection with his taut muscle. "The first question being, how could you sleep with me when you're engaged?" My voice was accusing as I glared at his sexy face.

"It's not exactly what you think."

"Oh?"

"We only got engaged this week."

"This week?" I frowned. "What?"

"Last weekend I did something I regret." His eyes bore into mine. "And something happened that made me realize that it was time for me to grow up."

"Last weekend you did something you regret?" I repeated, my face flushing. "Do you mean *me?*" I glared at him, as my stomach sunk. He regretted sleeping with me? I felt gutted at his words.

"I did do you last weekend, yes." He grinned. "But that's not what I'm talking about." He leaned forward and licked his lips. "That day is nothing I will ever regret."

"You're a pig." I shook my head, mesmerized by the movement of his tongue, so pink and pointy. I shivered just remembering it between my legs. I groaned inwardly as I recalled the feeling of it slipping inside of me. I know, I'm horrible. I should have been shouting at him or slapping him, but instead I was remembering every vivid detail of how rough and gentle his tongue had been. I was growing wet just remembering how much pleasure his seemingly innocent tongue had given me. I hoped that the moisture would cool me down in hell, because those fiery flames were exactly where I was headed.

"I don't oink." He teased me and for a second I thought he was about to kiss me.

"You sure about that?" I licked my dry lips and took a step back.

"Nervous Liv?" He raised an eyebrow at me and took another step towards me.

"Stop saying my name like that."

"Like what, Liv?"

"Like you're some sort of Spanish conquistador and I'm the conquest you're after."

"But I've already had you." He grinned. "The conquest is over. Done. Complete." He stepped back and looked around the room. "Nice." He nodded to the poster of the Backstreet Boys above my bed.

"Everyone I know has a poster of the Backstreet Boys." I muttered.

"Really?" He looked at me in surprise. "Everyone you know still has a poster of boy bands on their wall?" He wiggled his eyebrow and I made a face at him.

"Of course not now. This is my childhood room. This is where I slept as a teenager. I don't live here anymore. I have my own apartment and I don't have posters of the Backstreet boys up there." I said defensively.

"I think you're protesting a bit too much." He laughed. "Are you sure about that?"

"Of course I'm sure about that. I'm very sure I know what's hanging in my bedroom." I turned away from him, hoping he couldn't see the red in my face. I did have some photos of Matthew McConaughey in a scrapbook in my bedroom that I'd cut out from celebrity magazines. And those weren't from my teenage years. They were from the future husband scrapbooks Alice and I had made in college. Matthew McConaughey was my dream man. He was perfect: rough, handsome, had a sexy country drawl and he loved his mama. If he weren't married, I'd be on a plane to Texas or California doing whatever I could to meet him.

"Liv?" Xander's voice was hesitant. "Are you okay?"

"Yes, why?" I turned to look at him and his eyes were curious as he stared at me.

"You seemed to drift away just now and I was wondering what had occupied your thoughts so deeply? Surely not having day dreams about Justin Timberlake?"

"Justin Timberlake was in N'Sync, not the Backstreet Boys." I rolled my eyes at him and he laughed.

48

"Ask me if I care."

"I didn't say you cared. I was just correcting you because what you said was wrong. Ugh." I shook my head in frustration. "What do you want, Xander? You're annoying me."

"You. Again. In your bed. Under your Backstreet Boys poster crying out my name and singing 'Quit Playing Games with My Heart'."

"Oh." My jaw dropped at his presumptuousness and at the fact that he knew the name of a boy band song.

"Cat got your tongue?"

"You have five seconds to tell me what you really want, then I suggest you leave my room. I'm this close to telling my sister about you, you dirty pig."

"Telling your sister what about me?" He laughed. "That you met me at a wedding last weekend and then proceeded to have sex with me at the church?"

"We didn't have sex at the church." I protested. "We, we..." I sputtered out at him, not sure what to say. "You're a pig."

"You said that before." He grinned. "And I stand corrected, we didn't have sex at the church. Well, not technically. Not if you mean my cock in your——"

"Xander." I cut him off, my face officially the color of fire truck engine red. I could be in one of those picture books that they made for toddlers to learn the colors. When everyone thought of bright red, they would think of the color on my face during this conversation with Xander, miracle tongue worker and jerk.

"Yes?" He laughed. "I was just agreeing with you. Technically, my tongue inside of you doesn't qualify as fornification. Though what we did in the church is a type of sex right? If we're being absolutely correct, I believe that oral sex is still sex, but I don't know how technical we're being." His eyes mocked me as he continued. "So yes, you're correct we didn't have sex at the church. Not the full, we could be in a porn movie type of sex. However, we did have my mouth between your legs making you come quasi-sex and then we did have full on porno movie sex later that night, in my hotel room." He paused. "Does that make you feel better?"

"No, that does not make me feel better." I grabbed his arms and pulled him away from the door and closer to the bed. "And keep your voice down. What if someone hears you?"

"Would that be a problem?" He cocked his head.

"What do you think?"

"We're not back on that again, are we?" He grabbed my hands and pulled them up to his face. "Your nails need cutting." He studied them for a few seconds and I pulled my hands away from him.

"What?" I frowned, distracted by his comment. "What are you talking about?"

"I was just saying you need a manicure." He shrugged. "Your fingernails are longer and the nail polish is chipping off."

"Are you fucking joking with me right now?" My jaw dropped. "You're the most insufferable—"

"Pig, I know." He finished my sentence for me.

"No, I was going to say asshole." My eyes narrowed as I stared at the nonchalant smile on his face. "You're an asshole."

"That gives me an idea." He grinned and he grabbed my waist and pulled me towards him.

"Excuse me, what do you think you're doing?"

"Getting reacquainted with you." He laughed as he looked down into my face; his lips dangerously close to mine as his fingers slipped to my ass.

"Hey." I jumped back. "What do you think you're doing?"

"Well, I was touching your ass because you gave me an idea." His voice suddenly became seductively low.

"What idea?" I swallowed hard and then my jaw dropped. "Do you think I'm going to have anal sex with you? The day I find out you're engaged to my sister? Are you out of your mind? Did you really think I was going to let you—"

"Liv." He cut me off, his lips trembling.

"What?"

"I just wanted to feel your ass to see if it was as juicy and pert as I remembered." He winked at me. "I wasn't asking to take your anal cherry."

"You...wait, what?" I sputtered out, my heart racing. How had the conversation gone to sex again? Why oh why was he teasing me and making me feel so hot and bothered. He was the worst kind of man possible and yet, I was incredibly turned on.

"Anyway, let's not get sidetracked." He shook his head at me. "I'm sorry, but I didn't come to your room for sex."

"Say what?" I looked at him in confusion. "I never said—"

"I came because I wanted to explain to you that this is a delicate situation. I wasn't engaged when we made love. And I wasn't planning on becoming engaged either. However your sister and I have decided to get married." He studied my face for a few seconds. "I didn't expect to see you again." He shook his head and his face softened as he looked at my face. "You've made this all very difficult."

"What have I made difficult?"

"This arrangement between your sister and I…" He paused. "It's delicate. It's not a love match."

"Then what is it?"

Bang Bang.

"Liv?" Gabby's voice was soft. "Can I come in?"

"Just a second." I said, hoping my voice didn't show how panicked I felt. "Get under the bed." I pushed Xander down. "Now."

"Okay." He frowned as he got down on his knees and slithered under the bed.

"Liv?" Gabby's voice was louder. "Can I come in?"

"Just a second." I shouted and watched as Xander's legs and feet were hidden. I walked to the door and opened it, with a big smile. "Hey, what's up?"

"Can I come in?" Gabby seemed hesitant and I stared at her in surprise. My sister was never hesitant. She was beautiful, confident and always got what she wanted. Like my Mr. Miracle Tongue.

"Uh, what do you want?" Oh God, I couldn't look her in the face. I needed to make eye contact with her, but I couldn't. I was too ashamed of myself. What oh what was I going to do?

"Can I come in? I don't want anyone to hear." She pushed into the room and closed the door behind her. "What do you think of Xander?"

"Huh?" My face was hot. "Why do you ask?"

"I just wanted your opinion." She sighed. "I know you can read guys well."

"I, uh, I guess." I stared at her in shock. Since when did she think I could read guys well? Since when did Gabby ever want my opinion?

"I haven't known Xander long."

"Oh?" I bit my lower lip, wanting to ask her more, but I didn't because I didn't want Xander to think I cared to know about their relationship.

"I know, it's rash, but when he proposed I couldn't say no." She said breathlessly.

"How long have you known him?" I asked softly.

"I…that doesn't matter." She sighed. "The point is we're getting married."

"I mean if you love him." I shrugged. "Follow your heart."

"I'm pregnant, Liv." She burst out and the color drained from my face. "We're getting married because I'm pregnant."

2

"SHUT THE FRONT DOOR." I said in shock after I gasped for breath.

"I know." She sat down on my bed and I heard a groan. "Who thought I'd be having a shotgun wedding?"

"Not me." I said, heart racing. Oh my God, my sister is pregnant with Mr. Tongue's baby and we're going to be on Jerry Springer next week. I needed to call Alice right away. I needed to talk to someone about what was going on. The man I had slept with the week before, was about to have a child with my sister. Shit! I'd slept with my soon to be niece or nephew's dad. What did that make me? Some sort of Jezebel?

"I don't know him well," She made a face. "Am I making a mistake marrying him?"

"I just met him, Gabby. I don't know what to say." I wanted to shout, don't marry him, don't marry him. He was obviously a big jerk, who couldn't keep it in his pants, but now he was going to be a father, to my sister's kid, I didn't know what to say. Did I want to ruin their family before the kid was even born?

"When did he propose to you?" I asked softly. If it was before he'd slept with me, I would tell her, but if it was after, I wouldn't.

"Two days ago." She offered me a small smile and showed me her fingers. "Do you like the ring?"

"It's big." I said, not knowing what else to say. The ring was beautiful. It was the sort of ring I'd like to receive when I got engaged. If that ever happened.

"It was his grandmother's." She said softly and gazed at it. "I'm not keeping this one. He's going to take me to Tiffany's and let me choose one I like better."

"You don't like that?" I frowned as I stared at her. "It's gorgeous and it was a part of his family. That means something, Gabby."

"I don't want a used ring." She jumped up and frowned.

"You can't look at it as if it's used."

"I want my own ring. I've already seen the one I want: it's a Princess cut, 5 carat diamond, platinum and about thirty grand."

"Gabby." I said shocked. "That's a lot of money."

"So what? He can afford it."

"Oh Gabby." I sighed. "Can I ask you something?"

"Yeah, what?"

"Do you love him?"

"Do I love him?" She looked at me like I was crazy. "Oh Liv, you need to get your head out of the clouds. People don't get married because they're in love anymore. They get married because it makes sense. They get married because it's better than being single. There are tax breaks and all sorts of benefits to come from getting married."

"So you don't love him?"

"I love that he's a millionaire. I love that he's hot. I love that he proposed to me." She shrugged. "Seems good enough to me."

"But you're really not sure if that's enough, if you're in here asking me what I think."

"I don't even know why I'm in here." She sighed. "I think it's my hormones." She made a face. "Being pregnant sucks."

"Do mom and dad know?"

"Of course not." She scoffed. "I'm not about to tell them I'm knocked up." She stared at me intently. "And you better not say anything either."

"I wasn't planning on saying anything." *Trust me, dear sister. I want nothing to do with your sordid setup.* All of a sudden, I didn't feel so bad for Gabby. If anything, I felt bad for myself. I was the innocent party in this setup.

"I know you've always been jealous of me, Liv." Gabby fluffed her hair and stared at me with a sad expression. "But I do hope you can grow out of those feelings. We're adults now."

"What are you talking about?" I shook my head annoyed. "I'm not jealous of you. What do I have to be jealous of you for?"

"I have a good job. I have my own house. I'm beautiful. And now I'm pregnant and getting married to a millionaire."

"So?"

"Well, you have a shitty job that pays you what? Like ten dollars an hour?"

"I make thirty grand a year." I glared at her.

"And you live with roommates."

"I share an apartment with my best friend, not some random Joe from the street."

"And well, you've always been jealous that I'm a natural blonde and you're not."

"Is this a joke?" I looked around the room. "Am I on Candid Camera? Is that show even on anymore?" My jaw dropped as she acted liked the Gabby I'd remembered from my teenage years.

"What are you talking about?" She stared at me blankly. "Anyway, Liv. I wanted to say I want us to move on from whatever kept us apart all of those years. You're going to be an Aunt now."

"So?" I scratched my head.

"So you need to be more responsible now."

"What does you having a kid got to do with me?"

"I don't want you being a bad influence on my——"

"Gabby, I think you need to leave my room right now." I marched to the door and opened it and stared at her. "I'm not going to be responsible for what I say next if you don't get out of here."

"Liv, don't be like that. I was just trying to say that——"

"Honestly, Gabby I don't care." I shook my head. "I just need to be by myself."

"Fine." She huffed as she exited the room. "I just thought you'd be happy for me."

"I'm very happy for you, Gabby."

"Good." She smiled at me. "And if you play your cards right, maybe I'll hook you up with Henry."

"Henry, Xander's brother?" My eyes widened.

"Yes." She grinned. "He's very handsome and well, wouldn't that be fun if we were married to brothers?"

"Oh yeah, oodles of fun." I smiled weakly. *Here we come, Jerry.* I groaned inwardly. There was no way in hell that I wanted to be hooked up with Henry. Talk about creepy and gross.

"I'm pretty sure he's single."

"That's good." I said and then sighed. "Um, we'll chat later yeah?"

"Okay." She nodded. "And don't tell mom and dad about the baby, okay?"

"Okay." I said and then closed the door, my heart racing as I stood there taking everything all in. I watched as Xander squirmed out from under the bed and stood up.

"So then." He stared at me with an expectant look.

"So what?"

"Now you know why we're getting married."

"I can't believe you want to marry her after listening to all that."

"Why?" He frowned.

"She's a gold digger." I made a face. "And God forgive me, for saying that about my sister."

"She doesn't hide what she's after." He shrugged.

"You're okay with that?"

"Gabby and I haven't lied to each other about anything. We know what this is about."

"So she knows you slept with me?"

"No." His eyes narrowed. "But then I didn't know who you were until about an hour ago."

"Are you going to tell her now that you know?"

"No, of course not." He paused. "That would unduly complicate things."

"Because they're not complicated now?"

"Well, not really." He brushed some lint off of his jeans. "Nothing is really complicated right now. Though they could become more complicated if you still want to sleep with me; which I think you do." He stared at my breasts.

"You what?" My jaw dropped at his audacity. Was he for real? I stared at the smirk on his husky face and I tried to ignore how sexy he looked. *He's a jerk, Liv. He's not a sexy male God with a miracle tongue. Oh, I was going to miss his miracle tongue. No, stop it Liv you must forget his miracle tongue.* I groaned.

"Something wrong?" He asked softly.

"No." I snapped and glared at him.

"You still want me, don't you?" His eyes danced.

"No." I said adamantly.

"Okay, if you say so. Though I think you're lying." He grinned and licked his lips again. This time his tongue was sticking right out as if to taunt me even more. "Some people say I'm cocky." He said after a few seconds.

"Who you?" I feigned shock. "Who would ever think that?"

"Are you laughing at me?" His eyes were light as he studied my face.

"Does it sound like I'm laughing? Can you hear the sound of laughter coming out of my mouth and falling into your ears?"

"You think you're funny, don't you?" He took a step towards me.

"I'm not a comedian and have no aspirations to be one, so no, not really."

"So are you trying to say you don't think I'm cocky?" He tilted his head and smiled at me. I didn't want to stare back at him. I mean who can resist a hot guy with a cute teasing smile? His green eyes sparkled in mischief as he questioned me. The moment was light and silly and I so badly wanted it to be dark and stuffy. I didn't want to like Xander. I had every reason to dislike Xander, but I was finding it very hard to follow through on my dislike when he stood so close to me.

"What do you want from me Xander? This is highly inappropriate as I told you before."

"Why?" He took another step towards me and this time I could feel his thigh grazing against my leg.

"You're engaged to marry my sister."

"Yes, but we don't love each other."

"So you're not going to marry her then?" I asked softly and hopefully. I know it was wrong of me to be hoping for him to say he was going to call off the wedding. "You're going to call off the wedding?"

"Why would I do that?" He put his arms around my waist and pulled me to him. I could feel his erection pressing into my stomach.

"Are you seriously turned on right now?" I asked, shocked.

He grinned at me wickedly, not answering me. His eyes laughed into mine and he grabbed my hand and held it.

"What are you doing?" I asked softly, my heart racing at the fact that I was so close to him.

"Answering your question."

"What question?" My brain was fuddled.

"This one." He took my hand and placed it over his crotch and squeezed my fingers together gently so that I was grabbing his hardness.

"What are you doing?" I gasped as my fingers held onto his thick manhood.

"You asked me if I was turned on and I figured show was better than tell." He winked at me and I pulled my hand away quickly, images of his naked cock in my mouth and hands flashing through my head. We stared at each other for a few seconds and I knew I was in big trouble. I still wanted this man and he wanted me and I had no idea what I was going to do about it.

"You should leave." I looked at my bed instead of his face. All I wanted was to crawl under the sheets and groan.

"We haven't finished talking." He shook his head.

"There's not much left to say, Xander." I took a deep breath. "I'll keep my mouth shut, but only because I don't want to have to discuss exactly what happened between us."

"Don't you even want to know about Gabby and I?"

"No, why would I want to know about you and Gabby?" A sharp pain twisted in my stomach as I imagined them together. My head started pounding and I knew I was jealous. I didn't know why I was jealous. I didn't even think I'd see him again. Well, that was partially true. I hadn't thought I would see him again, but I had had a daydream running through my head all week. I'd kind of hoped that he would find me- you know what I mean, in a romantic movie sort of way. He'd ask people from the wedding about the beautiful girl in the light pink dress and he'd figure out who I was and come and find me. I'm not talking Lifetime Stalker movie either. He wouldn't become obsessed with me and stalk me and then kill me. I'm talking sweet romance movie moment. He'd find me and serenade me with a cassette player, remember those? And he'd have a bouquet of flowers and he'd tell me that the night we'd spent in the hotel was the best night of his life and that he couldn't stop thinking about me. So yes, while I didn't expect to see him again, I had hoped in the back of my mind that he'd find me. For a brief second when I'd seen him in the living room, I'd thought, maybe my dreams had come true, but of course they hadn't. Because that's just how my life goes. I never meet the romantic men. I never meet the men that want to woo me and sweep me off of my feet. I never meet the Prince Charming's of the world. I always meet the garbage men pretending to be Prince Charming, but then you figure out how much they stink and want to slap yourself for ever thinking they had more to offer.

"Are you listening to me Liv?" Xander's voice interrupted my thoughts and I looked up at him with a wry smile.

"No, sorry." I said and flashed him my teeth.

"You seem preoccupied." He said with a frown and I have to admit my heart jumped for joy for a little bit. Yes, I know I'm slightly immature, but it pleased me that he knew that he wasn't eating up my thoughts. I mean he was, but I'm pretty sure he thought I was preoccupied by something else. "What's on your mind?" He said softly. "Is it me?"

And then, because my feelings were hurt, and because I wanted to see if I could make him jealous, I said the one thing I could think of to try and rile him up.

"Oh no." I said sweetly. "I was thinking about Henry." I looked down with a fake demure smile. "Gabby mentioned that he was single and a nice guy and I was thinking, maybe I should get to know him better."

"You what?" His eyes narrowed and my heart jumped for joy at the displeasure on his face. "My brother Henry?"

"Yes." I pushed my breasts out slightly. *Look at what you're missing buddy.* "That's not going to be a problem, is it?" I licked my lips slowly and grinned. "After all, you're seeing my sister." He stood there for a few seconds, his eyes searching mine and then he went to the bedroom door and exited my room without a word. *Score one for me*! I thought as I stared at the open door. I stood there for a few seconds and then sighed. My victory felt very hollow. I hadn't really fixed anything. My wedding hookup. My Mr. Miracle Tongue was engaged to my pregnant sister. My bitchy, thinks she's better than me, sister. And all I could think about was how quickly I could leave the house and get away from them all. I was scared about what would happen if I stayed. I could still feel his hardness in my hands. He was a grade A jerk. How could he still be coming on to me if he was engaged to my sister? And how could I still be liking it? What was wrong with me? I was a home wrecker...well, a soon to be home wrecker. I was one of those women that Alice and I hated. One of those women that didn't care if the man was taken. Okay, so I didn't know he was taken when I first met him. The first night of sex wasn't my fault. But if it happened again. If I hooked up with him, I'd be the biggest bitch this side of the Atlantic. My brain was screaming at me for even thinking it could happen again, but I knew that Xander made me weak. Very, very weak. It was in that moment I knew that I was very far from being a winner. And I knew that I couldn't stand around and just wait for something to happen. I couldn't find myself waking up next to him in bed again. It wouldn't be right. I'd have to come up with a plan.

3

"YOU DIRTY DOG YOU." ALICE squealed in delight as I finished telling her about my meeting with Xander in my bedroom, and the way he'd stood so close to me and grabbed my hand.

"I'm not the dirty dog." I said annoyed. "He is. He's the cheat. He's —"

"Don't get me wrong. He is definitely a dirty dog." Alice agreed. "Maybe he's a dirty Rottweiler, or wait, what's a bigger dog than a Rottweiler? Maybe a St. Bernard? Are they bigger?"

"Who cares if a St. Bernard is bigger?"

"The dog in Beethoven, what breed was that?"

"Alice, I have no clue." I knew I sounded exasperated. "And I don't care. I have more pressing issues to discuss. Like what to do."

"That's why you're a dirty dog." She giggled.

"What do you mean?" I frowned into the phone, annoyed at her attitude. Didn't she realize how serious this was?

"I mean, you're asking me what to do. How can you be asking me what to do? You know what you should be doing as a good sister. There's no question about it."

"So I should tell Gabby?"

"No, you shouldn't tell Gabby. I don't know." Alice sighed. "That's awkward. I would normally say yes, but she's knocked up and that just seems wrong."

"I know. The pregnancy makes it harder."

"Oh my God, I just thought of something." Alice's voice sounded shocked and I sat up, my heart pounding.

"Oh, what is it Alice?" I groaned. "And please don't tell me that you slept with him as well. I'm not sure I could take any more surprises like that."

"No," She giggled. "What if you're pregnant as well? What if he knocked you both up? Wouldn't that be crazy?" She sounded excited.

"Alice, that's not something I even want to consider. Plus, he used condoms."

"Condoms aren't foolproof."

"I thought you were going to make me feel better." I wailed. "But instead you're making me feel worse."

"You know what I wish?" Alice said without even acknowledging what I'd said.

"What?" I sighed, knowing she was going to tell me whether I cared to know or not.

"I wish that you'd had sex with Luke." She mentioned her ex-boyfriend that we both hated; me even more now that I'd slept with Xander at his wedding. "Could you imagine what Joanna would say if she found out that

Luke got you pregnant at the wedding. That would be priceless. I'd pay good money to see that."

"How much? Ten dollars?" I said sarcastically.

"No, I'd pay a grand." She said seriously. "Yes, I would dip into my savings just to witness that."

"You're sick, you know that right? Really, really sick?"

"I know." She giggled and then let out a deep breath. "I'm a sicko and you love it."

"You're lucky I love you or I would have hung up the phone already." I shook my head, smiling slightly at the thought that someone had brought Joanna to her knees. Even though, the hypothetical person was me and it hadn't happened.

"You know I'm sorry." She sighed. "I am shocked for you. I don't even really know what to say. Where have all the good men gone?"

"I wish I knew." I groaned. "Maybe they're all gay now."

"Half are gay." Alice said. "And a quarter are married."

"So where are the other quarter?"

"If I knew I wouldn't be on the phone here with you." She laughed. "I'd be at the back of some limo having my brains fucked out."

"A limo?" I giggled. "Why a limo?"

"Because if I've waited this long to find Mr. Right, he better be fucking gorgeous and rich to make up for all my misery."

"Xander's rich." I wasn't sure why I'd brought it up, but it seemed fitting in the moment.

"Lucky bitch."

"I'm not really a lucky bitch because he's not mine. Gabby's the lucky bitch."

"No." Alice said simply. "She's just a bitch."

"Alice."

"You know it's true." Her voice rose. "I know she's your sister and you love her and yada, yada, yada, but she's still a bitch, b, i, t, c, h, b, i, t, c, h, b, i, t, c, h and bitcho was her name-o."

"Alice." I giggled. "You're horrible."

"I know, it's the way I was born. My mom must have had me under a full moon or something."

"Yeah, I guess so."

"So are you coming home tomorrow then?"

"No." I sighed. "My parents have some weekend activities planned for all of us."

"Boring."

"You know they love that shit."

"Any of your brothers going to be there?" Alice asked innocently and I smiled to myself.

"Yes, all of them are going to be here. It's going to be a big family celebration. Me, Gabby, Scott, Chett, and Aiden. And then Xander and his brother Henry and the 'rents." I took a deep breath. "We're all going to be one big family."

"Sounds fun." Alice said wistfully, having grown up an only child to two parents that loved to jet set around the world.

"You know you totally have to come up tomorrow morning right and stay the weekend with me." I said softly, wanting her to know that I wanted her there, but not wanting her to think it was a last minute pity invite.

"No, I can't intrude. It's Gabby's big weekend."

"You have to come." I said quickly. "You'll stay in my room and be like my bodyguard. What if Xander tries to sleep with me again and my whole family walks in on us in the bedroom, playing Cowboys and Indians?"

"Oh my God, so you would say yes if he tried to hook up again."

"No." My face reddened at my slip. "I mean, yeah, maybe, I don't know. I know I'm evil personified to even think that could happen, but he's just so gosh darn sexy."

"And you know they're not in love."

"Yeah." I sighed. "Not that that really excuses anything. If I slept with him again now, knowing what I know, I'd be a bitch. A big bitch. A bigger bitch than Gabby."

"That is true."

"Thanks Alice." I pouted into the phone.

"I'm sorry, but it's true. You can't sleep with your sister's baby daddy. That would just be plain wrong."

"I know."

"It would be worse than Jerry Springer wrong."

"Nothing's worse than Jerry Springer." I laughed at her comment, remembering why we were such good friends. We were on the exact same wavelength.

"True." She giggled. "So what time should I come tomorrow?" She asked casually.

"Well the brothers are all coming early and we're all going out for a pancake breakfast."

"I love pancakes." She said eagerly.

"So then come early."

"Are you sure?" She said, hesitant once again. "I don't want to impose on family time."

"Alice, you are family." I said softly. "You're my best friend and my parents look at you like a third daughter and my brothers look at you as another sister." *Shit, why did I say they looked at her as a sister?* I knew Alice had a crush on one of them, but I wasn't sure which one.

"Well, thanks, I guess." She sounded sad. "I'll be there at 9am."

"Great, I can't wait to see you."

"Now don't do anything I wouldn't do tonight."

"I'm not going to do anything." I said lightly and looked at my bedroom door. "I'm going to bed and I'm not leaving my room until you get here."

"You're silly."

"That's why you love me."

"I'm going to go and pack now. I'll see you in the morning, okay?"

"Okay, bye Alice." I hung up and lay back down on my bed and groaned as I stared at the ceiling. Images of Xander popped into my mind as I lay there. Where was he right now? What was he thinking? Was he thinking about me? I rolled over and buried my head in my pillow. I needed to stop thinking about him or I was going to drive myself crazy. I sat up in bed and decided to leave my bedroom. I wasn't tired as yet and being in my bedroom was making me think of things I could do in my bed; naughty things that I shouldn't be thinking about. I decided to go down to grab a coke from the kitchen and then go into the backyard and rock in the rocking chair that my grandmother had given us when I was a kid. I loved the rocking chair, it made me think of my childhood and how happy I'd been rocking on my dad's leg, or even one of my big brothers, when they had time for me. I'd had a happy childhood, asides from the fact that my sister had driven me up the wall for most of my teenage years. I wasn't sure if we'd ever have the kind of relationship that Alice and I had and that made me sad.

"TURN AROUND AND I'LL BE the one you want to boom boom boom." I made up words to the catchy song that was playing on the radio as I swung on the rocking chair on the back porch of my parents' house. The night air was cool and I was grateful that it wasn't another humid balmy Florida night. "Take me away and we'll boom boom boom on the moon moon moon." I giggled as I sang along to some girl crying out about not having a candy pop or boyfriend. I felt that my lyrics were far superior to hers. "You'll boom boom boom before you com com com." I sang out and then screamed as I felt a hand on my shoulder. "Argh."

"Liv, it's just me." Xander's voice was smooth behind me as he spoke and my body tensed up immediately.

"Oh, hello." I turned around and offered him a weak smile, ignoring his eyes and his chest. I stared at a spot on his ear and focused on that.

"I didn't know you were a singer."

"Huh? What?" I said stupidly.

"Have you hit any charts?"

"Charts?"

"Billboard? International? iTunes?"

"What?" I was so confused that my eyes left his ear and found his eyes. "What are you talking about?"

"I'm talking about your singing career." He asked with a small smirk. "Have you hit any bestselling charts or won any Grammys or anything?"

"You're an asshole." My eyes shot daggers into his as he tried not to laugh.

"It was an honest question. You did seem to be into that song you were making up." He grinned and I shook my head.

"Whatever." I couldn't stop myself from responding to his smile. "I know I can't carry a tune, but that doesn't mean I can't sing."

"I didn't say you should stop." He nodded in agreement. "It was quite pleasant to listen to."

"Sure it was." I laughed. "My brothers pay me to stop singing." I smiled at the memories. "In fact my brother Scott once gave me twenty dollars."

"Twenty dollars? Wow." Xander tilted his face. "He must really hate your singing."

"I think it was the song and the occasion." I giggled. "He was eighteen and had brought home his first proper girlfriend for Thanksgiving." I thought back to the holiday. "They were sitting out here talking about some class they were taking and I came out and started singing, "Love is a truly splendid thing." I started laughing harder. "You should have seen the look on his face when I burst into the chorus and started throwing ripped up pieces of paper on them."

"Ripped up pieces of paper?" Xander asked with a look of surprise.

"I didn't have rose petals." I giggled and started rocking back and forth. "If looks could have killed, Scott would have committed murder that night. Instead he gave me $20, so I made out pretty well."

"See your singing career has been profitable."

"Yeah, I guess you could say that." I sighed as I rocked back and forth. I could no longer see Xander, but I could still feel his presence behind me.

"Sounds like you were a troublesome child." He said lightly and I stopped rocking and looked back at him again. This time I didn't bother hiding my smile or laughter.

"It doesn't seem to have ended though, does it?" I raised an eyebrow at him and he looked back at me in surprise. I knew that he was shocked at my laughter and that I was able to laugh at the situation we were in, given how dramatic I'd been earlier, but really how could I not laugh.

"Are you okay?" He frowned at me and I could see him searching my face as I laughed harder. He most probably thought that I was crazy or having a melt-down. He wouldn't be far off of the mark.

"I'm fine. Why?" I said, finally calming down.

"I don't know, you just seemed like you were losing it."

"I'm fine. I just thought your comment was ironic; considering the mess we're in."

"I see." His lip twitched. "It is slightly unusual isn't it?"

"You can say that again." I laughed and his eyes fell to my lips and then back up to my eyes. His gaze was intense and searching and my breath caught as we stared at each other, the only sounds in the air were our breathing and a distant bird calling out to its lost mate.

"The baby isn't mine." He said simply as he gazed at me.

"What?" I frowned, my heart racing. Was he telling the truth?

"Your sister's baby. It's not mine." He looked away then. "I wasn't meant to tell you that."

"Why not?"

"It's complicated." He sighed and looked back at me. "I'm sorry. I shouldn't have told you that."

"Have you slept with Gabby?" I asked breathlessly. Please say no, please say no, please say no.

"Liv." He started to speak and the stopped himself. "I should go inside now."

"But you just came out." All of a sudden I didn't want him to leave. All of a sudden I wanted us to have this conversation. All of a sudden, I felt light-headed and giddy. Maybe, just maybe, I wasn't so in the wrong after-all. Maybe I didn't need to be on an episode of Jerry. Maybe I wasn't a backstabbing bitch.

"Liv, does it matter?"

"It matters to me." I nodded and bit my lip.

"Then no, I haven't slept with Gabby." He said seriously. "But I expect that to change once we're married."

"You're still going to marry her?" My heart was jumping for joy, but my stomach was still in the pits.

"Why wouldn't I?" He frowned as he gazed at me.

"I don't know. Maybe a simple thing like you slept with me." My voice dropped as he looked at me, his expression not changing. Why was he making this so difficult? Why couldn't he just tell Gabby he made a mistake and then ask me out on a date? I'd be willing to forgive him the transgression of asking Gabby to marry him. He hadn't really known me then. But he knew who I was now. Why would he still want to marry Gabby? After we'd had such amazing chemistry together.

"So?" He said simply and then turned around. "Good night, Liv. Have sweet dreams, my dear."

I didn't answer him. My face was burning with embarrassment and shame. "Try not to boom boom boom with too many moons." He said again with a light laugh and I sat back in the rocking chair and moved back and forth quickly, trying to forget our whole conversation.

4

"YOU DIDN'T HAVE TO COME at six am." I yawned as I opened the front door for Alice. "Scott, Chett and Aiden aren't home yet." I blinked at Alice as she beamed at me. "And why do you look so chipper and made up." I frowned and leaned towards her. "Are you wearing fake eyelashes?" I peered at her longer, thicker and blacker than normal lashes. "And hair extensions?" My jaw dropped open. "At six am?"

"Shh, I just wanted to look good." She blushed. "Go back to sleep."

"I think not." I headed towards the kitchen. "Let's have some coffee and talk?"

"Okay." She nodded and followed behind me. "Also, I came early to help you."

"To help me?" I looked back at her incredulously. "How is waking me up before the roosters helping me?"

"In case you were in bed with Xander, he could leave your room before Gabby woke up."

"Ugh, don't even." I made a face.

"You didn't sleep with him, did you?" It was her turn to look shocked. "Liv!"

"Liv nothing." I rolled my eyes and turned on the kettle. "I didn't sleep with him again." I took out two cups and yawned again. "And trust me, I never will again. He's an asshole."

"Ooh what did he do?"

"What do you mean, what did he do?" I turned away from her and opened the fridge. "Milk and sugar?" I said into the fridge.

"You know I want both. Now spill it Taylor, what did Mr. Tongue do?"

"His name is Xander." I groaned as I took the milk out and turned around.

"He was Mr. Tongue first." She grinned. "If I do recall he was Mr. Miracle Tongue, he was the—"

"Enough." I groaned again. "He is not anything to me."

"What happened?" Her eyes lit up.

"I'll tell you what happened on one condition?" I bit my lower lip and grinned at her.

"What condition?" She frowned and leaned forward. "I'm not sleeping with him as well."

"I'm not asking that." I rolled my eyes. "Tell me who you like."

"What?" Alice sat back, her face growing pink.

"Do you like Aiden, Scott or Chett?" I leaned on the countertop and stared at her. "Tell me which one of my brothers you like and I will tell you what happened with Xander."

"I don't like any of them. What are you talking about?" Alice stuttered as she avoided my eyes and I smiled to myself. Alice was such a poor liar and she knew that I knew the truth. I scooped some of the ground beans into the French press and then poured the boiling water inside the glass container and put the top on.

"Chett, Scott or Aiden?" I asked softly as I turned back to face her. "Let me think, I doubt it's Chett. You're not into blond guys and he's the blondest guy I know. And you're not into Nascar and he loves it. Let's see, so it's between Scott and Aiden. Hmm." I stared at her as she glared at me and I grinned. "Both are hot, though they're my brothers so I feel icky saying that. Let me think, who do I think you're after?"

"It's Aiden, okay." She blushed. "And I just think he's cute. I'm not after him."

"You like Aiden?" I made a face. Aiden was the eldest of all of us and he was my bossiest brother. Out of all of my brothers, he was the least fun and sometimes felt more like a second dad to me. "You don't seriously like Aiden, do you?"

"I knew you would say that, that's why I didn't tell you."

"It's just, Aiden." I made a face. "Imagine if you dated him and we had to double date." I shuddered. "It would be like double dating with my dad, he'd be trying to tell me what to order and not to stay out late, and God forbid my guy kisses me or something."

"Is the coffee ready?" Alice looked at the French press pointedly.

"Let me check." I sighed and pressed it down before pouring the coffee in two mugs and turning back to her. "You're not really interested in Aiden, are you?" I gave her a hopeful face. "Is this a bad joke?"

"How many bad jokes do you think are being played on you this weekend, Liv?" Alice laughed as she heaped sugar into her cup. "And yes, I like Aiden.

And no, he's nothing close to being your dad. He's only twenty-eight and he's gorgeous, and funny, and sweet, and well, yes, I have a small crush on him. I have for a long time, if I'm being honest." Alice took a deep breath. "You better not tell him."

"What am I going to tell him?" I rolled my eyes. "He'd just find a way to lecture me."

"So now it's your turn."

"My turn to do what?" I took a sip of my coffee and coughed. It tasted gross. I must have put too much coffee and not enough water in the French press.

"What happened with you and tonguey?"

"Don't call him tonguey. That sounds gross."

"What he did with it wasn't gross though was it?"

"It doesn't matter." I looked around the kitchen. "He's not into me."

"I'm sorry." She gave me an apologetic look.

"He's not the father, you know. He hasn't even slept with Gabby. Yet, he still wants to marry her."

"Does he love her?" Alice looked shock. "And wait what? They've never had sex?"

"I know. I was shocked as well." I tried another sip of coffee and then put the cup down. "Let's go to my room and talk there. I don't want anyone to hear us."

"Okay." She nodded and stood up. We walked to my bedroom and I noticed she had left her coffee sitting on the countertop as well. I closed the bedroom door behind us and then jumped back into bed. "You coming?" I asked her and patted the space on the mattress next to me.

"I don't know if I should lie down." She sighed. "I spent an hour flat ironing my hair this morning and what if my makeup smudges on the pillowcase?"

"Ah, come on Alice. Your hair and makeup will be fine."

"Fine." She yawned and took off her shoes. "I guess, just for a little bit, while we talk."

"Uh huh." I laughed. "You look tired. How much sleep did you get last night?"

"Two hours." She yawned wider and longer this time. "I was so excited that I couldn't sleep and now I'm absolutely exhausted."

"Oh Alice." I shook my head as she plopped down next to me. "Why didn't you tell me that you liked Aiden?"

"Because I knew you would react as you're reacting now." She rolled onto her side and looked at me. "Completely over the top."

"I was hoping you liked Scott." I grinned. Scott was my youngest brother and the one most like me. He was happy-go-lucky and always up to something. He'd gotten into so much trouble as a kid and I'd loved him telling me all his tales. I'd been the good child, but only because I always had my parents and Aiden down my back. There were many activities and tricks I would have liked to have gotten into, but never had the chance.

"Scott's a goof, I love him, but he's a goof." Alice laughed. "He can't keep serious for two minutes."

"That's why you should date him. You'll always be having fun. Aiden on the other hand, ugh." I sighed, still remembering all the times I'd gotten in trouble due to him telling my parents I was up to something.

"I'm sure he doesn't want me anyway." Alice rolled her eyes. "So don't worry."

"I'm not worried, I'm just——"

"Liv, do you want to talk about Aiden or Xander?" Alice interrupted me and I sighed.

"I don't really want to talk about either of them." I made a face. "Xander's a big jerk."

"Why?"

"I kinda let him know that I wouldn't be opposed to him no longer being engaged to my sister."

"What?" Alice's eyes almost popped out in shock. "You did not say that?"

"Well not in those exact words, but basically I told him that maybe he didn't want to get married now that he had met me and he wasn't the father of my sister's baby and basically he looked at me like I was crazy and walked away."

"Oh wow." Alice made a sad face. "He sounds like a dick."

"He is a dick." I closed my eyes, reliving my embarrassment. "And he has a small dick too."

"Oh really?" Alice's voice was amazed.

"No." I opened my eyes and looked at her. "He doesn't really have a small dick." I groaned and buried my face in my hands. "Why, oh why, did this have to happen to me? Do I have some sort of bad luck sign on me?"

"It's not your fault. I mean you did kind of know that he was an asshole after you guys hooked up at the church right?"

"Yeah, I could tell he was arrogant, cocky, full of himself—"

"And yet, you still went back to his hotel room."

"Well, you know I'm only human." I laughed and closed my eyes. "I don't want to talk about him anymore. Let's get a quick nap in and then deal with him and Aiden later."

"That sounds like a plan to me." Alice yawned again, her eyes closing as she snuggled into the pillow. "Night Liv."

"Morning Alice." I giggled and we both drifted off to sleep.

"WAKE UP, WAKE UP." SCOTT'S voice bounded into my bedroom as he banged on my bedroom door and opened it.

"What?" I groaned as I opened my eyes slowly and saw my brother's big blue eyes gazing down at me as he stood over my bed.

"Wake up Liv." He pulled the duvet off of the bed and I growled at him. "Or should I say wake up doggie."

"Asshole." I jumped out of bed and glared at him for a second, before laughing. "It's good to see you too, Scott."

"Come here." He gave me a big hug and then looked down on the bed. "Who's in the bed with you? Are you a lesbian now?"

"Scott!" I shook my head at him. "It's Alice."

"You and Alice are dating now?" He grinned as he wiggled his eyebrows.

"Don't be disgusting." I glared at him and Alice moaned as she rolled over in the bed, still sleeping and oblivious to the noise in the room.

"Just checking." He grinned and looked down at Alice in the bed. "Wakey wakey Alice."

"Don't wake her up." I punched him in the shoulder. "She didn't get much sleep last night."

"Why, what was she doing?" He licked his lips slowly and I punched him again.

"Ugh, what's that noise?" Alice opened her eyes slowly and then screamed.

"What?" I frowned as I stared down at her. "It's just me and Scott."

"No, there's a caterpillar on my face." She screamed again and jumped up out of the bed.

"What?" I stared at her and burst out laughing.

"Take it off of me."

"I'll get it." Scott laughed and pulled her towards him. He then reached to her face and pulled one of her cheap fake eyelashes off of her face. "I don't think it was a caterpillar." He dangled the eyelash in front of her eyes and she blushed.

"Oops." She grinned. "My bad."

"You're silly, Alice." I laughed and we all stood there for a few moments just grinning at each other.

"Why do the three of you always look like fools?" A loud imperious voice rumbled into the room and I turned around with a glare.

"Why do you always look like you have a stick up your ass, Aiden?" I asked him with a small smile.

"I see you still haven't left your teen years." He looked at me with a twinkle in his eye.

"And you're already fifty."

"Not quite yet." He walked into the bedroom and gave me a quick hug. "Hello, Alice, it's nice to see you."

"Hi Aiden." She said softly, her face pink as she gazed at her crush. I looked at Aiden critically then. I guess I could see his appeal. He stood tall at about six feet, with a muscular lean build, he had dark brown chestnut hair and sparkling blue eyes that seemed to gaze into your soul. All in all, he was a handsome man. Just not the man I would have set my best friend up with.

"What's going on in here? An orgy?" Xander walked into the room with a huge smile and I froze. He wasn't wearing a shirt and I couldn't stop from looking at his perfectly chiseled chest. His six-pack looked even more defined than the last time I had seen it naked.

"Nothing." I looked away from him and I saw that Alice was grinning from ear to ear, instead of glaring at him like I was. Why was she being such a traitor? How could she be smiling knowing what sort of man Xander was? Or more importantly how he had dissed me. I was still feeling the burn of his rejection.

"Who are you?" Aiden turned towards Xander with a disapproving look in his eyes and then he looked at Alice. "Is this a friend of yours?"

"No." Alice squeaked out and I stared at Aiden's face carefully. Had he smiled when she'd said no? My mind was racing as I gazed at my brother. Did he have a thing for Alice as well?

"Oh okay." He made a face. "I was about to say you really need to stop being a bad influence over my sister."

"Aiden." I shouted at him, horrified at his words. I guess I was wrong. Maybe I'd imagined the smile. "Stop being so rude."

"It's okay, Liv. I don't need you to fight my battles." Xander smiled at me with a twinkle in his eyes and turned to Aiden. "I'm Xander, Xander James. I'm your sister's fiancé."

"What?" It was Scott's turn to be shocked. "Liv, you didn't even tell me."

"Is this true Liv?" Aiden turned to me with a frown.

"I, uh, no." I shook my head, my face red. "He's not talking about me. I don't even know him. I haven't even, uh, kissed him, let alone, uh, slept with him." I stammered, my face bright red as I kept rambling on. "I wouldn't get engaged to Xander even if he paid me." I finished and I could see that both of my brothers were staring at me in confusion as Alice made a face at me.

"I guess I didn't make much of an impression on you then." Xander's voice cut the silence and then laughed. "I'm Gabby's fiancé." He said simply and smiled. "I assume you two are her brothers?"

"Yes." Aiden spoke up and stepped forward. "I'm Aiden, the eldest. This is Scott. That's my sister Liv and her best friend Alice. And our brother Chett hasn't arrived home yet." He looked Xander up and down and frowned slightly. "And you're marrying Gabby?"

"Yes." Xander nodded. "I think she's still in bed."

"Sounds about right." Scott scoffed. "It isn't noon yet."

"Scott." I rolled my eyes at him and giggled.

"You know Queen Gabby doesn't arise before she has to." Scott grinned at me and we giggled. We both felt the same way about Gabby and that was just another reason why he was my favorite brother.

"Are you two still harping on about Gabby?" Aiden sighed and shook his head.

"Why shouldn't we?" Scott squared his shoulders and confronted Aiden. "You might be the oldest, but you're not the boss of us all Aiden. We're not kids anymore."

"Then stop acting like one." Aiden looked at Xander. "Sorry about Liv and Scott, they're both rude and I don't think that will ever change."

"That's okay." Xander laughed. "I have a younger brother and I know what it's like dealing with impertinence."

"Ooh, I have to go and see if Henry is up and well." I said sweetly, my stomach churning in anger at Aiden and Xander. "I should see if there is anything I can do for him."

Xander's eyes narrowed as he gazed at me and his expression changed to one of annoyance.

"Henry is fine." He said shortly.

"I'm sure he is, but it doesn't hurt to check and see if he needs a helping hand." I smiled again and I could see Alice giggling from the corner of my eyes. "I want to make sure all his needs are taken care of."

"What are you talking about Liv?" Aiden frowned at me.

"Nothing to worry your sweet head about." I turned and smiled at him. "Excuse me folks, I need to go and perform one of my womanly duties." I brushed past Xander and I heard his sharp intake of breath as my breasts rubbed against his upper arm. My nipples tingled at the touch, but I made sure not to react. I hurried out of the room and down the corridor with a small smile on my face. That would teach Xander. He wanted to act like he was some hot shot and better than me. Well forget him. I didn't want him, need him or care about him. He could have Gabby and deal with her crap. I didn't care if she spent all of his money and then left him when he was broke. It would serve him right. I was fuming by the time I reached the end of the corridor just thinking about Xander. How dare he barge into my room and then say I was impertinent. I could have wiped that smug smile off of his face if I'd told my brothers that I'd fucked him last weekend. I could just image the shock on all of their faces. Aiden would most probably kill me and Scott would laugh. I should have told them everything. That would teach him to mess around with me. How dare he insinuate I was impertinent? And how dare Aiden act like he was some leader of the world. Grr. They both made me so angry. I had no idea why Alice was interested in Aiden. I was going to urge her to change her mind and to focus on someone else. There was no way I wanted my best friend dating my bossy older brother. And there was no way I was ever going to sleep with Xander again, not even if he begged me. Not that I really foresaw that happening. Xander had no interest in sleeping with me again. He just wanted to torture me.

5

I STOPPED OUTSIDE OF HENRY'S bedroom and stood there like a fool. I didn't really have anything to say to him. And I certainly wasn't going to offer to do anything for or to him as I'd insinuated to Xander. I stood there for a few seconds and was about to turn back around when I saw Xander coming towards the room with a sneer on his face.

"Did Henry throw you out already?"

"Excuse me?" I glared at him.

"You're standing in the hallway looking embarrassed." He shrugged as he stood next to me. "I assumed that you got blown off."

"Men don't blow me off." My head tilted up as I avoided looking at his chest.

"True, you're not really the sort a man would blow off." He licked his lips. "I think—"

"Can I help you Xander?" I cut him off, not wanting to go down the flirting road with him again.

"You look sexy this morning." He looked down at my tank top and short shorts.

"Okay and?" I would not let myself get caught up in this man again.

"And it makes me want to kiss you."

"I don't want to kiss you." I sneered at him. "I don't go back for seconds unless the meal was really really good." I looked him up and down. "And you, Xander James were just not that good." I lied, but pride making me try to hurt him.

"I wasn't good?" His eyes widened and he smiled. "You call every guy you meet Mr. Tongue?"

"You're good to go down on me." My face reddened. "But that's about it. I wouldn't sleep with you again."

"So the only good part of me is my tongue?"

"Yup." I nodded. "And every man has one, so it's not even that special."

"So I'm an average man with average tongue skills and bad fucking skills?" He cocked his head to the side and studied my face.

"Yes, average tongue skills and F grade skills in bed." I lied, unable to say fucking to him out loud. I wondered if my face was giving me away. Xander had A plus tongue skills and A plus fucking skills. My body was burning up as we spoke, reminding me that I was lying out of my ass.

"Average and an F now?" His lips thinned. "Hmm, I'm going down on the scale."

"Sorry, I didn't want to be rude before, but you know how it is."

"I do." He nodded and grabbed my hand and then opened Henry's bedroom door and pulled me into the room with him.

"What are you doing?" I gasped as he pushed me back against the door and positioned himself in front of me. He didn't answer me, but instead his eyes mocked me as his face moved closer to mine.

"What are you doing?" I gasped again as he lowered his mouth to mine. His lips were firm as they crushed into mine and his tongue slid into my mouth easily. I moaned as his hardness pressed into my belly and I kissed him back for a couple of seconds before I remembered where we were. Oh shit, what must Henry be thinking?

"What do you think you're doing?" I pushed him off of me and looked around the room wildly, my face a deep red.

"Henry's not here." He raised an eyebrow at me and laughed. "You can stop pretending to be affronted now."

"I'm not pretending anything." I frowned. "Where is he? And if you knew he wasn't here why would you say he blew me off?"

"Don't play games with me, Liv. I'm not the sort of guy that takes kindly to games."

"What games?" I said in a heat. Did he know that I had no interest in Henry? How embarrassing.

"Look, I know this is an uncomfortable situation and I know that your feelings are likely hurt, but I made a promise and a commitment to your sister. Even if I wanted to back out, it wouldn't be the gentlemanly thing to do."

"But you're not a gentleman."

"I wasn't one, no." He sighed. "I'm used to getting what I want when I want it and if it doesn't come easily I just take it, but life is about more than my ego."

"Okay." I took a step away from him as he looked as if he were going to kiss me again. "Good for you and your perfect life."

"Liv, I'm just saying there's no need to pretend you're into Henry."

"I'm not pretending." I shook my head at him, annoyed by his arrogance. "He's handsome, single, by all accounts a lovely man. I'm interested in getting to know him. What's so hard to believe about that?"

"He's my brother." He frowned, the smug smile completely gone from his face.

"So? Gabby's my sister." I looked him in the eyes. "You didn't seem to have a problem with that. I find it hypocritical that you would have a problem with me dating your brother."

"Why date my brother when it's me you want?"

"I don't want you. You seem to be the one that wants me. What do you think Gabby would say if she knew you had just kissed me?"

"I do not care." He growled. "What Gabby and I have is a business relationship."

"Well good for you."

"You don't understand." He shook his head and grabbed me around the waist and pulled me to him. "What happened to the carefree fun-loving girl I met last weekend?"

"She left the building when you were introduced as my sister's fiancé."

"What can I do to change this?" His fingers brushed the loose hairs away from my face. "I don't want us to argue about this anymore."

"I'm not arguing, I'm just stating facts." I shrugged and tried to push him away from me, but this time I couldn't move his body. My hands were flat against his naked chest and I swallowed hard. Why was he making this so difficult? Why wouldn't he just leave me alone?

"We still need to be friends, Liv." His fingers traced my lips. "We're going to be family."

I nearly vomited at that point. I mean, was this guy for real?

"Xander," I looked up into his eyes. "I don't intend on ever seeing you again after this weekend, asides from at your wedding. We do not need to be anything."

Our eyes met and we looked at each other for a few seconds and I could see that he was thinking hard. I waited for him to tell me that I was being stupid. That of course we'd see each other at other times. I waited for him to scold me and tell me I was being immature. I waited for him to tell me that I was acting like a silly schoolgirl. I knew that there was obviously no way I'd only be able to see him at the wedding. For all of our squabbling and quarrels, my family was close-knit and my parents would not allow me to blow off every dinner and get-together, even if I wanted to. I stood there with my shoulders squared and waited for him to tell me off for being immature, but instead he started laughing. I stared at him in amazement and shock as I watched the laughter fill his face: his eyes were bright, his mouth was wide and his head fell back as he laughed his head off.

"What's so funny?" I asked him softly, feeling even more annoyed at him. I hated that I didn't understand him and I couldn't read him. I hated that I loved that about him. I hated that I wanted to get to know him better. I hated that I would never have the chance to be more with him.

"You." He took a deep breath and finally stopped laughing. "You're a breath of fresh air." He smiled at me. "Yes, you're also a pain in the neck, but you're also a breath of fresh air."

"Okay, thanks, I guess."

"I want to make love to you again." He groaned, his expression turning to one of lust as he took a step towards me.

"No, we can't." I bit down on my lower lip.

"Oh, but we can do whatever we want." He grinned and turned around and locked the door before coming back to me.

"What are you doing?" I said in shock as he pulled his briefs down and stood in front of me naked; his cock already standing at attention.

"I'm showing you that I'm not an F in bed." He grinned and took another step towards me. "I like a good challenge."

"Xander." I groaned as he pulled me towards him. My body was trembling in anticipation and I felt guilty and confused. "We can't—" He cut me off by picking me up and throwing me onto the bed. His fingers pulled my shorts and panties off and he fell on top of me and kissed my neck. "Xander." I moaned and wriggled against him. "We can't do this."

"We can." His fingers slipped down my legs and rubbed me gently. I closed my eyes for two seconds and enjoyed the feelings of excitement as they swept through my body and then I pushed him to the side and rolled off of the bed. "What are you doing?" He blinked up at me in surprise as I picked my panties up off of the floor.

"I'm leaving." I rubbed my lips to get rid of his taste. "You can't just have me whenever you feel like it."

"Why not?" He frowned and I was about to protest when he laughed. "I'm not being serious." He sighed and sat up. I looked down and saw that his manhood was hard and sticking up. He looked down to see what I was staring at and he grinned at me. "Yeah, that's what you're leaving me with."

"Ask Gabby to help you out." I spat out, annoyed.

"This is always going to be an issue between us, isn't it?"

"What do you think?" I looked at him incredulously. For a smart man, Xander could be a real dummy sometimes. I watched as Xander jumped off of the bed, bent down, picked his briefs up and pulled them on. He then looked at me with a lazy smile and shrugged.

"So your parents seem nice and I think they like me." He said casually as if that were the most normal thing to say next in this situation.

"They are nice." I stopped myself from saying they wouldn't be so nice to him if they knew what kind of guy he really was.

"I think I'll quite like having them as parents."

"That's good."

"They'll make good grandparents."

"Yup." I looked away from him then as I wanted to slap the smug look off of his face. What was his problem? How could he try and sleep with me and then talk about my parents.

"You don't have anything else to say?" His eyes narrowed as he studied me.

"What else do you want me to say?" I looked back up into his face then.

"I don't know, something telling me I'm making a mistake." He shrugged nonchalantly.

"It's your mistake to make." I wasn't going down this road again. I wasn't going to make him think I wanted him.

"Ah ha, so you do think I'm making a mistake?"

"I don't care what you do." I lied and turned away. "I'm going to go back to my room now."

"But Alice is in there with Scott and Aiden."

"So?" I looked at him with a question.

"You don't want to cock block."

"Excuse me."

"Alice has a crush, doesn't she?"

"How did you know that?"

"It was obvious from the way she was beaming from ear to ear." He shrugged. "I didn't presume to think it was because of me."

"Not that that would be a problem for you right? You'd love three of the women in this house wanting you."

"So, are you saying two women in this house currently want me?" He smiled and raised an eyebrow at me.

"No." I said hurriedly. "Now tell me, who do you think likes Alice back in return?"

"Who?" He laughed. "I think Alice has herself a little problem."

"Oh?" I frowned and rubbed my forehead. "So you don't think Scott or Aiden likes her then?"

"Oh, quite the opposite." Xander rubbed his palms over his stomach as he stood there. "I think they both like her."

"What?" I frowned and looked into his eyes to see if he was being serious.

"I think both of your brothers have an interest in Alice." He nodded seriously. "Hopefully, they both don't make a play for her. She has an interest in one of them, doesn't she?"

"Yes." I nodded and bit my lower lip. How did he know that my brothers liked Alice and what did that mean? How would Scott feel if Alice and Aiden started dating because Alice liked Aiden and that was obviously who she would choose, wasn't it?

"Are you going to tell me which one?"

"No." I shook my head and turned back to the door. "That's none of your business."

"Are you always going to be like this, Liv?" He grabbed my shoulder. "Can't we just be friends?"

"No, we can't." I said as I opened the door and walked out of the room. Who the hell did Xander James think he was? Did he really think I could just forget everything and just be friends with him? Did he really think that was possible?

"Morning Liv." A soft husky voice made me jump and I blinked as I stared ahead of me. "Sorry," He smiled at me widely. "I didn't mean to scare you."

"It's okay." I smiled back at him. "Good Morning to you too, Henry." I looked into his eyes and I noticed that they were actually a lighter green than Xander's.

"Everything okay?" His perfect white teeth shone at me as he spoke and I really began to notice the subtle differences in his appearance to Xander's. Henry had slightly thinner pink lips and a rather deep-set dimple in his right cheek. His hair, though also dark, held light streaks of brown as well and it was slightly more unkempt than Xander's was.

"I'm fine. It's just been an exhausting morning already and we haven't even had breakfast." I laughed and rolled my eyes.

"I am hungry." He nodded. "I'm just coming back from my morning run and am ready for pancakes and bacon."

"That sounds good to me." I nodded eagerly. "Banana chocolate chip pancakes with lots of syrup and bacon."

"I'm a blueberry pancake guy myself." He smiled and ran his hand through his dark hair, "Though I wouldn't mind some chocolate chips. Maybe we can share?"

"Sounds good to me." I said and adjusted my top as I stared at him. "As long as you don't want some of my bacon as well."

"Don't worry, I never attempt to take bacon off of anyone's plate." He laughed and I stared at his lips for a few seconds as I laughed along with him.

"Good or I'll have to kill you." I giggled and poked him in the shoulder with two fingers sticking out like a gun.

"Uh oh, the warning has officially been issued."

"Yup." I said and winked at him.

"What's going on here?" Xander's deep voice was directly behind me and I couldn't believe that I hadn't heard him come out of the bedroom and down the corridor.

"Liv is going to share her pancakes with me, but she's warning me to stay away from her bacon." Henry answered his brother with a laugh. "I said that's a fair price to pay to share breakfast with a beautiful woman."

"Hmmm." Xander said in reply as my stomach flipped. Henry had called me beautiful. I had to admit that his words made me happy. Maybe I would try and get to know Henry a bit better this morning. "Maybe you shouldn't be sharing everything with everyone, Liv." He said to me obnoxiously as he looked down at me with a sneer.

"Excuse me?" I glared up at him, my mind off Henry as I gazed into Xander's dark green eyes.

"Maybe you shouldn't be so easy and willing to give it up." He said softly as I gasped. He paused as he looked me up and down and then he grinned. "Your pancakes I mean. I wouldn't be so easy to give them up. Henry's a pig. He'll gobble them all down before you can blink. And then you'll regret having given them up."

"I don't think I'll regret sharing my pancakes, though there are other things I regret." I tried to remain civilized, though it was difficult. I didn't want to embarrass myself in front of Henry or make him suspicious, but I so badly wanted to smack Xander. Hard.

"Oh?" He cocked his head. "Like what?"

"Xander, don't badger the girl." Henry gave his brother a reproachful look. "She just woke up."

"I'm not badgering her." Xander gave his brother a sharp look.

"I'm just saying you just met her and she doesn't know your sense of humor, so go lightly on her." Henry grinned at me. "We're not family yet."

"Thanks Henry, I appreciate it." I smiled at him warmly.

"Shouldn't you be getting in the shower or something?" Xander's eyes narrowed at me. "We wouldn't want you to hold up our getting pancakes."

"I'd worry about your fiancé, as opposed to me." I looked at him distastefully. "I'm pretty sure she's still in bed."

"Well I do wear women out." Xander said smartly and I gasped, all color leaving my face as jealousy stirred in my stomach.

"Xander." Henry chastised his brother. "Ignore him, Liv. Xander and I shared a room last night, he wouldn't dare disrespect your parents in their own home."

"I wouldn't be shocked if he did." I gave Xander a disparaging look and then looked back at Henry. "It's good to know one of the James brothers is a gentleman. Thank you."

"Any time." Henry bowed his head down and grinned. "Now hurry and shower so we can go and get those pancakes."

"Will do." I giggled and then hurried off to my bedroom. I could feel both brothers staring after me as I entered my room.

"There you are." Alice said melodramatically as I walked into the bedroom. "Where have you been?"

"You do not want to know." I closed the door behind me and fell to the bed. "You will not believe what just happened."

"What?" She stood next to her overnight bag and gazed at me with questioning eyes.

"Well—" I started.

"Oh my God, Aiden looked so hot this morning, didn't he?" She cut me off before I could tell her what had happened. "I need to change. I can't let him see me in the same clothes I was wearing this morning."

"He won't notice or care." I said quickly. "But get this, Xander pushed me into Henry's bedroom and threw me on the bed and—"

"Should I wear a skirt or a dress?" She held up a short black skirt and a red slinky dress as she cut me off again. "Or are they both too trampy?"

"Yes, they are both trampy." I nodded and continued. "He threw me on the bed and pulled his boxer shorts off and then he pulled my panties down and——"

"Okay, what about this blouse?" She held it up to her face. "And a nice pair of white pants? Or should I wear my black skinny jeans."

"Then he shoved his cock up my ass." I said loudly as I jumped off the bed. "He ripped my clothes off, threw me on the bed, turned me over and fucked me up the ass."

"So you had anal?" Her jaw dropped. I had her attention now. "Did it hurt?"

"Alice, get it together." I walked over to her and grabbed her shoulders. "Your response to me telling you that my sister's fiancé threw me onto his bed naked and penetrated me is to ask if it hurt?"

"Well, I've always wondered." She shrugged. "I figured I might as well find out, so I know whether or not to have anal with Aiden."

"Oh my God, Alice." I groaned at her and she gave me a small smile.

"Sorry, I'm going crazy aren't I?" She let out a long sigh and gave me an apologetic face. "I'm just so excited. I'm finally an adult and he can take me seriously now. He can see me as a woman."

"Yeah, I guess." I made a face. "I was trying to tell you about Xander."

"I know, sorry." She dropped the blouse down. "Tell me about Xander and the anal sex, then I'll tell you about Aiden and ask you for advice." She walked over to the bed and sat down. "Now spit it out."

"We didn't have anal sex." I walked back over to the bed and lay back on the mattress. "He did take my panties off though and he was naked and I felt him right there." I gulped. "Ugh, he was so close to being inside of me, but then I felt guilty and jumped up and pulled my panties on."

"That's funny." Alice giggled as she looked down at me.

"What's so funny about that?"

"You most probably left him with blue balls." She giggled some more. "I bet he's got to go to the shower so he can whack himself off."

"Oh Alice." I started giggling as well. "You think so?"

"Of course." She nodded. "He was naked right? And his cock was right there?"

"Yup, his fingers as well." I sighed as I remembered the touch of his fingers as they'd rubbed me. "I wanted him inside of me so badly, but just felt like it was wrong."

"So imagine how bad it must have been for him? His dick was a mere centimeter, or even just a millimeter from entering you and reaching the Holy Land and instead of being taken to paradise, he found himself in blue ball hell."

"Oh Alice." I started laughing. "I love you, you know that? I'm so lucky to have a friend that I can talk about sex with candidly."

"So am I." She grinned. "How else am I supposed to know the difference between a circumcised penis from one that hasn't been circumcised?"

"The internet, silly."

"That's not as fun as having you describe the difference."

"I only knew from looking it up online." I rolled my eyes at her.

"I wonder if Aiden—"

"Stop." I held up my hand. "I'm cool, but I'm not that cool. I do not want to talk about my brother's penis or how good he is in bed. And I never want to hear about him going down on you, you hear me?"

"Liv." She made a face. "Not that that's ever going to happen."

"You never know."

"I doubt Aiden will ever give me the time of day, no matter what I wear." She lay back on the bed next to me. "He's just not into me."

"According to Xander, both Scott and Aiden are into you."

"What?" She rolled over and looked at me. "Are you joking?"

"Nope." I shrugged. "He said that he thinks they're both into you."

"What makes him think that? Did they tell him?"

"He's never met them before Alice." I shook my head. "I don't think either of them told him crap, it's just an observation he made from ten seconds of being in the room with all of us."

"Oh," She made a face. "So that doesn't really mean much then."

"Yeah, not really." I sat up. "Now go and show me your outfits and let me help you figure out what to wear."

"I suck."

"We both suck." I groaned. "I was flirting with Henry to make Xander jealous."

"Oh, Mr. Tongue's brother?" Alice's eyes widened.

"Yeah, he's a cutie." I nodded. "I think you might like him."

"I don't need a third guy to worry about."

"A third guy?" I frowned. "Who's the second?"

"Well you said Scott liked me..." She said weakly and made a face.

"Oh my God, Alice, do you like Scott as well?" I asked her. This time it was my turn to be shocked.

"No, yes, no, I don't know." She made a face. "He's nice as well."

"Alice, you're the dirty dog now."

"We're both dirty dogs." She giggled and held up two tops. "Which one?"

"Wear the white top with your skinny jeans. The blue ones." I grinned at her. "And wear your white, opened toed heels."

"Heels to breakfast?" She made a face. "Are you sure that's not too much?"

"Trust me, it's not too much." I held in a laugh. If she was willing to wear fake eyelashes, dark eyeliner and hair extensions, heels to breakfast was not too much at all.

"Okay, if you say it's good." She grinned at me. "Maybe Aiden will take one look at me and be like 'where have you been all my life?'."

"Yeah, maybe." I offered her a weak smile. I was pretty confident that Aiden didn't have a romantic bone in his body.

"So what else happened with you and Xander?"

"Nothing much. He's such a jerk, ugh." I groaned. "Why do I still have the hots for him?"

"Because he's hot." She made a face. "And he has a tongue that can make you come in seconds?"

"Alice!"

"What? I'm just repeating what you told me."

"That was when I still liked him. That was when he was the stranger I hooked up with at a wedding. That was when it was still exciting and I could remember and fantasize. Now I can't do either of them."

"Well you can do both, it would just be a bit weird."

"He's the one that tried to have sex with me again. Should I tell Gabby?"

"I think you should." She nodded. "He can't have his cake and eat it too. That would be wrong."

"You really think I should tell her?" I asked in surprise.

"Hell no." She made a face and frowned up at me. "If you say anything, Gabby will never forgive you and everyone in your family will think you're a slut and Aiden will think I'm a bad influence."

"Alice." I shook my head at her.

"And I just don't think it's a good idea, honestly, Liv. Just spend the weekend and we'll go home and forget him. Gabby deserves him. They're both jerks."

"Yeah, I guess."

"And I mean, we don't even know why they're really getting married."

"True." I nodded. "I have no idea why he proposed to her all of a sudden."

"Yeah, it all seems weird. Maybe he's some shady drug dealer or part of the mafia or something. Maybe Gabby is signing her baby away like Rumpelstiltskin or The Omen or something."

"The Omen?"

"Yeah, you know how that lady gave birth to Damian, the devil."

"She sold her baby to the devil?"

"No, her baby was the devil."

"Oh." I scratched the side of my head. "So you're saying you think Gabby is giving birth to the devil?"

"No, I meant more like maybe she's selling her soul to the devil and Xander is the devil."

"I wouldn't be shocked if I found that out."

"Imagine if you really had slept with the devil, you'd have to spend the rest of your life in church asking for forgiveness, just for a chance to get to heaven."

"Thanks Alice, that makes me feel a lot better." I groaned. "I'm doomed."

"You're not doomed. Maybe you'll like Henry, or we can find you another guy. We'll let Xander know he can shove his dick up his own ass."

"That would be funny." I giggled.

"Wouldn't it be?" She laughed with me and we both just stared at each other for a few seconds before she spoke to me again. "I have a feeling that this is going to be another crazy weekend."

"You and me both, sister. You and me both."

6

"LIV." GABBY'S VOICE ECHOED THROUGHOUT the restroom. "Are you in here?"

I froze at the sound of her voice and I could see that Xander was trying not to laugh as his hand covered my mouth.

"Liv? Are you in here?" Gabby said again. "Speak up if you're in here. We can't find you, Alice, Xander or Scott and mom and dad want to pay the bill and leave now."

I glanced up at Xander, my face burning a bright red and I could feel myself sliding down his body, until his hands slipped to my ass and he pulled me back up, so that once again I was nestled firmly against his body, his cock nestled in-between my legs.

"Liv? Alice?" Gabby said again sounding annoyed and I bit my lower lip in shame and listened to her as she exited the restroom.

"I'm a horrible sister." I groaned and then cried out as Xander ignored my comment and instead entered me again swiftly.

"No, you're not." He grinned, his fingers squeezing my butt cheeks as he moved in and out of me. I tightened my grip around his waist and bit down on his shoulder to stop myself from crying out in ecstasy.

I know you're wondering what happened at breakfast that would have me fucking Xander again, and in the restaurant restroom, of all places. First off, you have to know that I'm not the sort of girl that stole other girls' boyfriends. Not in high school, not in college. Not ever. I was never the girl to go after another woman's man. I just don't do that, but you have to understand that these were extenuating circumstances. Xander wasn't really Gabby's man and well, he just made it too damn hard to say no to. Way too hard.

I didn't leave the house expecting to have sex with Xander again. That was not part of the plan. Not at all. I was planning on ignoring him, but that all went downhill as soon as we got into the SUV to go to the restaurant two hours ago.

"I'M SO HAPPY THAT EVERYONE came home to hear my good news." Gabby grinned from the passenger seat of my father's Lincoln Navigator. "You guys, rock." She looked at me and then Alice. "I can't believe that even people that weren't invited showed up." She gave Alice another look and then turned back to Aiden who was driving the car.

"Why didn't you ride with mom, dad, and Chett?" I asked Gabby, annoyed by her already and we'd only been in the car for five minutes.

"Because I wanted to drive with my fiancé and his brother." She said as she smiled at Xander lovingly. "And I wanted to be in the Lincoln. It seats eight and I wanted the largest amount of people to enjoy my company while we celebrate this weekend."

"Yay us." Alice said and looked at me with a grin.

"Grow up." Gabby rolled her eyes. "You two are college graduates now, you're both twenty-two. Stop acting like you're twelve."

"Don't talk to Alice like that." I snapped at Gabby.

"Yeah, give it a break." Scott spoke up from the backseat. "No one wants to hear you lecturing all day." He continued.

"Scott." Aiden stopped at the traffic light and looked into the back. "This is Gabby's big weekend. Have some respect."

"Yeah yeah yeah. No one died and made you John Boy Walton, Aiden." Scott retorted and Alice and I laughed at his comments. Aiden looked at Alice for a second then and her face went red as her laughter died.

"See what you've done." I turned around and looked at Xander, who was sitting in the last row with a smirk on his face. Henry was sitting next to him and looked slightly uncomfortable.

"Liv." Gabby snapped. "Do not talk to my fiancé that way."

"Am I lying?"

"That's why you're still single and can't get a man." Gabby snapped again, her eyes flaring at me. "You do not know how to treat a man."

"And you do?" My jaw dropped at her rudeness.

"I'm the one that's engaged." She flashed her ring and I turned away, wanting so desperately to shout that I was the one that had fucked him the previous weekend.

"Girls." Aiden spoke up again. "That's enough Gabby."

"What? Liv is the one–"

"You're being rude to Liv and to Alice, just stop it."

The car was silent then. I don't think any of us could believe that Aiden had spoken like that to Gabby. He never told her off. The only two he seemed to ride were Scott and I, even Chett didn't get chastised much. I turned around and looked at Xander again, but stopped myself from glaring at him because Henry was there. We were all more than ready to arrive at the restaurant and Alice and I jumped out of the SUV quickly and walked towards the entrance.

"Who knew that Aiden would stick up for me?" She grinned and I tried not to roll my eyes.

"So we still sharing those pancakes?" Henry ran up to join us.

"Sounds like a plan to me." I nodded and smiled. "Just remember—"

"No bacon, I know." He completed my sentence for me.

"Hmm, I don't believe we've been formally introduced." Alice held her hand out. "I'm Alice, Liv's best friend and number one supporter."

'Hi Alice," He shook her hand. "I'm Xander's younger brother Henry and general underling."

"Nice to meet you underling." Alice grinned.

"Nice to meet you number one supporter." He grinned back at her.

"Alice, I was hoping to speak to you." Aiden was suddenly by her side and I saw her looking over at him in glee.

"So just why did you come this weekend?" I asked Henry as we walked into the restaurant to join my parents and Chett. I could hear Gabby and Xander talking behind us.

"Xander asked me to come." Henry lowered his voice. "To be honest, I've never heard of Gabby before this weekend." He looked behind us for a quick second. "And she's not the sort of girl I expected him to settle down with. I mean, I never thought he would get married, period." He laughed.

"Oh? Why's that?"

"My brother Xander is a playboy. A confirmed bachelor so to speak. He's always said he never had any intentions to get married or to have kids."

"Really?" I wanted so badly to turn around and ask Xander why he was marrying Gabby. "So why do you think he's marrying Gabby?"

"My mom said that Xander would marry when he fell in love." He grinned. "She always said that she didn't give birth to robots and the day would come when a woman would claim his heart and he'd never be the same again. I guess that day came."

"Oh wow. So you think he really loves her then?"

"What do I know?" Henry shrugged and looked away.

"What? What aren't you telling me?"

"I don't want to be rude." Henry made a face. "But I just didn't think that someone like Gabby would ever be his type. I know she's your sister and all, but she's just so..." His voice trailed off and I laughed.

"She's a bitch."

"I didn't want to say that."

"It's fine." I laughed and hooked my arm through his, genuinely happy that he was here this weekend. We walked over to the table and my parents stood up, while Chett chatted away to someone on the phone. "We all call her that." I whispered in his ear before we sat down.

"Really?" He looked at me in surprise.

"And by all, I mean Alice and me." I grinned as he laughed.

"What are you two laughing at?" Xander approached us with a frown.

"None of your business." I said smartly and then winked at Henry, who laughed again.

"Hmmph." Xander's throat made a noise, but he didn't say anything.

"I'll sit next to you." Henry sat in the chair next to me and I smiled happily.

"I guess I'll take the other seat." Xander said and plopped down next me on the other side.

"But Alice was going to sit there."

"Well, she's not, is she?" He raised an eyebrow at me.

"Whatever." I looked past him, up at Gabby who was staring at us with daggers in her eyes. "I thought you'd want to sit with your fiancé. There isn't a chair to your right." I said stiffly.

"Well you thought wrong, didn't you?"

"So did you sleep well?" I turned back to Henry and decided to ignore Xander. I wasn't going to let him rile me up at breakfast in front of everyone. I knew my parents would not be happy if they heard me calling him names.

"Yes, pretty good thanks." Henry nodded back. "What about you?"

"Yeah, I felt...argh." I jumped as I felt a hand on my leg. I looked over at Xander, but he was busy talking to my father across the table. I reached under the table and grabbed his hand and tried to remove it from my thigh, but it wasn't budging; if anything, it was moving higher up on my thigh. Why oh why had I let Alice talk me into wearing a skirt this morning?

"Stop it." I hissed at Xander, but he didn't pay any attention to me.

"You okay, Liv?" Henry asked and I nodded. How could I tell him that his brother's fingers were running up and down the inside of my leg and I was starting to feel turned on?

"Yeah, so I heard you're single?" I said and then realized everyone was looking at me as the table had gone quiet.

"Way to be obvious, Liv." Gabby shook her head at me.

"Obvious about what?" I looked at her with my best death glare.

"That you're interested." She shook her head. "Mom and dad really should have sent you to deportment classes, maybe then you'd have some class."

"You're talking to me about class?" I laughed and looked at Alice. "You the girl that used to sneak out to meet Tommy, the guy from the car wash on Friday nights so you could have sex in the back of rich people's cars?"

"Liv." My mother admonished me as her face went red. "That's enough."

"She started it." I protested.

"Liv." Aiden gave me a look. "Enough."

"Yes, dad." I rolled my eyes at him. "Oh wait, my dad is sitting next to mom. So who then are you, Sir?" I asked, my voice raising as Xander's fingers ran all the way up my leg and settled at the top of my thigh and inched their way inwards. I closed my legs together, but that was a wrong move, as I just trapped his fingers in-between my legs and I could feel him rubbing against my bud. Oh God, why did it feel so good? I wanted to tell him to fuck off, but I couldn't. A part of me was getting off on what we were doing. I know that sounds awful, but you had to be in the situation, with your bitchy horrible superior sister sitting opposite you with a look on her face like I was a piece of dog poop on the bottom of her Jimmy Choo heels.

"Enough Liv." My dad finally spoke up. "This is not the time for you and Gabby to bicker."

"I'm not bickering. I'm just stating the….agh…" My voice trailed off as I felt Xanders index finger tapping and rubbing my clit. I was going to kill that man.

"You're such a jealous little—" Gabby started with a look of rage on her face.

"Come on guys." Scott cut her off. "We have guests. We don't want Xander and Henry to think we're all crazy."

"What about what I think?" Alice asked him with a small smile.

"You already know how crazy we are." He winked at her and she laughed. "That's true."

"Are you two done?" Aiden glared at them and I looked over at Xander's smug face in shock. Had he been right? Did both Scott and Aiden have crushes on Alice? Oh my God, how much crazier could our family get.

"Please do not worry about us." Xander spoke up as his finger kept rubbing me gently. "My brother and I are happy to share in all experiences with your family. We lost our parents a few years ago and we're happy to be a part of your family structure now."

"So you're orphans?" I asked him, my heart suddenly aching for him.

"We have a grandfather that is still very much alive." He looked over at me and smiled. "He's actually still working at the family business and making all sorts of demands."

"Oh?"

"He wants us to provide heirs for the company." Henry said with a laugh. "Antiquated isn't it? He said he won't pass on our shares until he sees us both getting married and having kids."

"Wow." I looked at Henry then. "That's crazy." Of course, I'd be lying if I said my mind wasn't ticking a million miles a second. Was this why Xander was marrying Gabby?

"It's a good thing that you're already pregnant then, isn't it Gabby?" Alice suddenly spoke up. "Xander will have both a wife and baby to show to his grandfather." There was silence at the table after Alice spoke and I watched as her hand flew to her mouth and she looked at me with wide eyes. She had forgotten that my parents weren't supposed to know about the baby.

"What baby?" Aiden frowned and looked at Gabby.

"I don't know what she's talking about." Gabby's face was bright red. "Let's order please."

"Is that why you're marrying her so quickly?" Scott spoke up and looked at Xander.

"Enough." My dad frowned and looked at his menu. "We are not going to have this conversation at this table."

"You really need to get over your jealousy, Liv." Gabby glared at me. "And stop gossiping about me. I know you have no life, but that's not my fault."

My jaw dropped at her words and I couldn't stop myself from what I did next. I opened my menu and as I gazed down at it, I reached under the table and started rubbing the front of Xander's pants, ensuring that my hand made solid contact with his manhood. I felt him looking at me as he sat back and I unzipped his pants slowly and reached my hand in so that I could have bare contact with him. I could feel him shifting in the chair as my fingers grabbed ahold of his naked cock and I smiled to myself as I felt him growing hard in my fingers. I looked up and glanced at Gabby who was a mere couple of yards away and had no idea what was going on.

I looked back down at the menu and decided to be even more daring. I slipped Xander's cock out of his pants completely and I heard him groan slightly as my hand moved up and down quickly. I felt his hand grab my wrist and he leaned forward and whispered in my ear lightly.

"You need to stop Liv."

"Stop what?" I turned to look at him and gave him a small smile.

"Stop." His eyes burned into mine. "Don't play with fire if you don't want to get burned."

"I've already been burned. What's another scar?" I said softly and then gasped as I felt his fingers slip under the sides of my panties and start to rub my clit with vigor.

"It seems like you have enough wetness to put out the fire already." He muttered as he continued to rub me. "You're ready for me already, aren't you? You dirty girl?"

"You're a pig." My fingers moved up and down faster as he rubbed me.

"So what are you getting?" Alice asked me from across the table and I looked up at her with a guilty look on my face. I was so scared that someone at the table was going to realize what we were doing. If someone knocked something off of the table and bent down to retrieve it they would see my hands gliding up and down his cock and they would see his fingers in-between my legs moving underneath my panties.

"Not sure." I said, breathlessly.

"Why don't you get pigs in a blanket?" Xander said and I looked over at him with a small glare. I removed my hand from his cock and tried to shift away from him. All of a sudden, the complete danger of what we were doing had hit me tenfold. Why was I taking these risks?

"I don't care for pigs." I glared at him. "They don't taste good."

"Oh?" He sat back and I felt his fingers sliding out of my panties. I quickly pushed my skirt back down and shifted to the left.

"Yeah, I prefer sausage to bacon." I had no idea what I was saying, but I just needed to control my breathing.

"I like both." He said. "In fact I can eat anything as long as it tastes good." He brought his fingers up to his face causally and I watched as he sucked my juices off of one finger at a time. "Taste is very important." He winked at me as he licked his lips and I turned away from him, suddenly feeling even more turned on than I had before.

We all ordered our meals next and the table was pretty quiet. The conversation was mainly between my dad and Xander and talk about stocks and bonds and other boring stuff. I kept my mouth closed and just ate my meal; though I did notice that both Aiden and Scott were making conversation with Alice and she seemed to be loving the attention. I was going to have to ask her what was going on when we got back to the house.

Henry and I shared our pancakes and I was starting to wish that I had met him before Xander. He seemed like a much nicer guy than his big brother.

"Excuse me, I'm just going to the restroom." I stood up and left the table and hurried to the ladies room after I'd finished my pancakes. I gave Alice a look that was a signal for her to follow me to the bathroom and then walked away. I went straight to the mirror as I entered the restroom and refreshed my lipstick and fluffed up my hair and waited. A couple of minutes later, the door opened and I looked to the side with a smile expecting to see Alice coming in.

"What are you doing in here?" I gasped as I stared at Xander.

"What do you think?" He strode towards me with an imperious look.

"You can't be in here."

"Why not?" He stopped in front of me and licked his lips as his arms crept around my waist and pulled me to him.

"Xander." I groaned as he pulled my t-shirt up and pulled my left breast out of the bra cup. "What are you doing?"

"What do you think?" He bent down and sucked on my nipple. I moaned as his teeth nibbled on my breast and he sucked hard.

"Xander." I moaned. "We can't do this."

"Come." He grabbed my hand and led me to one of the stalls and locked the door behind us. His hands crept up to my breasts and he played with both of my nipples as we stood in the small space, the sound of my heavy breathing the only sound in the quiet bathroom.

"This is so wrong." I groaned as I felt his hands slip up my skirt and start to squeeze my butt cheeks.

"Why?"

"You're engaged to my sister."

"We're more friends than anything else." He leaned down and sucked on my neck, his teeth biting into my skin. I grabbed his hair and then ran my hands across his shoulders and up the inside of his shirt so that I could touch his bare chest.

"Why are you marrying her?"

"It's a business transaction." He grabbed my face and then kissed me, hard. His tongue slid into my mouth easily, taking control of my tongue and possessing me. His lips were rough as he kissed me and I kissed him back passionately, unable to resist him and his presence. He was my lord and I was his peasant and that was how it should be in that moment. He lifted me up then and I wrapped my legs around his waist. I was so caught up in the moment that I didn't even think to stop him. I felt his hand run down between our bodies and he undid his zipper, his cock thrusting out with power, letting both of us know exactly who was running the show. His hand slid behind me and I felt him moving my body up a little higher, before he moved his hand and moved my panties to the side.

"Xander," I looked into his eyes with a question.

"Yes?" He grinned and I felt him thrust his cock inside of me in answer.

"Oh." I moaned as I cried out. He pushed my back against the door and moved back and forth.

"Hold on tight." He grunted as he entered me over and over again.

"Oh." I screamed as he slammed into me and he paused.

"Shh, honey." He laughed. "Bite down on my shoulder if you have to, but you can't scream out loud."

"I'm trying not to." I moaned as he slid into me easily again. I could feel him going deep inside of me and I could feel my climax building up quickly. I was almost at the top of the mountain and I knew that the ride down was going to be explosive.

"You're so sexy." He kissed me as he moved in and out of me, slower now. "Look at me." He commanded and I stared into his eyes. "So, so sexy." He groaned as he adjusted his position and increased his pace slightly.

"We shouldn't be doing this." I protested weakly, knowing I didn't want him to stop.

"Why not?" He groaned as he lifted my ass up higher as I'd been slipping down.

"Because…" I started and then closed my mouth as I heard the restroom door opening.

"Liv, Liv, are you in here?" Gabby's voice resounded through the restroom and I froze. I could see that Xander was trying not to laugh. What man thinks it's funny to nearly being caught by his fiancé as he fucks her sister in a public restroom? He's sick, I tell you. I know I'm preaching to the choir and I'm not making it any better by allowing him to fuck me. I mean, I should have stopped him when he started playing with me under the table, but she had just made me so mad.

"We're going to hell." I whispered in his ear as he continued to fuck me after Gabby left the restroom.

"Speak for yourself." He groaned as he increased his pace and slammed in and out of me harder. I felt him explode inside of me a few seconds after I climaxed. My body shook violently against the door and his body as we came together. I was panting in ecstasy as we stood there for a few seconds just allowing ourselves to enjoy our mutual orgasms. Then I slid down his body and stood up on my own two feet, feeling guilty as hell as I stared at him. He reached up, pulled my bra up properly to cover my breasts and then pulled my top back down.

"I love breakfast." He said with a grin as he stared at me.

"Excuse me?" I looked into his eyes. "What are you talking about?"

"I love a good fuck for breakfast." He leaned forward and kissed me. "I'm sorry I didn't get to do any tongue work though. Maybe later."

"You're such a pig." I shook my head. "Do you have no shame?"

"Shame? Me?" He laughed and ran his hands through his hair as he adjusted his shirt and pants. "Not really." He opened the restroom door and stepped out. I stood there and watched as we walked to exit the bathroom. He stopped at the main door and turned around to look at me. "Oh by the way, Liv. Stop flirting with Henry. That's never going to happen."

"Excuse me?" My jaw dropped.

"My brother doesn't want my sloppy seconds." His eyes narrowed. "So stop flirting with him."

"You jerk." My heart raced thunderously at his words. In that moment I hated both him and myself. "How dare you?"

"How dare I what?" He looked me up and down. "Leave my brother alone."

"I'll do what I want."

"We're just as bad as each other, Liv. You can't act all high and mighty now. You just had sex with me in a bathroom stall while your sister waited outside. You know the score now and you still did it. I'm not the only pig in this bathroom."

"How dare you?" I was close to tears. This was not how I'd expected this to go down, at all.

"I know you don't understand my reasons for marrying Gabby, when I don't love her." He shrugged, his eyes burning into mine. "But that's not for you to understand. Some of us know that love is the stupidest reason to get married."

"What?"

"I told you that I proposed to Gabby last week because I did something I regretted last weekend. You asked me if that was having sex with you." His eyes were dark as he gazed at me. "And the answer is yes. I regretted fucking you last weekend. It was you that made me decided to propose to Gabby. Not because you're her sister. I didn't know that then."

"What did I do then?"

"It doesn't matter." His face softened for a moment as he gazed into my face. "All that matters now is that I am engaged to her and you're just going to have to deal with that."

"I hate you." I said, with my stomach rumbling in disappointment and rejection. What I really meant was that I hated both of us. I hated that I'd been so weak that I'd slept with him again.

"No you don't." He laughed as he turned around. "You just hate how I make you feel. You hate that you can't control yourself when you're around me. You hate that the feeling of me inside of you feels like you're finally complete. You hate that your body belongs to me."

"What?" My voice dropped. "Why would you say that?"

"Because that's exactly how I feel as well." He gave me one last glance and then exited the restroom, leaving me standing there in a daze.

7

"WHERE HAVE YOU BEEN?" ALICE asked me as I walked out of the restaurant.

"You don't want to know." I made a face. "Where were you?"

"You don't want to know either." Alice made a face and we just stared at each other for a few seconds.

"Oh Alice. I'm so dead."

"What did you do?"

"I was in the restr—"

"There you are." Gabby rushed out of the restaurant. "I've been looking for you." She gave me a disapproving look.

"I'm here. What do you want?" I asked her and looked at the side of her head. I was too embarrassed to look into her eyes. I didn't want her to see my shame.

"I wanted to say sorry." She bit down on her lower lip and I looked up at her in shock. Say what?

"Huh?" I looked at Alice who also looked like she was in disbelief.

"I wanted to apologize to both of you." She sighed. "I've been a bitch and been rude to both of you." She looked into my eyes and I was surprised to see a look of sincerity as she gazed at me. "I guess I've always been **jealous of your friendship and I lashed out this morning. I shouldn't have.**"

"What?" I said and swallowed hard. Why did she have to choose today to change into a loving and changed big sister? Why did she have to choose the moment right after I'd betrayed her? Why oh why?

"I've been rude and mean." She grabbed my hand. "I'm sorry. I shouldn't have said those things this morning or the other day."

"I, uh, what brought this about?"

"I had a talk with Chett." She said softly. "He knew about the baby before. And he knows it's not Xanders." She bit down on her lower lip. "I'm in a really lucky position to have found a man like Xander."

"Oh?" I smiled weakly. Please do not say that you're in love with him now. Please, please, please.

"He didn't have to take on me and a baby that wasn't his." She nodded. "I know that, but I'm so grateful that he is——"

"I'm so excited for you." Alice interrupted her and I was never more grateful to her than I was in that moment. I wasn't sure I could stand there and listen to Gabby go on and on about Xander any more without throwing up. "You must be so excited to plan the wedding."

"Yeah, I am." Gabby nodded and sighed.

"Must feel nice to know that a handsome man like Xander wants to date someone like you?"

"What the fuck does that mean?" Gabby snapped and I froze at her tone. Alice and I looked at each other for a few seconds and I knew we were both thinking the same thing. Had Gabby really had a change of heart or had someone put her up to this?

"There you are." Xander and Henry walked out of the restaurant and I avoided his glance as he looked my way. "Did you speak to your sister, Gabby?" Xander asked and I knew that he had put her up to her apology.

"Yes." Gabby snapped and Alice and I smiled at each other.

"Good." Xander walked over to me and tapped me on the shoulder. "You had us all worried."

"What? Why?"

"You just disappeared." His eyes burned into mine.

"Disappeared."

"Yes." He gave me a small smile. "I was worried you had disappeared or fell into a hole or something."

"Yeah, I'm sure you were."

"She's fine." Alice stepped forward with a frown and glared at Xander. "There's no need to worry."

"Okay." He looked at Alice and back at me and I knew he was wondering why she was being so cold. To be honest, I was surprised as well. I'd never seen Alice look at someone like that before.

"Let's go and wait by the car." Alice grabbed my arm and we walked away from Xander. I could feel him watching us as we walked away.

"What was all that about?" I asked her with a side look.

"I don't like him." She made a face. "He shouldn't be playing you and your sister. He's a dick. I don't like him trying to rile you up."

"Yeah, I don't know what game he's playing at." I nodded.

"Just stay away from him." She looked at me as we reached the car. "He thinks he can have his cake and eat it too, I think not. I mean he was cool for a wedding hookup, but you deserve more than the crap he's dishing out right now."

"Yeah, I can't believe I just had sex with him again."

"You what?" Alice's jaw dropped.

"Yup." I nodded with a red face.

"Where?" She shook her head and looked around.

"In the restroom." I whispered.

"I'm not even going to ask." She giggled. "Oh Liv."

"What?" I groaned and buried my face in my hands. "I suck, don't I?"

"I don't know. Did you?" She giggled again and wiggled her eyebrows.

"No, I did not suck him off in the bathroom." I laughed. "And no he didn't get a chance to use his miracle tongue either."

"Just his miracle dick?"

"Alice." I bit my lower lip and groaned again. "Shit, it was so hot. So hot and so bad."

"That's because bad is always hot." She looked around before speaking again. "Was it as good as last time?"

"It was even better." I wailed. "Why, why, why? Why did this have to happen to me?"

"It's not your fault."

"I always meet the shitty guys."

"Yeah, but at least this guy is shitty and good in bed."

"Or in the public restroom." I laughed.

"I don't understand why we can't meet good guys." She sighed. "What's wrong with us? We're good women. We're pretty. Honest. Fun loving. Shit, if I was a lesbian I'd date both of us."

"You'd date yourself?"

"Hell ya." She grinned. "I'm pretty awesome."

"That is true."

"I just wish someone other than the two of us knew that." She sighed and leaned back against the car. "What's wrong with us Liv? Why do we always find ourselves in these messes?"

"What happened with you?" I asked softly. "I told you about me and Xander, but what happened with you just now?"

"I was flirting with the waiter to try and make Aiden jealous and well the waiter tried to kiss me and Aiden saw and gave me a look that made me feel like a tramp."

"Oh Alice." I sighed, glad that she hadn't been flirting with Scott. Imagine if she had caused some sort of fist fight between them. That would have made my family a sideshow circus. Not that we weren't already half way there.

"I know. I'm a mess."

"We're both messes." I laughed.

"What are we going to do?"

"We need to forget about all of them. Let's go out tonight and meet some new guys and have some fun."

"You want to?" Alice didn't look enthused about the idea.

"Yes! We don't need them! We're two hot girls. We need two hot men that will appreciate us."

"I don't know." She made a face. "When we went out in college, we never had much luck."

"That's because we were nerds." I giggled. "And we didn't know how to play the game. We both played it safe and settled for losers. You dated Luke and now he's married to Joanna, our ex-roommate. And I dated Justin and Evan and well, we both know how great they were."

"Evan was addicted to his PlayStation." Alice giggled.

"And my panties." I shuddered. "And not in the sexy way either."

"There's a sexy way?" Alice looked at me curiously.

"Yeah, the steal and sniff sexy way." I made a face. "Okay, that sounds perverted when I say it out loud, but that's kinda sexy because you know you turn your man on. I mean, if you're going to steal my panties, do it because you're sniffing them or whacking off into them. Don't do it because you want to wear them."

"I wish I would have seen his face when you caught him in your black thong and red lipstick."

"He ruined the lipstick as well. It was the Chanel tube as well. I spent $42 on that lipstick and he didn't even replace it."

"I dare say he stretched out the thong as well." Alice giggled.

"He did." I giggled as well. "I gave it to him as a parting gift when we broke up."

"Oh Evan, I thought he was a weirdo from the beginning." Alice said. "I mean what guy brings over his PlayStation and games every time he's staying at his girlfriends' house?"

"A loser guy, that's who!" I groaned. "Not that Justin was any better."

"True." Alice agreed with me. "What was up with his hair?"

"His hair was the least of his problems." I giggled as I remembered my other ex. "Remember when we caught him using your concealer to cover up his acne."

"I know." She groaned. "I caught him using my toothbrush once as well. He was so gross."

"Ugh, I always seem to pick the worst guys."

"Don't look now, but the posse is headed towards us." Alice said softly.

"Ugh, I don't even want to see Xander or Gabby's face. Please say we can go out tonight."

"Fine." She grinned. "Let's see how much more trouble we can get ourselves into.

"LET'S PLAY SCRABBLE TONIGHT." SCOTT popped his head into my room later that afternoon.

"Sorry, we're going out." I looked up at him from my vanity.

"Going out where?" He frowned. "That's no fair."

"Alice and I are going out to meet some men as we don't want to end up as old maids."

"It's too late for that." He grinned and I poked him in the abdomen. "Ouch, that hurt."

"Good." I made a face at him. "Now scram, Alice and I are trying out my different eye shadows."

"You both look like clowns." Scott said with a straight face as he looked at me and then at Alice. "Clowns that should stay home and play scrabble tonight."

"Nope." I shook my head and stood up. "Not going to happen."

"Hey guys, we're playing scrabble tonight." Aiden walked into the bedroom and I groaned loudly.

"Alice and I are going out tonight. We will not be partaking in the family scrabble tournament."

"What do you mean, you and Alice are going out?" Aiden looked at Alice and frowned. "This is meant to be a family weekend."

"I've had enough family for the day." I walked to my closet and opened the doors. "Tonight I need to forget about family."

"Liv," He started and I turned around to look at him with fire in my eyes. If he dared to try and tell me I couldn't go, I was going to hit him. "Fine, have fun." He said simply and my jaw dropped open in shock.

"What, that's it?"

"You're an adult. You can do what you want."

"Oh my God, it's the end of the world." I looked at Alice with a smile. "Aiden is not trying to tell me what I can and can't do."

"I guess miracles do happen." She said softly and I watched as Aiden laughed.

"I guess so." I pulled out a black slinky dress that I'd worn in college and showed it to her. "Should I wear this tonight?"

"That's hot." Alice nodded. "Definitely wear that dress."

"Okay, this is my cue to leave." Scott hurried out of the bedroom and Aiden, Alice and I all looked at each other.

"So where are you two going?" Aiden asked softly and I gave him a weird look. Why was he still in the room? Why did he care where we were going?

Men are so difficult to understand. I had no clue what Aiden was up to and he's my brother.

"Not sure yet. That's all Liv's decision."

"Oh okay, you trust her?" Aiden joked and my jaw opened even wider. Was that my brother teasing Alice?

"Yeah, I trust her." Alice smiled and blushed.

"What sort of place are you guys looking for?" Aiden asked again.

"We're looking for a place with hot men that will devour us." I said with a laugh.

"Hmmm." Aiden looked at me with a disapproving look. "I know a nice wine bar if you guys are interested in that?"

"No, we're going to dirty dance and grind. Maybe we'll drink some wine as well, but we want loud music and fast men." I danced around and started moving my body back and forth. "I want a man that knows how to move to some hip hop, baby."

"Okay." Aiden frowned. "That sounds like fun."

"It will be." I smiled at him sweetly.

"Maybe I'll come as well."

"What?" My smile left my face. "No, you can't come."

"Come where?" Xander walked into my room.

"What is going on in here?" I turned away from him. "Why does everyone think they can just walk into my room?"

"Maybe because you have an open door policy?" Xander answered with a smirk and I just rolled my eyes. What had I ever seen in this insufferable man?

"It's not open to you."

"What do you want Xander?" Alice glared at him and a surge of happiness washed through me. This was why Alice was my best friend. This was why I trusted her with my life. She always had my back.

"Girls." Aiden frowned as he looked at us. "Why are you being so hostile to Xander?"

"I don't think we're being hostile." I said sweetly and turned to Xander. "Do you think we're being hostile?"

"No," He stared into my eyes. "I don't."

"So how can I help you, Xander? Did you get lost? Do you need me to help you find Gabby's room?" I turned back to my closet and picked up a red dress. "Or this one?" I showed it to Alice and she nodded enthusiastically.

"Maybe try them both on and let me see what they look like."

"You're wearing a dress to play scrabble tonight?" Xander looked confused. "A bright red dress with a long slit. What kind of scrabble game is this?" He grinned and looked at Aiden.

"They're going out dancing." Aiden shook his head as if to say typical girls.

"Dancing?" Xander looked at me. "I didn't know we were going dancing tonight."

"We're not going anywhere. Alice and I are going."

"Just you and Alice?" Xander looked at Aiden. "Is that safe?"

"What do you mean is that safe? We're women, not little girls." I growled at him.

"I wanted to go with them as well, but they said no." Aiden said softly and I saw him looking at Alice.

"Well I suppose you guys can come." Alice said weakly and I gave her a death glare.

"Sorry guys, you're not coming. It's a girls night out." I put my hands on my hips. "Alice and I need to meet some hot guys."

"What?" Xander frowned again. And this time his green eyes looked at me furiously. "Is that a good idea?"

"Yes, why wouldn't it be?" I asked him with a sass I never knew I possessed before.

"I just don't think it's a good idea." His lips thinned.

"And you thought I was overprotective." Aiden laughed then. "Looks like you have another big brother who is going to boss you around, Liv."

"Oh yay, another annoying big brother." I groaned and then walked over and gave Xander a quick hug and a kiss on the cheek. "Welcome to the family, big bro."

"Thanks." Xander looked at me with a weird expression on his face. I could see that I'd knocked him off of his feet slightly. I didn't know what he was thinking, but I did know that he wasn't acting as cocky and confident as he had before.

"Now scram, I want to try on my dresses."

"Yeah, I want to try on my dresses as well." Alice said and looked at Aiden. "Please vacate the room."

"We're out of here." Aiden grinned at her and I felt like puking. It looked like it was really going to happen. Alice was going to end up dating Aiden and they were going to get married and I was going to have to be around him forever.

"Or we can help you both decide." Xander said, not moving.

"Huh?" I looked at him with narrowed eyes, my heart racing "What do you mean?"

"We can tell you which dresses look best."

"This isn't Pretty Woman." I scoffed. "We don't need your help."

"Fine." He shrugged. "No hair off my back."

"See ya then."

"Let's go, Xander." Aiden walked out of the bedroom and Xander followed behind him.

"He's a hard guy to figure out isn't he?" Alice sighed.

"Yes, he is. I just don't get him at all."

"Is it sad that all I can think about is what it would be like to kiss him?" Alice said wistfully and I froze.

"You want to kiss Xander?"

"What? No. I'm talking about Aiden."

"Oh, sorry. I was talking about Xander."

"Ugh, men!" She shook her head and I made a face.

"I'm going to go to the study to read for a bit." I said. I needed to get out of the room and clear my thoughts as I felt confused and muddled about my feelings.

"Okay. Sounds good. We can try on the dresses in a couple of hours?"

"Yes! Let's do that."

"Okay, I'm going to have a nap now then." She yawned. "I'm still a bit exhausted."

JEALOUSY IS ONE OF THOSE emotions that I love to hate. I hate feeling jealous because it makes me feel inadequate, but I love it when a guy is jealous over me. It's a weird thing, jealousy. There is such a fine line to walk without seeming crazy. I have to admit I was jealous over the relationship my sister had with Xander, even though they had never had sex. *Supposedly*. I don't know any platonic friends that get engaged. It makes me burn inside. I mean, it's not like he's mine, but I kinda had a thing for him. I wanted him to want me to be his fake fiancé. Why couldn't he have asked me to marry him? Though that could be more complicated for us. Seeing as we had sex and all. And seeing as I had real emotions for him. I just didn't know why they were getting married; especially because she was pregnant with another mans' baby.

"What you reading?" His deep voice interrupted my thoughts as he walked into the study and sat next to me on the couch.

"Hemingway." I said the first name that came into my head. "Ernest Hemingway. For Whom The Bell Tolls." I continued, not sure where the lies were coming from as I hid the cover of my Fifty Shades of Grey book. I didn't need him thinking I was a nymphomaniac. I didn't know what ideas he might get into his mind if he knew I was reading a book about BDSM. I did not need him tying me up on my father's desk and fucking me with my ass in the air as he spanked me for being a naughty girl. I didn't need him doing that at all, though I had to admit that the thought of that happening was quite exciting. Maybe we could role play: he could be Christian Grey and I could be Ana. Only I didn't want to do any of the hardcore stuff like being whipped. I wasn't sure I'd enjoy being whipped. Though I wouldn't mind being spanked with his hot sexy firm hands.

"Oh really?" His eyes looked impressed as he gazed at me and I wondered if he looked at my sister like that as well.

"Oh really what?" I said distracted by his gaze.

"Oh really, you're reading Hemingway." He grinned. "Which book again?"

"The Old Man and The Sea." I said quickly and then swore under my breath. "I mean For Whom The Bell Tolls." I blushed and looked down. That was why I wasn't going to let him tie me up and have sex with me in the study. When I was around him, my brain went to shit. Who knew what would happen if we got really down and dirty?

"Oh what's it about?"

"What's what about?" I asked him blankly as I imagined him spanking me lightly and then a little harder. I wondered how into the spanking he would get. Would my ass sting from his touch or would it merely tingle.

"The book." His eyes teased me as he sat there.

"Oh it's about a man waiting by a church." I said weakly. "He goes to the church every day and waits for the bell to ring."

"He goes to wait for the bell to ring?" Xander's lips twitched.

"Yeah." I nodded. "It's a magical book and it only rings for wizards. Like Harry Potter, you know?"

"Hmm, I see." He grinned and then grabbed the book from my hand. "Fifty Shades of Grey?" He said as he looked at the cover. "Is this a new one by Hemingway then? One I haven't heard of before?"

"Give it back." I snatched it back from him, my face a deep, dark red. "What are you doing in here anyway? Haven't you bothered me enough for the day?"

"I didn't know you'd be in here. I thought you were doing your fashion show with Alice."

"Ha ha, fashion show indeed. We're just trying on outfits and deciding what we both look best in."

"If you say so." He opened the book. "Now tell me what this book is about."

"It's just a romance book." I blushed and reached over for the book. "Give it back to me."

"I have a question." He hands me the book, his eyes sparkling.

"What?" I snapped, embarrassed that he'd called me out.

"What's a Christian Grey-flavored popsicle?" He asked with light eyes.

"What?" I frowned at him and then hit him on the shoulder with the book. "You're a pervert."

"I'm the pervert?" He grinned. "I'm not the one reading porn in the middle of the day."

"I'm not reading porn." I growled at him.

"I mean if you're feeling horny, I can help you out."

"Help me out?"

"With my miracle tongue." He grinned and then flicked his tongue back and forth at me. I have to admit that the sight of his long pink tongue moving sensually across his mouth did turn me on. A lot. I could feel it in my panties and in the heaviness in my breasts.

"Xander." I shook my head. "Have you no shame?"

"No." He leaned forward and I felt his tongue in my ear. "I have no shame at all." He whispered and then sucked on my earlobe. "Let me make you come, Liv. Let me take your panties off with my teeth and let me take you to the top of the cliff and back down with my tongue. He wants to be inside of you as much as you want him inside of you."

"Actually." I jumped up off of the couch and dropped the book into his lap. "I don't care about your tongue at all. I don't need your tongue inside of me. And I certainly don't need to be taken up and down a cliff, thank you very much."

"Are you sure about that?" His fingers ran across my trembling lips. "Climbing cliffs is very enjoyable."

"Yeah well, I've been down that road and have no need to go back." I pushed his hand away and quickly walked out of the study, my heart racing at his touch. Why oh why did Xander affect me so badly. He was like a drug my body desperately craved that I knew was very bad for me. He was slowly, but surely making me an addict and I knew that my addiction was leading me nowhere good. I knew I had to wean myself off of him before it was too late. I was not going to let Xander and his miracle tongue bring me down, any further than I already was.

8

"HOLD STILL, LIV." ALICE STOOD in front of me and styled my hair with her curling iron. "If you keep moving I'm going to burn you."

"Don't you dare burn me," I warned her. "This is boring."

"I'm nearly done." She sighed. "Just be patient."

"I've been sitting here for twenty minutes." I sighed. "What sort of hairstyle are you creating?"

"A seductive, sensual one." She grinned. "All the men in the club will be all over you."

"All but one, you hope." I laughed. "If I get them all, who are you going to have?"

"I'll find someone." She giggled and flicked her long brown hair with blonde streaks back.

"Oh boy." I laughed. "And you're sure my makeup doesn't look too slutty?"

"Is there such a thing as too slutty?" She asked as she stared at me face.

"Yes." I nodded. "I don't want anyone to think they can offer me twenty dollars and take me behind the trashcan for a blow job?"

"What about for a hundred?" She wiggled her eyebrows at me and we both laughed.

"Tonight's going to be fun."

"We deserve some fun." She stepped back and looked at me for a few seconds before grinning. "You look beautiful."

"You think?" I jumped up and ran over to the mirror and stared at my reflection. My long, brown hair hung in loose waves surrounding my face and down my back. My brown eyes sparkled with excitement and my smoky eyes made me look like a sexy vixen. "Do you think this lipstick is too red?" I asked as I pouted into the mirror.

"No way. Red is hot."

"I suppose so."

"And it matches your red dress perfectly. Slip it on now."

"Okay." I hurried to the bed and picked up my newly ironed dress and quickly took my clothes off and pulled it on. I had to suck in my breath to get it past my waist and down my hips. "This dress is a lot shorter than I remember it being." I looked down at my exposed thigh and gulped. "I'm not sure about this, Alice. I'm not a stick you know. Girls like me, with curves shouldn't wear skintight clothing."

"Says who?" She shook her head. "You look hot, sexy, beautiful, amazing, and perfect." She pointed her finger at me. "Fuck those skinny bitches. Every man wants a woman with curves."

"I don't know about that." I laughed.

"Well if he wants a stick, then he's not for us." She grinned and pulled on her short, black dress.

"True."

"Any guy looking for a stick will be disappointed with me." I giggled. "I'll never be a stick, my boobs are way too big."

"Men love big boobs."

"Well mine haven't helped me much yet."

"They will tonight." She gazed at my partially exposed boobs. "Vaboom vaboom."

"Thanks, Alice." I shook my head.

"I'm ready, I think." She pulled on her heels and then looked at me. "What about you?"

"Yeah, I guess I'm ready." I nodded and grabbed a handbag from the closet and then slid my feet into my black stilettos. "I hope I don't fall in these. My feet are already killing me." I moaned.

"You'll be fine. Just hold onto my arm."

"I need alcohol." I giggled as we made our way out of my bedroom.

"Me too." She agreed. "I want to get drunk tonight."

"I want to get slizzard." I said.

"What's slizzard?" She asked me in confusion and I looked and her and laughed.

"I have no idea." I shrugged. "I just heard that term recently and thought it sounded good."

"It does. It sounds cool. Here's to us getting slizzard."

"Slizzard baby." We linked arms and made our way to the front door.

"Liv." Aiden's voice boomed through the house as I opened the front door.

"Yes." I stopped and rolled my eyes.

"Come into the living room please."

"Why?"

"We want to see you before you go out."

"Ugh." I looked at Alice and we both made faces at each other. "He is so frigging annoying. He needs to get married and have kids already. Oops." I made a face as I looked at Alice.

"It's fine." She gave me a lopsided smile. "I'm sure he'll make a good father."

"Let's face the army and then leave." I said with an exasperated sigh and we walked towards the living room. "Good evening everyone." I said as we walked into the room. All eyes fell to Alice and I and I almost laughed at the different expressions on everyone's faces. Aiden looked stunned, Henry looked impressed, Gabby looked pissed, Chett looked bored, Scott looked excited and Xander, well Xander looked brooding. I could feel his eyes surveying my entire body and I had to tell myself to resist looking at him again.

"So where are you two off to then?" Aiden stood up and walked over to us.

"A bar."

"What bar?" He asked, this time his eyes looked slightly angry. I wondered if he would ever get over the need to have to know everything.

"I think we're going to Beach Lagoon." I said finally.

"Okay, down on Fifth Street?" He asked again.

"Yes Sir." I nodded and then saluted him.

"Funny."

"If mom and dad don't find the need to stay up and ask me, why do you care?"

Aiden stared at me for a few seconds and then turned to Alice. "You look very nice this evening."

"Thanks." She blushed as she answered him.

"Are you going to be warm enough in that dress?" He stared at her long expanse of naked leg and bare shoulders and she nodded.

"I'm pretty sure the alcohol will keep me warm."

"Who's DD?" He looked back at me with a frown.

"We're going to take uber there and back." I tried not to roll my eyes. "We're not irresponsible you know. We did make it to twenty two with some brains."

"I just wanted to make sure you didn't want a ride there and back."

"I can drive you if you want." Xander spoke up then and stood up.

"Oh you don't need to do that." Gabby sounded annoyed as she glared at me. So much for her I'm sorry shtick. I knew she wouldn't be able to fake a sweet personality for long.

"I don't want you girls to get taken advantage of." Xander stood next to Aiden and stared into my eyes. This time I couldn't avoid his eyes. His irises looked furious as he gazed at me. I wasn't sure what his problem was, but I couldn't stop myself from shivering as I stood next to him. I could feel the electricity flowing between us and I took a step back.

"I think we'll be fine." I licked my lips nervously.

"Yeah, we'll be fine." Alice repeated and I could see her and Aiden giving each other small looks back and forth.

"Trust me Xander, Alice and Liv won't have any problems." Gabby jumped up and walked over to us. "They both pro's at looking like sluts and not getting bothered."

"Gabby." Aiden admonished her.

"What?" She shrugged. "It's true." She looked at Alice and I and then at Xander and Aiden. "I mean come on. You don't go out in heels as high as those, with dresses as short as that and not expect that some creep is going to try and slip his hand between your legs or down your top."

"Gabby, shut up." Scott shouted. "What is your problem?"

"Maybe it's pregnancy brain?" Henry said and gave me a small smile.

"Yeah, but she hasn't been pregnant all her life." I muttered. "That doesn't excuse her lifelong bitchiness."

"Liv." Aiden gave me a look and I turned to Alice.

"Ready?"

"Yes." She nodded eagerly. "Let's go."

"Wait a second." Aiden caught her wrist. "Can I speak to you for a second please?"

"Uh okay." She looked over at me and made a face and followed him to the corner of the room.

"I need to speak to Liv as well." Xander said to Gabby and he grabbed my upper arm roughly and pulled me outside of the room with him.

"What do you think you're doing?"

"Where do you think you're going in that outfit?"

"To a club."

"It's not appropriate." He shook his head as he glared at me.

"Appropriate for what?"

"It sends the wrong signals." He gazed down at my heaving breasts.

"What signals are you talking about?"

"The 'I'm looking to get fucked' signal." He muttered as he took a step towards me and pushed me back against the wall.

"Who says I don't want to give off that signal?" I said with a gasp as he grabbed my hands and pressed them back against the wall, next to my head.

"Is that what you want?" He leaned in and kissed my neck softly.

"Xander." I gulped as he kissed down my neck to my collarbone and the top of my breasts. "Stop it, anyone could come out of the room and see us."

"What do you care?"

"Xander, don't." I moaned as his hand ran down the side of my body and stopped on my thighs.

"Don't what?" He pushed his hardness into my stomach and moved back and forth. "Don't show you what you're doing to me in that sexy almost nonexistent outfit."

"Was there anything else you needed to say to me?" I turned my head away from him as he leaned forward to kiss my lips.

"Why are you trying to bewitch me?"

"What are you talking about?"

"Nothing." He sighed and stepped back. "Why did you have to be Gabby's sister?"

"Why did you have to be her fiancé?"

"You don't understand." He frowned. "This isn't just for me. This is to help protect someone that I love."

"I don't understand what you're talking about."

"It doesn't matter." He shrugged. "It is what it is."

"Can I ask you something?"

"Sure." He nodded and I saw his eyes fall to my breasts.

"Are you marrying her so you can gain your inheritance?" I said softly. "Does that have anything to do with it?"

"Why do you care?" He asked me angrily and that made me even madder. I couldn't believe he had the gall to ask me why I cared when he was still trying to get into my pants. Didn't he realize how fucked up this situation was? What sort of girl did he think I was, if he thought this was okay? What part of this situation was okay in any way?

"I don't care, Xander." I huffed out. "Just leave me the fuck alone, okay. You're the one that keeps coming after me. I'm not the one coming after you. I'm done with your bullshit okay? It's not cool for you to keep trying to get into my pants and then question me when I try to figure out what's going on with you and Gabby."

"You didn't care who I was or what I was doing last weekend."

"That was last weekend." I folded my arms. "This is this weekend. And this weekend, I'm not interested in you and your crap."

"Me and my crap?" His lips twitched as if he wanted to laugh and that infuriated me even more. How dare he think that this was a funny situation! How dare he look so superior and smug while I was fuming on the inside. My fingers itched to slap him. He wouldn't be looking so cocky if he had my palm print across his cheek.

"Leave me alone, Xander. I am done with you." I poked him in the chest. "I'm going out in my slutty dress and I'm going to do what I want. Maybe I'll meet an even better man and then I can hook up with him and forget I ever met you."

"I wouldn't recommend that." His lips thinned and he grabbed my wrists. "That's not the answer to any of this."

"Well that's not your problem, is it?" I smiled at him widely. "I can do what I want."

"Liv." He said my name slowly and his gaze was intense as he stared at me.

"Yes, Xander?" I said lightly. I'm not going to lie. I was getting off on our conversation. I was getting off on the fact that I could rile him up by talking about other men. I was loving the fact that he was acting jealous. The only problem was, he wasn't giving me what I really wanted. He wasn't breaking up with Gabby and telling me he had fucked up. He wasn't pulling me towards him and telling me he wanted me and only me. He wasn't telling me that Gabby and his family fortune meant nothing to him. All he was doing was showing me he was horny for me. And well, I already knew that. I wanted more than that from him. I wanted him to look at me with more than lust. I wanted to look into his eyes and see something akin to love. I know that was an unrealistic expectation. He barely knew me and I barely knew him, but that's what I wanted. That's what I hoped to see. I wanted to see a real emotion. A real, pure and heart stopping emotion that had nothing to do with lust.

"Have a good evening." He said finally and turned away. "Don't do anything I wouldn't do." He said and then walked back into the living room. I stood there feeling gutted and rejected. I could still feel his lips on my neck. I still felt branded by his touch and I hated myself for it.

"You ready?" Alice walked out of the living room, her eyes bright and I nodded.

"What did Aiden say?" I whispered to her as I pulled up the Uber app on my phone.

"Nothing good." She sighed. "He just asked me to make sure that you didn't get into too much trouble."

"What?" My voice rose. "I swear he's the most annoying man. I know you like him, but ugh, Aiden is so annoying."

"I think it's cute that he's so protective." Alice looked wistful.

"Trust me, Alice. You won't think it's that cute, if you're dating him." I shook my head. "He's bloody annoying."

"CHEERS." ALICE GIGGLED AS WE took another tequila shot and then rose our glasses of vodka coke up in the air. "Here's to the men we've loved, the men we've lost, the men we've screwed and the men we've booed, here's to the men to come and the men to make us come."

"Alice." I laughed out loud. "You're so bad."

"I'm not done." She winked at me and her voice rose above the sound of the music. "Here's to the men to come and the men to make us come. Here's to the men that last all night, and the men who make our days bright, here's to the man we'll ultimately marry, but his cock be bigger than a ferry."

"Bigger than a ferry?" I said and then chugged my drink down along with her. "How can a cock be bigger than a ferry?"

"I don't know what else rhymes with marry?"

"What about, hmm, let me think?" I paused and danced along to the music in the club, my mind spinning as the alcohol settled in my bloodstream. "What about dairy?"

"Dairy?" Alice giggled. "How can a man's cock be bigger than a dairy?"

"You know what I mean, may his cock be bigger than a dairy cows." I laughed hard then. I felt someone behind me start to dance against me and I twisted my head to see if he was cute. It was an older man, with a buzz cut and bad acne scars and I was about to push him away, when I decided to just let him dance with me. What harm was there in that.

"Bigger than a dairy cows, ha ha." Alice started laughing really hard. "That's funny."

"What's your friend laughing at?" The man behind me whispered in my ear and I felt his hand creeping around my waist.

"You." I elbowed him and moved away from him. "Let's go dance on the dance floor." I said to Alice and grabbed her hand.

"I want another drink." She hiccupped and I shook my head.

"Not yet, we don't want a hangover tomorrow. Let's dance and then get one."

"Fine." She nodded and we made our way to the dance floor. I looked back towards the bar and I saw the older man with the buzz cut walking towards the back of the bar with someone and he didn't look happy. My heart thudded as I wondered what was going on, but tried to forget it as the music changed to one of my favorite Jay-Z songs.

"I think Jay-Z and Justin Timberlake should collaborate on every song." Alice shouted as we moved our hips in beat to the music. Or as in beat as we could.

"I thought you wanted Jay-Z and Taylor Swift to make a song."

"Well they can all make a song. That would be cool."

"Yeah, it would be." I nodded in agreement and then closed my eyes and danced along to the music. I loved being in night clubs, they always made me feel so alive. Being on a crowded dance floor, dancing along with the crowd to different songs was such a collective high. I raised my hands up in the air and sang along to the song as I moved. Alice grabbed my hands then and we jumped around together singing loudly.

"Oh my God, I love this song." Alice screamed as an old Backstreet Boys song started playing.

"Me too." I screamed as well and we giggled, both drunk enough to be really enjoying ourselves. I started gyrating my hips and dropping to the floor and I could feel a couple of different guys staring at me. That encouraged me to start moving my body even more, copying moves that I could remember from Britney Spears music videos. I was even starting to forget Xander and his arrogance. I grinned when a hot blond guy came up to me.

"Hey." He said as he started dancing next to me.

"Hey," I said back.

"What?" He shouted and moved closer to me.

"I said hey." I shouted back as I gazed into his deep blue eyes.

"Oh." He laughed. "Want to dance?"

"Sure." I nodded and he grinned and moved behind me. Alice grinned at me and I winked at her as I felt his hands on my waist lightly moving behind me. I continued dancing to the music and watched as a gorgeous guy, with a bodybuilder's body, grabbed Alice and pulled her to him. I giggled as she started dancing with him and closed my eyes again, losing myself to the music. However, it only took a few minutes for me to start feeling uncomfortable. I opened my eyes and looked around the crowded club carefully. The hairs on the back of my head were standing on end and I felt like someone was staring at me. I ignored the feeling and continued dancing, but I wasn't as into it as I had been earlier.

"Do you want to get out of here?" The man behind me shouted into my ear and I felt his hands moving up my stomach towards my breasts. I grabbed his hands once they reached my ribcage and shook my head.

"Don't be a tease." He shouted and I felt him gyrating behind me.

"I'm not." I shouted back at him, annoyed.

"Let's get out of here." His right hand fell to my hip and I was about to push his hand away again, when I felt him suddenly pulled away from him.

"What?" I turned around with a frown and saw Xander standing there, holding the guy back in a tight grip. "Xander! What are you doing here?" I muttered, angry and excited at the same time.

"Is this guy bothering you?" He squeezed the man's arm tightly and I shook my head quickly. "Get out of here." He pushed the guy away. "And don't bother this girl again, you hear me?"

"I wasn't bothering her." The guy looked angry. "She wanted it."

"Get out of here." Xander pushed him again and I was scared that a fight was about to break out.

"What are you doing here?" I shouted.

"What?" Xander moved closer to me. "I can't hear you."

"What are you doing here?" I shouted again, this time into his ear as he stood next to me.

"Aiden and I wanted to make sure that you and Alice were okay."

"What?" I frowned, even more pissed now. "We're not kids."

"Well you both act like kids." Xander's body was touching mine now and I shivered. "We wanted to make sure those two dresses didn't get you both into trouble and it looks like we arrived just in time."

"Whatever." I said and looked around. "Where's Aiden?"

"Gone to make sure Alice is okay with Hulk Hogan's cousin." He winked at me and I couldn't stop myself from laughing.

"You're stupid."

"Is that any way to thank your savior?"

"My what?" I scoffed as I licked my suddenly dry lips.

"Your savior." He grinned and moved forward so that his lips were resting gently against mine. "Do I get a kiss as a thank you?"

"No, you do not." I swallowed hard, but didn't move back. I felt the tip of his tongue licking my lips and my whole body trembled at his touch.

"Please." He said, his eyes daring me to kiss him back as he pushed the tip of his tongue into my open mouth slightly.

"No." I shook my head and my lips closed on his tongue for a few seconds and sucked.

"There you guys are." Aiden and Alice approached us and I jumped back from Xander quickly. "It's time for us to go."

"What?" Both Alice and I looked at him in shock.

"It's time to go." Aiden looked mad, madder than I'd ever seen him before. I looked at Alice's face and she looked pissed off. I stared at them for a second and I wondered if their relationship was over before it even started. That would serve Aiden right. He was acting like a real idiot. I was used to his imperialist nature, but I knew Alice was getting her first real glimpse of it and was likely not appreciating it.

"Aiden, we're not leaving." I shouted at him, letting him bear the brunt of my anger. "You two shouldn't have come here."

"We wanted to make sure you were both okay." He looked over at Alice and frowned as she smiled at some guy that was dancing next to her. "Two single girls have to be careful these days."

"We know how to take care of ourselves." I sighed and then looked at Xander. "Where's Gabby?"

"She's with Henry." His eyes bore into mine. "Do you wish she was here instead?"

"No do you?"

"No." He said simply and my heart thudded away dangerously as I gazed into his eyes. What was it about this man that he could pierce my heart and soul with a glance and leave me aching with want and need at just one touch.

"Please leave." I said softly. "This night is for Alice and me. I don't want this headache, Xander." I rubbed my forehead as the beginning of a headache was about to set in. "I can't have you showing up like this. It isn't fair to me."

"Just one dance." He said, his eyes never leaving mine.

"What?"

"One dance and I'll leave and take Aiden with me."

"Why do you want a dance?"

"Who wouldn't want a dance from a sexy siren like you?" He winked at me.

"I'm not a siren." I shook my head with a blush.

"When you dance, I couldn't stop myself from looking at you. I think that makes you a siren." He pulled me towards him. "Dance with me, Liv."

"What about Aiden and Alice?" I nodded towards them next to us and he shrugged.

"What about them?"

"Fine, one dance." I sighed. "Don't try any funny stuff."

"What funny stuff would I try?" He looked at me innocently and I laughed.

"Don't try and slip your hands up under my skirt." I whispered in his ear and he laughed and pulled me closer to him.

"I can't make any promises." His arms went around my waist and we started dancing together. It felt nice and warm and oh so dangerous as his hands moved up and down my back and ass, until they settled on my lower back. We danced in silence, our bodies moving together in harmony as if we'd danced a million different times to a million different songs. His body against mine felt like home and I allowed myself to relax into him, I put my arms around his neck and rested my head on his shoulder. We moved slowly as if at a ball; our dance was totally out of place in the packed club, but neither of us cared. We were surrounded by people, but in that moment there was only us. I was surprised that he didn't try to touch me sexually again. His hands remained where they were and his lips never ventured towards mine. I could feel his heart beating in his chest, steady and solid, reminding me that he was only a man; just like me. I pulled back slightly and looked into his face to see if I could figure out what he was thinking. He stared back at me with intense eyes, no smile on his face. We just studied each other as we moved, as if we were trying to remember every single detail of each other's face. I felt as if he were my husband going off to war and this was the last dance we were promised before he shipped out. We stared at each other, just taking each other in. It felt like it was the first time we were actually seeing each other. It was the first time we were in each other's presence without fucking or arguing. This moment was for us. For the people we could have been in different circumstances. In different circumstances, this moment could have felt magical, but instead it was tarred. It was tarred by the fact that we weren't just two strangers getting to know each other. We were already tied together, in ways that we'd never be able to erase or forget. We were each other's dirty little secret and as I continued to stare at him, I felt a wave of crimson shame ripple through me. What was I doing dancing with this man I could never have? How many times was I going to put myself through this?

"The dance is over." I stepped back and gave him a short smile. "You should leave now."

"What if I don't want it to be over?" He said as he gave me the most drop-dead smile I'd ever seen on his face.

"Then I'd say I'm sorry." I shrugged and hurried over to Alice before he could stop me. I pushed my way through the crowds and grabbed her arm. "Let's get a drink."

"I was wondering where you disappeared to." She said and sighed. I saw that Aiden was standing there with a disapproving look on his face and I knew that their conversation hadn't gone well.

"What happened with Aiden?" I said as we made it to the bar, where it was quieter.

"He told me that he was disappointed in me. And that I hadn't shown common sense by dancing with a man that looked like he could bench-press three hundred pounds." She made a face.

"What?"

"He said there was no way I'd have been able to beat the guy off if he tried something with me and I tried to say no."

"Are you joking?" I groaned and rolled my eyes. "I swear Aiden is an idiot."

"I just don't know why he has to be so rude to me." Alice made a face. "It's like he thinks I'm ten."

"It's not just you, Alice. Trust me." I shook my head. "What do you want to drink? They're on me."

"Let's get another round of Vodka and cokes and you can choose the shots."

"Let's get some blowjobs." I laughed and signaled to the bartender. "My friend and I want two vodka's and cokes and two blowjob shots please."

"Coming right up." He grinned. "I wouldn't mind a blowjob as well."

"I'm sure you wouldn't." I flirted with him and he stopped and leaned forward.

"How's about I give you the shots for free."

"That sounds good to me." I grinned and licked my lips.

"All you have to do is stand on the bar and dance a little as you down it."

"I think I can do that." I nodded in agreement. "And so can my friend."

"Okay great." He laughed. "Come round to the side and I'll lift you both up."

"Okay." I nodded. "Come on Alice, we can get free drinks if we dance on top of the bar."

"Are you sure?" She asked me skeptically and I nodded.

"I'm sure." I grabbed her hand. "Let's go and show Xander and Aiden what they're missing."

We walked around to the side of the bar quickly and the hot bartender helped us up the bar. I looked out at the crowds of people and for a second I thought about getting back down. I wasn't so sure this was a good idea, but then Alice grabbed my hands and started dancing and so I went along with her.

"Here are your shots girls." He handed us the glasses. "No I want to see you drinking them as if they were really blowjobs."

"Okay then." We both laughed and grabbed the glasses. I closed my eyes and sucked on the glass and downed the drink quickly and then started swaying back and forth. I could hear some guys whistling and hollering at us and I moved my hips in a more pronounced manner so that I could give them a show. Before I knew what was happening, I felt a pair of strong arms around me and pulling me off of the bar top. I opened my eyes and saw Xander's fuming face in front of me.

"You are determined to make me blow up tonight, aren't you?" He growled as he set me down on the ground.

"I didn't ask you to do that."

"You looked like you were about to fall, Liv. What were you thinking?"

"What are you talking about? We just got two free shots for—"

"Dancing on top of the bar like some hooker." He cut me off and I saw him shaking his head. I looked behind me and noticed that Aiden had picked Alice off of the bar and seemed to be giving her a similar lecture.

"I'm not a hooker."

"Come with me." He lifted me up again and carried me through the crowds and outside of the club. "What are you doing Liv?"

"What do you mean what am I doing?"

"Why are you teasing me?" He ground out and leaned forward and kissed me roughly, his lips brushing against mine as his fingers ran through my waves and brought my head towards him.

"I'm not." I mumbled as I kissed him back. He tasted and smelled like lazy sex on a Sunday afternoon and I ran my hands through his hair and held onto him for dear life as he sucked all the air out of me.

"I want you so badly." He groaned as his hands fell to my ass and he cupped my butt cheeks. "I want to fuck you right here, right now, in front of everyone." He muttered as he sucked on my lower lip. "I want everyone to know that you're mine and that I'm the only one whose hands and cock will be getting under that short skirt tonight."

"Xander." I moaned, turned on by his guttural talk. My hands flew to the front of his pants and squeezed his already hard cock. I was about to unzip his pants, when something inside of me snapped and I took a step back and pushed him off of me. "No, stop." I gasped, wiping my lips in haste. "We can't do this."

"What?" He groaned, his eyes dark with desire.

"You can't keep playing hot and cold with me and I can't keep letting you. I don't know what's going on, but the fact of the matter is, I'm not your plaything. I'm not going to fuck you whenever you want me to. We hooked up last week and you regretted it so much that you proposed to my sister. Well, you know what Xander, you can go and fuck her. I'm done. I'm over this. You can just leave me alone, okay."

He looked shocked at my outburst. It was as if he finally understood that I was not cool with this whole sordid mess. It was as if his cock had just figured out that he couldn't just play around inside of me whenever he wanted. I was not going to be that girl. Not with him. He was about to say something when Aiden and Alice came out of the bar.

"There you are." Alice ran over to me and she looked furious.

"Everything okay?" I asked her quietly.

"Your brother is an asshole. End of story." She muttered and looked away.

"You guys need to leave now." I said loudly and glared at them both. "And when I say now, I mean that if you aren't gone from this street in thirty seconds or less I will scream so loud that the police will come running and arrest you both."

"Liv." Aiden started to say something and then stopped himself. "I'm sorry." He sighed and I just shook my head.

"It's too little too late." I took a deep breath and looked at Xander as I spoke. "You can't treat me like this anymore. I'm not going to take it. Just go home and leave us well alone." I turned around and grabbed Alice's arm and we walked back into the club, both of us knowing that our fun girls night out had already been ruined, but neither one of us wanting to admit it and go back home.

9

"WELCOME HOME." SCOTT OPENED THE front door as we arrived back at the house few hours later.

"Yeah thanks." I muttered and brushed past him, not in the mood for small talk.

"I'm going to hop in the shower, is that okay, Liv?" Alice asked me softly and I nodded.

"Yeah, I'm going to grab some water and go out to the rocking chair in the back yard. I'll be up in a bit."

"Okay." She nodded and I watched as Scott escorted her down the hallway. I sighed and then walked to the kitchen and looked through the fridge for some food. I grabbed a bottle of water and some string cheese and headed out to the backyard to rock my bad mood away. The sky was beautiful tonight, almost majestic in its' deep velvety blackness. I stared at the twinkling stars and sat back, enjoying the cool breeze that caressed my face.

"So you made it home safely, I see." Xander's deep voice interrupted my thoughts and I groaned out loud.

"You, again." I turned to look at him and almost groaned again. He was bare chested again and just wearing his boxers. "What do you want?"

"I wanted to apologize." He stood next to me. "I'm sorry about tonight."

"It's fine." I shrugged and looked away from him.

"Can we go and sit on the grass?" He asked softly. "I feel weird standing while you're sitting."

"I don't want to sit in the grass." I said petulantly.

"I'd like to have a talk with you, Liv and I'd rather we both be in a comfortable position."

"Fine." I jumped up. "I have to go in and get a blanket then. I can't sit on the grass in this dress."

"I brought one with me." He held it out in front of him. "Just in case you were out here."

"You were waiting up for me?"

"Yes." He nodded. "I felt like we needed to talk."

"Okay then."

"First, I want to apologize again for Aiden and I just showing up at the club. I know that was a bit of a crazy thing to do."

"Yeah, just a bit." I said sarcastically and watched as he lay the blanket down on the grass. Then we both sat down and got comfortable.

"It was a shock for me, you know, seeing you here." He said, abruptly changing the subject and I looked down at my legs. He thought he'd had a shock? What about me?

"Yeah well, I wasn't exactly over the moon to hear the news either."

"It's your fault that we're even in this position." He grabbed my hands. "Look at me, Liv."

"It's my fault?" My voice rose. "Is that supposed to be a joke?"

"You left me and when I woke up and you were gone, I felt empty, lonely and sad." He sighed as his fingers played with mine. "I've never felt that way before."

"What do you mean I left you? I've never left you."

"Last weekend." He made a face. "We made love all night in the hotel and when I woke up you were gone. No note, no number. I didn't even have your name. And I was upset. I wanted to spend the day with you. I wanted to get to know you."

"So you proposed to my sister because you were upset that I hit it and quit it?" I bit my lower lip to stop myself from laughing. I wasn't sure why I had said 'hit it and quit it', but it made me want to laugh.

"Did you just say 'hit it and quit it'?" Xander's eyes were laughing at me.

"Yes." I nodded and smiled. "I'm not sure why I said that."

"Maybe because it's true." He grinned. "That is what you did, well technically I hit it, but you were the one to quit it."

"Xander." I raised an eyebrow at him and sat back. "You can continue with what you were saying."

"Sorry, I got distracted." He licked his lips. "I was just remembering how deep and hard I was hitting it. I was hitting all the right spots, wasn't I?"

"Xander." I blushed, not wanting to tell him that he had hit spots I didn't even know existed before.

"Sorry." He chuckled. "It's hard to forget the best sex of your life."

"I was the best sex of your life."

"Yes." He had a devilish look on his face as his thumb traced up and down my wrist and palm. "And I think that's why it hit me so hard when you weren't there that morning, no pun intended. I," he paused and gazed into my eyes. "I was angry, Liv. I was angry that the first time I ever felt something the morning after a night of passion was the first time a woman had hurt me. I reacted rashly. It's hard to realize that meaningless one night stands don't always stay meaningless."

"What do you mean?"

"I mean that you were something different. What we had...that spark in the church and then in the hotel, well it was special. It made me feel different, weird, I don't even know how to explain it. I didn't like that feeling. I still don't like that feeling. I don't like being here with you and feeling like I'm flying. I don't like touching you and feeling like we're connected. I don't like looking at you and feeling like smiling. I'm not that kind of guy. I don't want these feelings. I've treated you poorly and for the first time in my life I'm ashamed of my actions. I'm ashamed of making you feel like a piece of meat. Because for the first time in my life, I realize that sex and women aren't just there for my pleasure. You've made me feel that and I don't know how to feel about that."

"What are you saying Xander?" I breathed out, my heart racing fast. I'm going to be honest now and admit that I thought he was going to tell me he loved me. I know, I'm crazy, he barely knew me and yet, I wanted him to tell me he loved me. And if I'm even more honest, I wanted him to propose to me. I wanted him to say that he needed me so badly that he wanted to spend the rest of his life with me. I even half thought that was coming.

"I met Gabby a few weeks before the wedding through Luke and well, the day after he called I met up with her, Luke and Henry."

"Luke that just got married?" I frowned. "Luke from the wedding?"

"Yes." He pursed his lips.

"Didn't he go on a honeymoon with Joanna?"

"The honeymoon was postponed."

"I didn't know Gabby knew Luke." I sat back and thought. "I mean she might have met him through Alice, but that was a while ago."

"That's beside the point, Liv." He sighed. "When I met up with Gabby, she was upset because she had just found out she was pregnant and the father didn't want to marry her and she was worried her family would be disappointed and she made a comment that she wished she had a fiancé to take home. And Henry reminded me that our granddad was holding control of the family business until I got married and well, the idea just came to me." He shrugged.

"You're engaged to Gabby because you felt bad for her and because you want control of your family company?"

"Basically." He nodded.

"And you won't end the engagement?"

"It would be stupid of me to let one night with you influence me into changing my plans, Liv. I'm not trying to be cruel, but Gabby and I have a business arrangement." He sighed. "One that will benefit both of us."

"What about me?" I said softly.

"I don't know what to say, Liv." He sighed. "I know I've been a jerk and I can't change that. I can only apologize, but I don't know what else to say."

"I guess there is nothing else to say." I sucked my breath in to hold back my tears of disappointment. What was the point of expressing my emotions and hurt? He would only think I was a psycho. The only one who would understand my feelings right now was Alice.

"I wanted to explain to you why Gabby and I were engaged. I didn't want you to think that I was some sort of bastard that would be chasing you and your sister. I don't feel anything for your sister except friendship. I don't have that sort of chemistry with her."

"You told me you wanted to have sex with her." I bit my lower lip, jealousy bursting to make its way out.

"I'm not sure I said that, but maybe I intimated something about making the marriage a complete one. I was only saying that to get a rise out of you."

"Well that's nice."

"I act stupid when I'm around you. I'm not myself."

"Who are you then? ET?"

"Quite possibly."

"That's what I thought." I nodded thoughtfully. "You're an alien from outer space."

"And you're from inner space."

"Something like that." I said with a smile and then he started tickling me. I fell back on the ground giggling and tried to push him off of me, but he continued tickling me under my arms, on my stomach and by my knees. "Xander, don't." I gasped as we rolled around on the blanket.

"I didn't know you were so ticklish." He grinned down at me, his eyes light as he gazed at my face.

"Well now you do."

"Yes, I do." He leaned down and gave me a quick kiss on the forehead and then lay down on the blanket next to me, so that our shoulders were touching. "It's not all about the money, you know."

"What?" I said softly as I stared up at the stars in the sky.

"I don't want the company so that I can make more money. I already have a lot of money."

"Okay." I said softly, hoping he would tell me why he wanted the company.

"I have a nonprofit in Africa. We help to purify water with chlorine machines and we dig wells." His voice was soft. "Right now, I'm only able to donate a million dollars a year through the company foundation, but if I took charge of the company, I could change the rules."

"You don't have shareholders?"

"We're a privately held company. We have a board, but it's not large and I can control them." His voice was passionate. "I want to be able to do this. My family has a lot of money. I want to be able to do some good with it. It's really important to me."

"I understand." And I did. It was a worthy cause. A very worthy cause. A cause that surprised me if I was honest. I felt guilty then. I realized that I wanted this handsome, sexy man to want me, to tell me that he loved me and I didn't know a thing about him. All I knew was that he was good with his tongue. I felt ashamed of myself. "So how long have you had the nonprofit?" I asked softly as we lay there staring up at the night sky.

"Since I was 17." He said and I could feel him looking at the side of my face. "I started it my last year of high school with some money my dad gave me. He said I could have a car or I could use the money for something good."

"And you turned down the car?"

"Yes." He said, his voice low. "I had just done a science project on cholera and water borne diseases and there were all these people dying in different African countries just from drinking water." He sighed. "I didn't think it was right."

"So you wanted to help?" I asked softly.

"Yes. I knew I had to help." He said passionately. "It was actually something I could help to fix. People dying of diseases in water is preventable. It's not like strife in the Middle East or wars. This is something tangible. This is something that can be fixed. And we know how to fix it. They know how to fix it." He rolled over and I looked at him then. His eyes were blazing. "When I got into the family business, I made sure my father invested in some different water purification systems. We were going to use them in…" His voice trailed off. "Sorry, I'm boring you."

"Not at all." I shook my head and touched the side of his face. "What happened?"

"My parents died in a car crash and my grandfather was no longer interested in helping; at least not without a set of rules."

"Like you getting married?"

"Yes." He sighed. "I resisted as long as I could and I tried to use my own money, but my trust is tied up in so many ways and there are restrictions on how I can use the money. I don't have full access to it until I'm 35."

"Oh wow."

"So I finally said, fuck it. If I need to be married to do what I need to do, then I need to get married. And then your sister needed a husband. So we came to an arrangement. It seemed smart. It seemed practical. And it was safe. There were no feelings to complicate matters or make anything messy."

"That's good." I looked down, trying not to show him how hurt and confused I was again.

"I really like you, Liv." His fingers grabbed my chin and he made me look at him. "But I don't even know you, you know. I don't understand why or how I could feel so close to you. Or how I could miss you that morning when you were gone. I'm a practical guy. A resourceful guy, but I don't do relationships or emotions. Or feelings. They're not to be trusted."

"I understand."

"Do you really?" His eyes searched mine.

"Yes." I leaned forward and gave him a light kiss. "I understand Xander."

"I can't just let this craziness between us change everything. I can't let my emotions influence this decision." He sounded as if he were trying to convince both of us.

"You need to do what you need to do." I pulled back slightly and blinked rapidly. I would not let myself cry in front of him.

"Will you spend the night with me?" He asked softly. "We don't have to have sex. I just want to hold you in my arms. I just want to feel your heart beat next to mine. I just want to wake up with you still there next to me."

"No, sorry." I shook my head and stood up slowly. "I'm sorry, Xander, but like I told you before, I'm not that kind of girl. Thank you for explaining why you're marrying Gabby, but that doesn't change anything. You're still her fiancé and she is still my sister and I'm still me. And I don't want to be the other woman in any sense of the word." I straightened my dress and looked down at him, trying to remember the look of hurt on his face. I was pretty sure I'd never see this side of him again. "You're a great guy Xander, but you're not my great guy. Good night." I said and nodded my head and walked back across the lawn and into the house. *Don't trip, don't trip* was all I could think as I hurried away from him, with my heart racing and tears streaming down my face.

10

"DO YOU THINK YOUR PARENTS are going to be pissed?" Alice asked me as we crept into our apartment early the next morning.

"Nah, they most probably won't even notice we aren't there." I lied.

"I'm glad you wanted to leave early as well." Alice sighed. "I've got a splitting headache."

"Me too." I sighed and rubbed my forehead. "I didn't want to deal with any of them this morning."

"Yeah, me either." She yawned. "It was a good idea to wake me up at four am so we could get out of there before anyone woke up, but I'm still tired."

"Are you saying you want to go back to bed?" I laughed and she nodded.

"I wasn't sure if you wanted to talk about what happened last night." She collapsed onto the couch.

"What do you mean?"

"I know something happened between you and Xander after we got back."

"How?"

"I just do." She wrapped her arms around her legs. "Now are you going to tell me or do I have to tickle it out of you?"

"Oh Alice." I groaned and sat down on the couch next to her. "It's such a mess."

"Oh no, what happened?" She looked at me with big eyes. "You didn't sleep with him again did you?"

"No," I shook my head. "We were in the backyard, Alice."

"Did you give him a blowjob?"

"No Alice." I rolled my eyes.

"Did he go down on you?"

"Nothing like that." I giggled. "He told me that he's raising money to help people in Africa so they can have clean drinking water." I sighed. "He's a really good man. Not as much of a jerk as I thought."

"Huh?" She sat up. "I'm sorry, but what? I'm confused. Why is that bad? Isn't that good? You found out that the guy you had a one night stand with is actually a really decent person."

"It should be good right?" I groaned. "But it's not good, that's why he's marrying Gabby. Supposedly by marrying her, he can gain access to more money at his family company and help more people or something."

"So why can't he just marry you then?" She shrugged. "Why does it have to be Gabby? I'm sure his grandfather didn't say, you have to marry the biggest bitch you can find."

"Oh Alice." I giggled. "I think he feels a sense of obligation to her."

"Hmm, okay." Alice frowned. "So his problem is that he's too nice a guy?"

"I guess." I leaned back and sighed. "Though I don't know anyone that would call Xander a nice guy. Sexy, yes. Hot as hell, yes. Good in bed, yes, but nice? I don't know." I giggled.

"Yeah, I wouldn't call him nice." Alice said. "More like jerk."

"So yeah, he said that he had a good time last weekend and that he missed me when I wasn't there in the morning and that he wasn't used to those feelings and that is why he proposed to Gabby."

"What?" Alice yawned and made a face. "Shut the front door! That is the stupidest thing I've ever heard in my life. He spent a night with a hot girl, having hot sex and because she left in the morning, he decided to propose to another girl? Is he on drugs?"

"When you put it like that, it does sound a bit stupid." I sighed. "But he explained it better, he said it was because he wasn't used to having that depth of feelings."

"What depth of feelings?" Alice looked at me like I was crazy. "Look, I'm not trying to be a bitch here and tell me if I'm getting something wrong, but all you guys did is fuck. He went down on you at the wedding and then you guys spent a night in his hotel room fucking like dogs right?"

"Yes." I nodded.

"Were there any late night deep conversations you didn't tell me about? Did you realize you were soulmates?"

"We spoke a little bit, but nothing major." I conceded, as my heart dropped. "So you think he was lying to me?"

"I don't know." She sighed. "It just seems weird. 'I had sex with you and you left and that made me sad' sounds fake. I think most guys would wake up feeling ecstatic if the girl they had just picked up was not there."

"Yeah, that's true." I sighed.

"And I mean, he's still with Gabby right? Did he say he would end things with her?"

"Nope." I said curtly. "He said he hoped I understood, but they had a business relationship."

"Bullshit." She said and rolled her eyes. "He's full of shit."

"Yeah, I guess so." I closed my eyes. "So that's why I wanted to leave this morning before everyone woke up."

"I understand." She said softly and reached over to hug me. "I'm sorry, Liv." She rubbed my back and before I knew it, I was crying. The tears poured out of me and I sobbed uncontrollably.

"I'm sorry," I hiccupped as she rubbed my back.

"Don't be." She said softly. "It's okay."

"I feel like such a fool. I don't know why I had my hopes up so high. I don't know why I thought this would be anything different." I spoke my thoughts out loud. "I just hoped that when he saw me again and touched me again, he would want me you know? I wanted to have that magical relationship that everyone else has, but me."

"I don't have it either." Alice said and I leaned back to see tears in her eyes.

"Oh Alice, what's wrong?" I stared at her face. "I'm sorry, I forgot to ask you what happened last night. Why were you so eager to leave early as well?"

"I don't want to talk about it." She bit her lower lip and looked down. "I made a mistake and I ruined everything."

"Oh Alice, what happened?" I said softly, my stomach sinking. What had she done?

"It doesn't matter." She shook her head. "I don't want to talk about it right now. I'll tell you later, okay?"

"Sure." I wiped a tear from her cheek. "I'm here for you anytime."

"I love you." She said with a sigh. "You're the best friend I could have wished for."

"You know I feel the same way about you." I smiled at her gratefully. "We may have lost the boyfriend lottery, but we own the friend lottery."

"Yeah, it's a pity we're not lesbians." She giggled through her tears. "Then we'd be able to live happily ever after."

"Are you hitting on me Alice?" I winked at her and she hit me on the shoulder.

"You never know." She giggled and wiped her eyes. "We'll find good guys one day."

"Yup, let's not look for them at the club though." I laughed as I remembered the previous evening. "I don't think we're going to meet any winners in the club."

"Yeah, ha ha." She stretched. "We can forget the guys at the club."

"Yay." I stretched and stood up. "Okay, I think it's time to go back to bed."

"Me too." She yawned again and wiped her eyes. "See you in a few hours."

"See you this afternoon." I giggled and walked to my bedroom. I dropped on my bed in a heap and before I knew it I was fast asleep, once again having dreams of my night with Mr. Miracle Tongue.

THE CONSTANT RINGING OF THE doorbell woke me up and I cursed into the pillow as I covered my ears. "Make it stop." I muttered to myself.

Ding Dong.

"I'm coming." I screamed as I jumped out of bed and hurried to the front door. It was during times like this that I envied Alice her ability to sleep through anything. "Yes?" I opened the door with an attitude and my heart dropped as I stared at Xander on the other side of the door, a huge grimace on his face.

"Hello Liv."

"Xander." I nodded and glared at him. "What are you doing here? You woke me up, you know?"

"It's Sunday afternoon, Liv." He pushed past me and into the apartment. "Why are you in bed still?"

"I'm tired." I muttered. "And come in, why don't you?"

"Why did you leave so early this morning?" He glared at me as we stood in the hallway.

"What?" I yawned and glared back at him.

"You and Alice left before everyone else woke up."

"We needed to get back. We had work to do."

"Who is it?" Alice chose that moment to exit her bedroom, rubbing her eyes.

"You were sleeping as well?" Xander asked Alice.

"Yeah, why?" She walked up to us and yawned again.

"So what work did you guys have to do, Liv?" Xander raised an eyebrow and looked at me.

"I don't have to tell you." I looked away from him. Why was he here? "How did you get my address?"

"Aiden gave it to me." He said shortly.

"I'm surprised he didn't come as well." I said annoyed.

"I don't think he wanted to come." Xander said and I looked over at Alice, who was blushing. What had gone down with Alice and Aiden? I stared at her for a few seconds, but she avoided my stare.

"I'm going to make some coffee." She said finally. "Anyone want some?"

"I'll take a cup." Xander said. "Black please."

"I'll have a cup as well, milk and sugar, you know how I like it." I said and she walked into the kitchen. "Shall we sit in the living room then?" I turned back to Xander. "I assume you're not going to leave before you have your coffee?"

"You assume correct." He said stiffly and he followed me to the living room.

"So what do you want, Xander?" I sighed. "I thought we said everything we needed to say last night."

"You didn't say goodbye."

"What?" I frowned at him. "What are you talking about?"

"You left this morning without saying goodbye." He stared at me and I wondered what I looked like. I was sure hot and mess would describe me pretty well. I hadn't bothered to take off my makeup the night before and I could feel that my hair was no longer a wavy cacophony of beauty, but more a frizzy bush.

"Are you fucking joking me? Why do I need to say bye?" I shook my head and tried not to notice how pink his lips looked this morning.

"Why do you have to be so immature, Liv?" He shook his head at me. "I thought we made up last night. I thought you understood where I was coming from. I thought we were friends."

"What do you want from me, Xander?" I groaned out loud, unable to stop my frustration from coming out. We stared at each other for a few seconds and he shrugged.

"I don't know." He sighed. "Nothing I guess."

"Then leave." I sat back and looked away from him.

"I don't want to leave." He said softly.

"I'm not having sex with you." I shifted away from him. "If that's why you're here."

"That's not why I'm here." He grabbed my hand and pulled me towards him. "I don't know what to say Liv. I don't know what you want from me. I don't even know you. I know nothing about you really. I can't just change my life for you."

"You already told me that." I sighed and pulled my hand away from him.

"I'm the guy that has sexual relationships. I'm the guy that goes after what he wants and gets it. I'm the guy that leaves in the morning."

"Well good for you." I jumped up as Alice walked into the living room with the coffee. "We're done here, Xander." I looked at him and folded my arms as I chose my words carefully. "It's like you said, you don't know me. If you did know me, you would know that I'm not the sort of girl that just has sexual relationships. I'm not the girl that is the fuck buddy. I'm not the girl that lets a guy trample all over her." I stared at his face and looked into his impenetrable green eyes. "I don't know what you want. And you don't know what you want. And that's just not good enough, Xander. I'm not going to settle to be second best, I don't care what your issues are." And then I walked out of the living room and directly to my bedroom. I locked the door behind me, turned on my laptop and played my music as loud as it would go and then walked into my bathroom and turned on the bath and poured some Epsom salts in and waited for the tub to fill up. I was not going to think about Xander. I was not going to let him get to me. I didn't care what he thought as he left. I didn't care if he thought I was rude. I didn't care. I didn't care. I didn't care. I kept repeating that to myself as I stripped my clothes off and settled into the bath. I sat back and closed my eyes and let the water calm me down. He was a jerk for playing with my feelings like this. Why couldn't he just leave me alone?

"WANT TO WATCH A MOVIE, Alice?" I exited my room about four hours later, feeling refreshed. I could hear the TV on in the living room and I made my way to the room, determined to keep my mind off of Xander.

"What do you want to watch?" Xander sat there next to Alice with a warm smile on his face.

"You?" I frowned. "What are you still doing here?"

"That's my cue to get up." Alice smiled at me. "I'm going to go and have a bath too."

"What's going on Alice?" I looked at her, hurt that she would sit and chat with him after everything he had done to me.

"Just talk to Xander." She rubbed my shoulder as she left the room. "He's not all bad."

"Whatever." I sighed and looked back at him as she left the room. "I thought I told you to leave."

"I don't actually believe you said that." He grinned at me and then pat the seat next to him. "Sit."

"What do you want Xander?" I could feel my blood pressure rising.

"I know your birthday is in September. I know you're a Virgo. I know you work for a small nonprofit doing marketing work. I know that you wish you were better in science because you wanted to be a vet. I know you love dogs, hate cats, and that you're deathly afraid of spiders and snakes. I know that you want to be on Survivor or The Amazing Race. I know that you think Matthew McConaughey is the best looking actor in Hollywood. I know that that you love cupcakes and French fries and that you hate vegetables, but you make yourself eat them because that's what you've always done. I know that you love your family, even though they infuriate you and I know that if you could have any car in the world, it would be a black sports Range Rover."

"A Range Rover isn't a car, it's an SUV." I said, feeling dazed.

"I know that you're a romantic and that you believe in true love and fairy tales."

"Alice told you that?" My jaw dropped. I was going to kill Alice.

"No." He shook his head. "Alice told me everything up to the car. I figured out the true romantic stuff."

"Oh." I said stiffly.

"Why did you ask her all that stuff?"

"You said that I didn't know you and you were right." He gave me a weak smile. "I wanted a chance to get to know you and I didn't think you were going to answer any of my questions."

"I see."

"Do you really?" He stood up and walked over to me. "Do you really see, Liv?"

"Not really." I shook my head, my heart racing as he grabbed my hands and pulled me towards him. "What's the point of asking her all those questions?"

"I don't know." He shrugged. "I don't really understand what's going on between us."

"Neither do I." I acknowledged.

"I just wish you would quit playing games with my heart." He grinned and then winked at me as I laughed.

"She told you that was my favorite song as well?"

"Yes," He laughed. "She did."

"I'm going to kill Alice." I sighed.

"Please don't." He leaned forward and kissed me. "Or at least not just yet."

"Okay then, I won't kill her yet." I kissed him back and whimpered as I felt his hands reaching up under my t-shirt and squeezing my bare breasts.

"No bra?" He groaned next to my lips as his fingers pinch my nipples.

"I'm at home, I don't need a bra."

"I need to be at your home more often." He grunted lifted my t-shirt up quickly before lowering his head and sucking on my right nipple.

"Xander, you can't do this." I moan as he sucked eagerly and pinched my other nipple.

"Yes, I can." He grinned up at me and switched to my other breast.

"What if Alice comes back out." I groaned as his teeth tugged my nipple gently and I ran my hands through his hair. "Xander," I moaned his name loudly.

"Let's go to your bedroom then."

"I don't know." I said hesitantly.

"Please." He licked his lips and then kissed me again.

"We haven't really solved anything though." I wasn't sure what to do.

"Do we have to figure it out now?" He kissed the side of my neck and then whispered in my ear. "My tongue wants to show you how badly he's missed you."

"You know just what to say to get me to say yes, don't you?" I giggled and grabbed his hand and pulled him towards my bedroom. "Come on, before I change my mind."

"We wouldn't want you to do that, would we?" He chuckled as we entered my room and I made sure to lock the door behind us. I did not need Alice walking in while Xander went down on me. Not at all. "Nice room." He looked around and grinned. "And no Backstreet Boys posters."

"Very funny." I laughed and leaned forward to kiss him again. "Keep it up and you won't make it to the bed."

"Oh really?" He laughed and grabbed me around the waist and picked me up. I started squealing and then he dropped me on the mattress and just looked at me for a few seconds. "I better get to work quickly then." He winked at me and reached down and pulled my top off. He stared at my breasts for a few seconds and licked his lips. "I like you with no bra." He said and then reached down and pulled my boy shorts off. "And no panties either, yummy." He moaned and spread my legs open before dropping to his knees. I groaned as I felt his face between my legs and I knew that he could feel my wetness, as his tongue ran back and forth on my clit as he gently sucked on it. My entire body felt on edge as his tongue continued to play with me and gently entered me.

"Oh Xander." I whimpered as he fucked me with his tongue. I had almost forgotten how delicious being with him felt.

"Turn over." He groaned as he rolled me onto my stomach.

"Why?" I cried out, not wanting him to stop doing what he was doing as I was already so close to a climax.

"Shh." He stood up and I twisted my head and watched as he pulled off his shirt and pants quickly. I took a deep breath as I stared at his naked cock, jutting out in front of him.

"What are you—" I started, but he slapped my bottom lightly.

"Shh." He said again with a grin and winked at me. "Put your head down, close your eyes and spread your legs."

"What?" I frowned as my heart raced.

"Don't ask any questions, just do what I say." He slapped me again, a little harder this time and I moaned as his finger slipped between my legs and rubbed my clit.

"Oh." I cried out and spread my legs.

"Good girl." He groaned as he lowered his head and bit my ass gently.

"What are you doing?" I groaned as I felt his tongue licking down my ass crack.

"No questions." He slapped me again on the bottom of my ass and rubbed my wet clit again.

"Okay." I cried out, my entire body on high alert.

"You're learning." He said softly and his hands spread my legs again. I felt his breath on my pussy and my body shivered as he licked my clit with his warm and ticklish tongue. I closed my eyes and moaned into the sheets as he licked me. It felt different from this position, but if anything it felt even more intense and exciting. And then I felt his tongue moving up higher and I froze. My eyes popped open as his tongue licked up my butt crack again. What was he doing?

"Relax." He groaned as he kissed up my back. I could feel his cock grazing my leg and I moaned.

"What are you doing?" I said softly as he squeezed my butt cheeks.

"Showing you how many miracles my tongue can perform."

"With my ass?" I whispered as I felt his tongue on my butt again, moving closer and closer to my anus.

"You just had a bath right?"

"Yes." I whispered. "Why?"

He didn't answer me with words, instead I felt his tongue licking me in a place I'd never been licked before. At first I was shocked into silence. I couldn't believe he was licking my asshole and I couldn't believe how wonderful it felt. I closed my eyes and gripped the sheets, feeling almost embarrassed at the amount of pleasure that was cascading through my body. And then he did this thing where he licked my clit for a few seconds and moved back up to my ass. The feelings were overwhelming. I could barely stop myself from screaming when he pushed the tip of his tongue inside both holes. I felt dirty and I loved it. And then his cock entered my pussy in one hard thrust and I couldn't stop myself. I came immediately and screamed out his name as he slammed into me, each thrust feeling deeper and deeper.

"Oh Xander." I screamed as he grunted behind me and filled me up.

"Yes Liv. Scream my name." He pulled out and flipped me over. "Scream my name, Liv." He grinned down at me and entered me again quickly. I moaned as I looked up into his eyes and he grabbed my hands and held them tightly as he started to move a little slower.

"Oh shit, Xander. I'm going to come again." I screamed as the tip of his cock kept hitting my g-spot every time he moved inside of me.

"Come for me, Liv." He groaned and then I felt his body shuddering as he increased his pace and exploded inside of me. He collapsed next to me on the bed after a few seconds and then kissed me on the cheek.

"Promise me something Liv." He whispered in my ear.

"What?" I asked him softly as he kissed the side of my face.

"Don't leave the bed until we both wake up."

"Okay." I nodded, my heart soaring as he pulled me into his arms. "I won't leave the bed until we both wake up."

"You can leave if you need the bathroom though, I don't want you to wet the bed." He said lightly with a laugh and I slapped his arm as I laughed with him and closed my eyes. I wasn't sure how he'd done it, but I was feeling a million times better about our situation now. I had faith that we'd figure out a way to make this work. He liked me, he really liked me and his staying and asking Alice all those questions had to mean that he wanted to see where we could go in our relationship. He was ready to give us a chance now. He had to be.

11

"MORNING." XANDER'S VOICE WAS WARM as I opened my eyes.

"Morning." I blinked and looked at the clock on the wall. "Wow, we slept the whole evening away?"

"I guess you were tired."

"You didn't sleep?"

"Not until night."

"Oh no, what did you do?"

"Watched you." He said and then laughed. "I didn't expect that to sound so creepy."

"It does sound a bit creepy, doesn't it?" I giggled and my heart soared as he stared at me and leaned down to give me a kiss.

"I'm not a creep." He kissed me harder and ran his hands through my hair. "I promise."

"Hmm, I'll take your word for it." I laughed. "You did kiss my ass yesterday." I flushed at the memory.

"I think I did more than kiss it." He winked at me as he ran his fingers down my stomach and between my legs and rubbed gently.

"Xander." I groaned and pushed his hand away. "Not now."

"Okay." He laughed and played with my breasts instead. "Did you sleep well?"

"Yes, I did? You?"

"Great." He nodded. "I figured out the secret."

"What secret?"

"The secret to making sure you're not gone in the morning."

"What's the secret?"

"Have sex with you in your apartment." He grinned and I laughed.

"You're an idiot." I ran my fingers down his chest lightly and played with his nipples.

"A sexy idiot."

"I guess." I leaned forward and kissed his chest lightly and he rubbed my back. "So what do we do now?" I asked softly and he froze. I looked up at him with a slight frown and studied his face. "Everything okay?"

"Yes of course." He nodded.

"So what do we do now then?" I asked again.

"I'll do whatever you want me to do, Liv." He kissed the top of my forehead and leaned back.

"Whatever I want you to do?" My heart thudded, those weren't the words I wanted to hear.

"Yes, if you don't want me to go through with the engagement, I'll end it." He nodded.

"What do you want to do?" I cocked my head and studied his face. Didn't he want to end the engagement? I could feel my body growing warm. I should have been happy that he was willing to do what I wanted, but I wasn't. I didn't want him to do what I wanted him to do. I wanted him to do what he wanted to do. I wanted him to be the one to decide to call off the engagement. I wanted him to be the one that made the decision because there was no other option in his mind.

"I don't care." He shrugged, his face indifferent. "Whatever will make you happy."

"Why do you like me, Xander?" I asked him softly. "I mean asides from me leaving you in the hotel room. Why do you like me?"

"I was intrigued by you the moment I saw you at the church." He stroked my hair. "And I thought you were beautiful and sexy as hell. And sassy too. And then you called me Mr. Tongue and I thought that any girl that has the confidence to hook up at a wedding and then give me a nickname had to be a girl I wanted to get to know better."

"I see." I said and sighed. I didn't know what I was hoping he would say.

"And I'm still intrigued by you. I'm more intrigued by you now, than I was before." He kissed me. "So tell me, Liv. What do you want me to do?"

"You said that you met up with Luke and Gabby and Henry that day?" I said and decided to ask him the questions that had been puzzling me. "How do you know Luke?"

"His grandfather and mine grew up together." He said right away. "I've known him since we were young."

"How come we never heard about you or met you when he dated Alice?"

"I don't know." He shrugged.

"How does Luke know Gabby?" I said softly. "And why do either of you care what happens to her and the baby."

"It's complicated," Xander made a face. "I don't think it's important."

"I just want to be able to understand." I sighed.

"Look, I have to go and meet Henry now." He sat up and pulled me up as well. He kissed me hard over and over again and then pulled back. "Henry and I need to meet up with Luke to discuss something this morning."

"Oh okay." I frowned and he kissed my cheek.

"Don't be mad at me, okay." He gazed into my eyes. "This whole thing will work out. You just tell me what you want."

"I want you to do what you want to do." I said softly. "I want you to make the decision."

"Okay." He nodded and got out of the bed. "I have to go now. Can I see you later tonight?"

"Yeah, call me." I said trying not to have an attitude.

"I'll see you later, Liv." He jumped out of bed and I watched as he pulled his clothes on and left the room. I lay back with a sigh and closed my eyes. Maybe one day we'd be able to get it right.

"SO YOU THINK LUKE MIGHT be the father of the baby?" Alice's jaw dropped as we sat in a booth at our local diner and ate mozzarella sticks.

"Yes, it's the only thing that makes any sort of sense." I nodded. "Every time I bring Luke's name up, he acts funny." I sat back. "Crazy right?"

"I can't believe it." She shook her head. "I knew he was a dog, but damn."

"I know, but we know he's shady because he cheated on you with Joanna."

"I wonder if he hooked up with Gabby while he was dating me as well?" She shuddered. "He's fucking gross."

"Tell me about it." I sipped on my coke. "She's such a slut."

"And now she's marrying my man." I made a face.

"Why is Xander marrying her again?" Alice made a face. "It's not like it's his baby."

"I guess he and Luke are good friends. And well it helps him out as well."

"They can't be that good friends." Alice said. "I never even heard his name before."

"I know, I was thinking about that as well." I said with a sigh. "So many things don't make sense."

"Oh my God." Alice leaned forward. "Don't look now, but Gabby just came into the diner."

"Oh no." I groaned.

"And she's with Henry."

"Henry?" My voice rose and I couldn't stop myself from looking over towards the entrance. My jaw dropped as I watched Gabby and Henry walking to a booth, with his arm on her back, tenderly stroking her. "What the fuck is going on?" I turned back to Alice. "Are we in the Twilight Zone?"

"Maybe?" She shook her head and I could see she looked dazed as well. "I'm seriously confused here."

"Me too." And then suddenly it hit me. "What if Henry is the dad?"

"What?" She frowned.

"What if Henry is the baby daddy." I nodded as the idea started to make sense. "Maybe Xander is marrying her because Henry doesn't want to, but they figure Xander can because of the inheritance and stuff and this way they make sure the baby is taken better care of."

"I guess that could make sense." She nodded. "I did wonder why Henry was there last weekend."

"It was odd right? And he kept talking about babies." I nodded. "Shit, I should become a detective." I said excitedly. "Frigging Henry is the dad."

"But what about Luke?" Alice frowned.

"Who knows?" I shrugged and we both looked at Gabby and Henry smiling and flirting on the other side of the restaurant. "Wait a second, I'm getting a call." I grabbed my phone from my bag and pulled it out. "Hello."

"Hey you." Xander's voice sounded smooth and sexy.

"Hey you back." I smiled into the phone. "It's Xander." I mouthed towards Alice and she grinned.

"What are you doing?"

"Alice and I are eating."

"Will you be done soon?" He asked softly. "I want to see you."

"Well, I'm with Alice…" My voice trailed off as I looked at my friend.

"It's fine." She mouthed to me. "I'm going to go home and do my nails."

"You sure?" I asked with a frown.

"Positive." She nodded. "Go and get the dirt from Xander."

"Okay." I grinned. "You still there, Xander."

"Yes."

"Okay, I'm downtown. Come and meet me at the bookstore on Steamer Avenue in an hour."

"Okay. I'll see you there in an hour." He said and hung up.

"We're meeting in an hour."

"Sounds good." Alice grinned. "I can't wait to find out what's going on."

"I already told you." I grinned back at her.

"Okay Sherlock." She laughed and I winked at her, excited to see Xander and find out what decision he had made.

"I MISSED YOU TODAY." XANDER kissed me and twirled me around.

"I missed you too." I said giddily, happy to see him. "So before we go any further, I have a question to ask you."

"Okay...?" He looked at me with a curious expression.

"Is Henry, Gabby's baby daddy?" I rushed out and Xander's expression looked shocked.

"How did you know?"

"I knew it!" I fist pumped. "Scotland Yard here I come."

"You're moving to England" He teased me.

"No." I rolled my eyes and laughed. "But seriously, he's the baby daddy?"

"We're not sure. We think so." He sighed. "Do not tell anyone this, but it's either Henry or Luke."

"What?" My jaw dropped. "They had a gangbang?"

"Liv." He laughed and shook his head. "No, they didn't."

"Then how?" I asked quickly.

"She slept with them both." He sighed. "But based on the dates, we're pretty confident that Henry is the father."

"Oh wow." I chewed on my lower lip. "That's crazy."

"I take it Gabby didn't tell you all this."

"No she didn't." I said with a laugh. "I didn't know she was such a slut."

"Liv." He admonished me.

"What? I'm just saying." I giggled as we walked through the bookstore.

"Well now you understand why this is all so complicated." He sighed as we stopped in the self-help section.

"No why?" I frowned.

"Henry slept with her, but he doesn't want a relationship with her. He doesn't want to be tied to her, but he does want a life with his kid. This seemed to be a perfect solution. I get to marry someone and gain control of the company and Henry gets to have a relationship with his child."

"Okay." My breathing slowed at his words.

"So this marriage really solves two problems."

"So what are you saying, Xander? You don't want to end the engagement?"

"We would only be married for a year. That's the amount of time I need to be married before I can gain control of the company."

"So you want to marry my sister and sleep with me on the side?"

"You wouldn't be on the side." He exclaimed angrily. "There is nothing between me and Gabby, you know that. This is just a business transaction."

"I don't believe this." I shook my head and sighed. "I can't believe you."

"What?"

"Nothing. I'm done." I took a step back. "I'm just so done."

"What? Look if you want me to end it then I will. I was just saying that—"

"Forget it, Xander. I don't want you to do anything you don't want to do. I want you to end the engagement with Gabby because you can't go on one more second living a farce. I don't want you to do it because I made you."

"Don't be mad Liv." He reached out to grab my arm and I pushed him away.

"Of course I'm mad." I shouted at him. "Just go home to Gabby and play happy families and leave me out of it." I ran out of the store and turned my phone off. Was it too much to ask for him to want to make the right decision by himself? Was it really too much to expect? Was I being unreasonable not wanting to share his bed while he was married to my sister? I mean really? Did he really think that was an acceptable solution? Who in their right mind would ever think that was a good plan?

12

ALICE AND I BOTH SIGHED as we walked up to the front door of my parents' house.

"Thanks for coming." I offered her a weak smile. "You really didn't have to."

"It's fine. I wanted to be able to support you today." She took a deep breath. "Plus who cares what Aiden or Xander have to say. We're here because your parents requested you. You're not here for them or even stupid Gabby."

"Let's do this." I opened the front door and we walked into the house. Everyone was there, including Henry and Xander. And I just stood there with a fake smile on my face. I wasn't going to act like I cared that he hadn't called me in the last two weeks. I didn't care that I hadn't heard from him since the bookstore. He could do what he wanted to do. He meant nothing to me. If he could forget me that easily, I could do the same. "Hey everyone."

"Hey sis." Scott jumped up and gave me a hug and then he turned to Alice and gave her a kiss on the cheek. I noticed Aiden glaring at them and wondered exactly what had gone down between him and Alice as she still hadn't told me.

"So what's so important that we had to come this weekend?" I looked at Gabby and she gave me an evil smile.

"I'm home." She smiled. "That's what's so important."

"What?" My jaw dropped. "I had to come home just because you're here."

"Yes." She grinned. "Isn't life grand, but just in case anyone wanted to hang out with me later today, I'm going out with a few girlfriends."

"Okay." I rolled my eyes.

"We're celebrating my upcoming wedding."

"Okay." I looked at Xander and he gave me a short smile. I turned away and looked at Scott. "So what plans do you have this weekend?"

"Whatever you want to do." He grinned and I smiled at him gratefully.

Ding Dong.

"Who's that?" Aiden jumped up with a frown. "Is anyone expecting anyone?"

"Not me." I shook my head and noticed that Alice was blushing. "Alice?" I asked her softly.

"Uhm, yes." She squeaked out.

"Who?" I frowned.

"Don't kill me." She mouthed and I scratched my head. What was she talking about?

"Liv." Aiden's voice sound stiff and angry as he walked back into the living room.

"Yes?" I snapped at him and frowned at the two burly guys behind him. "What?"

"These guys are here for you and Alice." He looked at her with a cold mask. "They said they're here to join you for the weekend."

"What?" I was confused.

"Brock and Jock, there you are." Alice ran to one of the big burly guys and gave him a kiss on the cheek. "We're so glad you made it, aren't we Liv?" She gave me a look and I nodded slowly.

"Uh yeah, sure." I walked over to Alice with a questioning look and she turned to everyone. "Brock and Jock are two guys we've been dating and we wanted everyone to meet them."

"Oh yeah, haha." I laughed and faked a wide smile. "So glad you made it Brock." I kissed the other guy on the cheek and he stared at me like a robot.

"I'm Jock." He said stiffly.

"I know that, I was just teasing you honey." I linked my arm through his and looked over at Xander who was glaring at me.

"Brock and Jock?" Gabby asked with a laugh. "Nice names."

"We're brothers." Jock said and I wished I could tell him to keep his mouth shut. Where had Alice picked these guys up from?

"And we love to double-date, don't we?" Alice said with a wide smile. "And have sleepovers." She said and giggled and I could see Aiden looking even angrier as he walked away from us.

"Good for you." Gabby flipped her hair. "I'm glad you two losers have found guys that can put up with you."

"Shut up, Gabby." I shouted at her and she looked at me with a raised eyebrow.

"Or what?" She said sweetly.

"Ugh." I groaned. "Nothing."

"That's what I thought." She laughed and then leaned down and gave Xander a kiss on the cheek. "I'm going out. See you later, okay baby?"

"See you, Gabby." He said, but his eyes never left my face. "Liv can we talk?"

"No." I shook my head. "Let's go out Jock and Brock. We'll be back later."

"You just got here." Scott said with a frown.

"Well we're going out now." I snapped and grabbed Jock's hand. "Let's go guys."

We all hurried out of the front door and I turned to Alice. "What were you thinking?"

"I was thinking we'd have two hot guys here to make us feel better and make those two fools jealous."

"And the best you could do were Brock and Jock?" I said quietly. "They look like mountain men."

"They're strippers." She giggled. "They were the best I could do."

"Oh Alice." I groaned. "What should we do?"

"Tell them to go home and go to the mall and then go and get a drink?"

"That sounds like a good idea to me." I nodded in agreement. We gave the two brothers $40 and then hopped into my car and drove to the local mall.

"I LOVE RETAIL THERAPY." I grinned happily as we made our way into the wine bar with our hands full of bags.

"So do I." She nodded. "Though my credit card doesn't agree."

"Neither does mine." I laughed. "But that's a worry for next month when the bill arrives."

"You speak the truth." She said and we ordered a bottle of Chardonnay. "Until the bill arrives then we are fine."

"Exactly."

"Oh my God." She groaned and I frowned.

"What?"

"You won't believe who's here?" She sighed.

"Who?" My face paled. "Please don't say Gabby and Xander?"

"No, well, you're half right. Gabby is here with a bunch of girls."

"Oh great." I made a face and then watched as Alice frowned.

"Okay, this is weird, but she's drinking wine, I think." Her eyes narrowed and she gasped. "She is definitely drinking wine."

"What the fuck?" I turned around. "She can't drink alcohol! She's pregnant."

"What's she doing?" Alice frowned. "She's such a selfish bitch."

"I'm going to go and tell her off." I jumped up, furious with Gabby. What the fuck was she playing at? "What do you think you're doing?" I screamed as I approached a giggling Gabby.

"Oh hi, Liv." She grinned. "I'm showing Shannon my ring."

"I don't care what you're showing her?" I shouted at her again and picked up her glass and sniffed. "This is wine. Why are you drinking?"

"What?" She frowned.

"You can't drink Gabby."

"What?" She grabbed her glass and sipped some wine in front of me. "Says who?"

"What about the baby?" I said softly. "How can you do this to the baby?"

"I'm not pregnant." She laughed and sat back.

"What?" My jaw dropped. "What about Xander and Henry and the baby and the engagement? What do you mean you're not pregnant?"

"Oh Liv." She shook her head. "You don't get it do you?" She sipped some more wine.

"Get what?"

"Luke and I had a relationship. Well, we had sex." She grinned. "Don't tell Alice, but it started when they were dating."

"Oh my God." My eyes widened. "What?"

"Yeah, he's pretty good in bed." She grinned. "Who was I to say no?"

"Oh Gabby." I shook my head.

"Well then he met that bitch Joanna." She got angry. "And instead of being with me, he dumped Alice and started dating her."

"I'm sorry."

"Don't be." She shrugged. "We still fucked. And I had hoped he would come to his senses."

"But then, what about Henry?" I asked softly.

"Oh, he was Luke's friend. I met him one night and tried to make Luke jealous." She shrugged. "He was okay. I didn't care about him."

"Why did you lie about the baby?"

"I wanted to make Luke call off the wedding." Her face grew sad. "I thought he'd call it off to marry me if he thought I was pregnant with his baby."

"Oh."

"But stupid Henry told him we fucked and somehow they ended up thinking it was his. And well, next thing I know Xander is offering me money to marry him as long as he and Henry can be in the baby's life."

"And you let them believe there was still a baby."

"He gave me this huge rock and promised me a lot of cash." She shrugged. "Who was I to say no?"

"But there's no baby, Gabby. You can't just lie and think that's okay."

"What do you care?" She drank some more wine.

"I can't believe you did that. I thought you were pregnant. Everyone thinks you're having Henry's baby."

"I'm not stupid, Liv. I'm on the pill." She tossed her hair. "Do you really think I'd have unsafe sex and risk having a baby and ruining my perfect figure right now?"

"You're a selfish bitch."

"Thank you." She grinned and drank some more wine. "And salute to you too."

"Whatever." I shook my head and walked away from her, my head thudding as I joined Alice again.

"What's going on?" She asked softly as I sat down with her. "What did she say?"

"She's not pregnant." I said in a daze. "She's not pregnant, Alice."

"No way." She looked at me with a shocked expression. "So she lied."

"Yes, she lied to all of us." I rubbed my forehead and closed my eyes for a second.

"Are you okay, Liv?" Alice grabbed my hands and I opened my eyes slowly and nodded.

"Yeah, I'm okay."

"You don't look fine."

"It's just something she said, it got me thinking."

"What's that?"

"I'm not on the pill."

"So?" Alice shrugged. "Does that matter?"

"I had sex with Xander."

"So? He used condoms right?"

"Not the last couple of times." I shook my head and buried my face in my hands and groaned. "How could I be such an idiot Alice? He came in me several times." I whined and then looked up at her. "Gabby's not pregnant, but what if I am?"

"What do you want to do?"

"Let's go home."

"To your parents' house?"

"No, let's go to the apartment."

"Don't you want to tell Xander what you found out?"

"No." I shook my head and stood up. "He made his decision. He can deal with the mess that his *business transaction* makes. That's his problem."

"Oh Liv." Alice sighed. "Promise me one thing though."

"What?"

"Take a pregnancy test."

"I'll get one this week." I nodded and we left some cash on the table and then walked out of the restaurant to the sound of Gabby and her friends laughing. I didn't know what to think or feel. A part of me wanted to be pregnant and the other part of me was scared stiff that I was. I wanted to tell Xander the truth so badly, but I didn't want to be the one that told him. I didn't want to be the girl that was chasing him and forcing him to be with me. That was no way to start a relationship. No way at all.

13

THERE WAS A BIG BROWN package sitting on my bed when I got home from work and I looked at it with a curious expression. Who was sending me a package? It wasn't my birthday and I hadn't ordered anything online in ages. I walked over to it eagerly, excited to see what was inside. I smiled to myself at my excitement. It was the first time in over two weeks I'd had anything to feel excited about. Alice and I hadn't gone back to my parents' house after the bar and no one had called or tried to find out what had happened.

I was sad that my family didn't even bother to find out why we'd left, but I was even more hurt that Xander hadn't called me or come over. I'd hoped that he'd show up that evening, but he hadn't. I didn't even know if he knew that there was no baby. I was confident Gabby wouldn't tell him. She had no morals and no conscience. She wouldn't care. I sat on the bed and opened the package quickly, ripping it open to see what was inside. I opened the box and stared at the contents with a frown. There was a tongue sitting there. I picked it up and then saw the note. It was from Xander and it read "Please call me soon. I want to talk to you." I threw the note and the tongue on the bed and hurried out of the room. Did he think that was funny? I walked to the kitchen to get some water and tried to calm my rapidly beating heart.

"Hey, I didn't hear you come in." Alice said with a small smile as she walked into the kitchen.

"Yeah, just got in." I said and took another sip of water. "I saw the package. Thanks for putting it in my room."

"No worries." She nodded. "Anything good?"

"No." I shook my head and then frowned as my phone rang. "It's Aiden." I rolled my eyes at her and answered the phone. "Hello."

"Liv, its Aiden." He said stiffly.

"I know, what do you want?"

"Are you coming home this weekend?"

"Nope."

"I think you should come." He said again, softer this time. "Gabby needs your support."

"Why?" I said shortly.

"Xander broke off the engagement."

"Really?" I said surprised, though I didn't want to admit it. I also didn't want to admit how happy that made me. "Why?"

"I guess it wasn't a real engagement." He sighed. "I think she was up to her old tricks or something."

"Oh?"

"Yeah, she's not really pregnant, but she'd lied and said she was having this baby and really needed support."

"Oh? Wow." I faked shock.

"Yeah, turns out he asked her if they could break it off that first weekend." Aiden continued talking. "He thought he'd made a mistake or something, but she told him mom and dad would disown her if she wasn't engaged. And that she'd move to France or something and take the baby with her."

"Oh wow." I shook my head. "That's crazy."

"Yeah, so anyways we're all getting together this weekend to make her feel better."

"I'm not coming, sorry."

"You should come, Liv. You and Alice."

"Alice and I are not coming." I said loudly and I saw Alice staring at me. I knew she was wondering what we were talking about.

"Please Liv."

"If you want to see Alice, just pick up the phone and ask her out or something."

"Liv." He groaned. "I don't want to date Alice."

"Uh huh. So why do you want to see her this weekend?"

"Liv, it's complicated."

"Aiden, grow up. I know you like Alice, just ask her out." I shouted into the phone and I saw Alice shaking her head at me.

"Liv, I saw Alice and Scott kissing." Aiden said softly. "There is nothing between Alice and I. She already made her choice."

"You what?" My jaw dropped. "You saw what?"

"That night we were all at the club. I was waiting up to apologize to Alice and as I walked to your room to say sorry, I saw her with Scott and they were kissing."

"Oh." My voice was a squeak and I could tell from the look on Alice's face as she stood there that it was true. "I didn't know."

"Yeah well, it is what it is."

"I'm sorry, Aiden." I said softly.

"It's fine." He sighed. "Maybe we can go and grab lunch soon."

"What? You and me?"

"Yes, you and me." He laughed. "I think we're old enough to be friends now, don't you think?"

"Yes, I'd like that." I said with a smile. "I'd like that a lot."

"Oh and Liv."

"Yes, Aiden?"

"Go easy on Xander." He said softly. "He's a good guy."

"What are you talking about?" I asked softly, my heart racing and my face red.

"You know." He laughed. "I'll see you soon." He said and hung up. I put my phone in my pocket and looked at Alice in silence, unsure of what to say.

"You kissed Scott?" I said finally and she sighed.

"No, yes, not really." She burst into tears. "He walked me to my room that night and he leaned in to give me a kiss outside the door. And I said what would one kiss hurt? You'd always told me to go for him. So I leaned forward and he kissed me, but I knew as soon as our lips touched that I didn't like him like that, but it was too late. As we kissed I saw Aiden in the corridor glaring at us and I just didn't know what to do." She sobbed. "Oh Liv, what am I going to do?"

"Oh Alice." I groaned. "We've really fucked this all up."

"I don't know what to do." She cried. "I really like Aiden and now he hates me."

"He doesn't hate you." I sighed. "I'll come up with a plan. We'll figure something out."

"Thanks, Liv." She rubbed her eyes. "I'm going to go and lie down now."

"Okay." I nodded and watched her leave the room. I stood there for a few seconds and then pulled my phone out and made a call.

"Hello." His voice was a sexy drawl and I felt my heart jump at the sound.

"It's Liv."

"I know." He laughed. "I take it you got my gift."

"Yes." I shook my head as I walked to my bedroom. "I did."

"What do you think?"

"I think it's perverted. Who sends someone a plastic tongue?" I laughed.

"Me." He said softly. "Have you used it yet?"

"Used it? What are you talking about?"

"Oh, you don't know what it is yet?"

"No, what is it?"

"Take it out of the box and look at it carefully."

"Okay." I grabbed the box and pulled the tongue out. I looked at it carefully and noticed a small switch I hadn't seen before. I turned it on and the tongue started vibrating back and forth. "Oh my God, is this a vibrator?"

"Yes." He laughed.

"Xander." I shouted at him. "How could you?"

"How could I what?" He laughed. "I figured if you couldn't have my miracle tongue, you could have second best."

"Wow, how nice of you." I laughed and lay back on the bed.

"I aim to please." He said with a chuckle. "I'm glad you called Liv."

"I heard about you and Gabby." I said softly.

"Yes, the engagement is over."

"I'm sorry about everything. I'm sorry she lied about being pregnant."

"I ended it before I knew she was lying Liv." He said softly. "I ended it the weekend you showed up with Brock and Jock."

"What? That was two weeks ago." I said, hurt he hadn't called me.

"I was mad at you Liv. I wanted to talk to you that weekend, but you went out with Alice and you never came back."

"I was too hurt and jealous."

"I understand why you were upset at me. I acted like an idiot." He sighed. "I shouldn't have expected you to be okay with me and Gabby being married; even if it was a fake engagement."

"It was crazy, but I could have been more understanding."

"We were both a bit crazy." He sighed. "But maybe more than anyone. I'm not even sure what I was thinking. All I can say is that the first weekend with you gave me some sort of brain damage."

"Oh Xander." I giggled.

"So are you going to test out the tongue?" He asked softly.

"What?" I said feeling a bit turned on.

"I want you to try the tongue and tell me if you prefer the real thing or not."

"Xander." I blushed. "I'm not going to do that?"

"Or maybe I can help you out and see for myself."

"See for yourself?"

"I can see if you scream louder with your present or with my miracle tongue."

"Hmm, I'll think about it."

"Make up your mind quickly." He laughed and then I heard the doorbell ring. "I'm here."

"You're here? At my house?"

"Yes. Now come and get me."

"Hold on." I ran out of the room and to the front door and there he was. "Xander, you're here."

"Yes, it's me, in the flesh."

"I don't know what to say." I blushed and he grabbed me and pulled me forward to kiss me.

"Say you want me to come in and visit your bedroom." He winked at me as he turned his phone off.

"Come in." I said weakly and we walked to my bedroom quickly. Xander closed and locked the door behind him and then pulled me in for another kiss.

"I've missed the taste of you." He said softly. "I've missed you."

"You didn't call." I said as I kissed him back.

"I wanted to give you time to miss me as well." He laughed. "Now, let's see that tongue."

"You want me to use it now."

"Oh yes." He laughed as his massaged my breasts. "I very much want you to use it now."

"Hmm, I'll think about it." I pulled his shirt up and touched his stomach, letting my fingers slip into his pants to touch his manhood.

"Oh, Liv." He groaned and grabbed my hand. "Don't start something you can't finish."

"Oh, I can finish." I grinned at him and licked my lips.

"I want you to come with me to a wedding this weekend." He said against my head as his hands slipped up my shirt.

"I'm not going to go just so you can have some more church sex." I giggled and lifted my arms up so he could pull my top off. He unclasped my bra and sucked on my breasts with vigor. "Oh Xander." I groaned as his hand reached down and undid the button on my pants.

"That's not why I want you to come with me." He muttered as he pulled my pants down.

"Uh huh." I said and watched as he pulled his shirt off.

"I want you to come as my date." He looked up at me with a smile as he pulled his pants down. "I want it to be our first official date."

"Hmm, really?" I gasped as he grabbed me and carried me over to the bed.

"I'm sure." He kissed my neck as his fingers slid down between my legs and rubbed me gently.

"Oh Xander." I groaned as he kissed down my stomach and then stopped right at my belly button.

"Yes, dear?" He grinned up at me.

"I've missed you." I said softly and ran my hands through his hair.

"I've missed you too." He kissed back up my stomach and stared into my eyes. "I nearly let my fear ruin the best thing that's ever happened to me."

"Oh?" I said softly as I gazed back at him. "What's the best thing that's ever happened to you? Hooking up at a wedding? Having a one night stand with me?"

"What we had was not a one night stand." He kissed my lips softly. "What we had was so much more. And I'm not just saying that. I'm not inviting you to the wedding so we can have hot sex in a side room. I'm inviting you because I want to have you by my side at a special occasion. I want to show my friends and my family that I have a girlfriend and I'm proud to introduce her to everyone I know and love."

"Oh Xander." I kissed him hard, my heart melting.

"And Liv, I want to make this vow to you." He grinned at me.

"What's that?" I asked, my heart beating fast.

"I vow that the next wedding we have sex at will be ours." He said with a deep voice, full of emotion as he gazed at me with love in his eyes.

"Oh Xander." I stared at him searchingly, not daring to believe what I was hearing.

"I love you Liv." He kissed my lips, and my nose and my cheeks. "I loved you the moment I saw you. You're the wind to my sails. You're everything to me. I never ever expected to feel this way. I've never wanted to wake up with someone before. It took me aback, but now I know how lucky I am. I love you, Liv and I know that I love you with all of my heart. I know you're the only one I want to spend the rest of my life with. I know that you're it for me. So know that I mean that vow with all my heart. I see us getting married, Liv. No one could ever love you more than I do because I love you with everything it means to love. We don't know each other that well yet, but we have the rest of our lives to get to know each other." He kissed me again softly and stroked my face. "Will you let me be your Mr. Miracle Tongue forever, Liv?"

"Oh yes, Xander." I nodded. "I love you too."

"Good." He said smugly. "And now it's time to conduct the test." He grinned. "I want you to close your eyes so you can't see if it's my tongue or the toy and then I want you to tell me which one you think is best."

"Oh Xander." I giggled and was about to say something else, but the sight of him wiggling his tongue at me shut me up. I mean, who was I to say no to the contest? I needed to concentrate hard and prepare myself for the orgasms to come. It's a hard job, but someone's got to do it.

Epilogue

THREE MONTHS LATER

SO I KNOW YOU'RE WONDERING about my being pregnant. How could you not be right? Well, I'm glad to say that Xander and I were not pregnant. I do want to have babies. I want lots of them, but not quite yet. Not until after we're married. Not until we know each other a bit better, because let's be honest, we don't really know each other that well.

So the other thing you should know is that Xander and I both lied. I told him that the tongue vibrator didn't come close to him and his tongue-work and well, if I'm honest, it did come pretty close. I hadn't expected it. Maybe it felt so good because I always closed my eyes and pretended it was Xander's tongue when I used it. I think he figured out that I lied because one day the tongue just disappeared and when I asked him where I could buy another one, he told me he wasn't sure. Likely story.

And Xander lied, when he said that the next wedding we would have sex at would be our own. That didn't happen. We've been to two weddings since that conversation and we had sex at the last one. Loud, obnoxious door breaking sex. And yes, I say door breaking for a reason. We were against a door and it broke as he pounded into me. We were lucky though. Only the bride saw us in all our glory. And she just rolled her eyes and walked away. Typical Gabby behavior, yes, I said Gabby. Yes, she did get married three months after her broken engagement to Xander. Don't be surprised. I'm not. She found some sucker on an online dating site and had a fake pregnancy scare with him. I guess she figured it worked once; so she'd try it again. Only this time, she told him the truth before he found out. She got lucky though, because he didn't care. Turns out he was hoping to get her pregnant anyway.

My family was also surprisingly cool about Xander and I getting together. It turns out that both Aiden and Scott had sensed there was something between us, Chett didn't care and Gabby, well Gabby had a few words to say to me, but she got over it pretty quickly. My parent's were the most surprised, but after having to deal with all of my siblings for all of their lives, me dating my sister's ex-fiancé wasn't even close to the top of the shocking things they'd had to deal with. Remember I have Gabby for a sister and boy did she know how to get into trouble. I think once you've dealt with one of your daughters hooking up with your pastor, you can deal with anything.

You should be pleased to know that Xander and I are going strong. You wouldn't think a relationship that had such auspicious beginnings would stand a chance in hell, but it did. We're very much in love and we're so happy I can hardly take it. Though, we do argue a lot about a lot of different things. He's still obnoxious and pompous and inappropriate and I still feel like slapping him every other day. But there's a good part to arguments, the makeup sex is great. And when I say great, I mean he proves to me night after night why he's my Mr. Miracle Tongue. I also call him Mr. Miracle Cock to Alice, but we decided it's best I don't tell him that. I don't want to make him any more arrogant. He's full of himself as it is. We're going to move in with each other in a couple of weeks. I'm so excited I can't stand it. I thought it was too fast to move in already, but he says he doesn't want to go another night and morning without me in his bed again. I rolled my eyes when he said that, but inside I was thrilled. I mean, that's the sort of romantic talk I was looking for. Only I don't tell him that. I've learned to let Xander come to realizations himself. It tests my patience, but our relationship is better for it. I got really lucky and I know it. I also know that we're both still a bit immature and a bit crap at dealing with relationship issues, so I just try to let him be. We've got a lifetime to get it right. And we're already making plans together; things we want to do and that kind of stuff. We've planned a trip to Paris, a sex-class we want to take (shh) and a special party for when we move-in. The party is for Alice and Aiden though; we're hoping to get them together. Well I am, Xander doesn't really care. You know how guys are! As long as he's getting regular sex he's happy to go along with almost everything I say. And I'm fine with that. I really am. My life is wonderful now. I feel content and I've got as much excitement as I can take. Who knew my one night stand would lead to the rest of my life?

Thank you for reading One Night Stand. I hope you enjoyed it!! If you did, please leave a review and recommend the book to your friends. Please also, join my mailing list so you can be notified when I have new book releases. If enough people want a book about Alice and Aiden, I might write one. So sign up so you will be notified if there is a book for them!
I also welcome emails, so feel free to email me at jscooperauthor@gmail.com with your thoughts at any time.

ALL JS COOPER BOOKS

Rhett
Illusion
Guarding His Heart
The Ex Games
Everlasting Sin
The Forever Love Series
Crazy Beautiful Love
Scarred Series

Made in the USA
Middletown, DE
10 June 2015